D0405062

Money Has No Smell

ALSO BY PAUL STOLLER

In Sorcery's Shadow (1987; with C. Olkes)

Fusion of the Worlds (1989)

The Taste of Ethnographic Things (1989)

The Cinematic Griot (1992)

Embodying Colonial Memories (1995)

Sensuous Scholarship (1997)

Jaguar (1999)

Money Has No Smell
The Africanization of New York City

Paul Stoller

THE UNIVERSITY OF CHICAGO PRESS | CHICAGO AND LONDON

The University of Chicago Press, Chicago 60637
The University of Chicago Press, Ltd., London
© 2002 by The University of Chicago Press
All rights reserved. Published 2002
Printed in the United States of America

18 17 16 15 14 13 12 11 10   5 6 7 8 9 10

ISBN-13: 978-0-226-77529-6 (cloth)
ISBN-13: 978-0-226-77530-2 (paper)
ISBN-10: 0-226-77529-1 (cloth)
ISBN-10: 0-226-77530-5 (paper)

Parts of this book appeared earlier in *Public Culture* 7 (1): 249–75 (©
University of Chicago, 1994); *American Anthropologist* 99 (4): 776–89;
Anthropology and Humanism 22 (1): 81–94 (© American Anthropological
Association, 1997); *New Immigrants in New York,* edited by Nancy Foner,
2nd ed. (New York: Columbia University Press, 2001), 229–49; and the
Journal of Contemporary Ethnography 30 (6): 651–77 (© Sage Publications,
Inc., 2001). They are reprinted here with permission.

Library of Congress Cataloging-in-Publication Data

Stoller, Paul.
    Money has no smell : the Africanization of New York City / Paul Stoller.
        p.   cm.
    Includes bibliographical references (p.) and index.
    ISBN 0-226-77529-1 (cloth : alk. paper) — ISBN 0-226-77530-5 (pbk. : alk.
paper)
        1. West Africans—New York (State)—New York—Economic conditions.
2. West Africans—New York (State)—New York—Social conditions.
3. Muslims—New York (State)—New York—Economic conditions.
4. Muslims—New York (State)—New York—Social conditions.   5. Street
vendors—New York (State)—New York.   6. New York (N.Y.)—
Commerce—Social aspects.   7. New York (N.Y.)—Social conditions.
8. New York (N.Y.)—Ethnic relations.   9. Globalization—Social aspects—
New York (State)—New York.   10. Transnationalism—Social aspects—
New York (State)—New York.   I. Title.

    F128.9.A24 S76   2002
    305.896′607471—dc21   2001053384

♾ The paper used in this publication meets the minimum requirements of
the American National Standard for Information Sciences—Permanence of
Paper for Printed Library Materials, ANSI Z39.48-1992.

Contents

Money Has No Smell

On a midtown Manhattan sidewalk just down the street from the Museum of
Modern Art (MOMA), an exceedingly "modern" space, an African merchant
from Mali sells "primitive" art. Based in West Africa, he spends several
months a year in New York City. Shoppers, mostly tourists, have been buying
many of his pieces during the busy 1995 Christmas season, and he will soon
return to Mali to buy more masks and statues. The shoppers tell him that
his pieces remind them of what they have just seen in the museum. "This
is a good space," he says, "but sometimes the police fine me and threaten to
take my goods."

Several paces closer to the MOMA an American street merchant is also
selling African masks and statues. Amid his display of exotic wooden objects
there are placards with photographs of him buying art in Africa. As he hawks
his pieces, he talks about his travel experiences.

The West African merchant, who is a Muslim, refers to the statues and
masks as "wood."[1] For him art is simply a commodity, like any other, that he
hopes will bring a good return in the New York market. Necessity compels
him to sell idolatrous objects, which, according to a strict reading of the
Qur'an, is forbidden. With the proceeds of this sacrilege, he feeds his family
in Mali and buys more "wood." For this trader, money, as the West African
adage says, has no smell.

The American merchant presents his masks and statues as products of
a personal journey: the objects embody narratives of travel and adventure.
For some shoppers these narratives render the "primitive" more attractive,
comprehensible, and interesting—if not authentic.

AFRICAN ART FOR SALE ON 53RD STREET, MIDTOWN MANHATTAN, SUMMER 1997. (PHOTO BY
JASMIN TAHMASEB MCCONATHA)

• • •

These displays of sidewalk "wood" embody multiple narratives of primi-
tivism and modernity, objet d'art and commodity, business and romance,
Islam and tourism—all in the space of a hundred meters of Manhattan sidewalk, all in the shadow of one of the art world's most hallowed institutions.
This confluence of symbolic contradiction is a small reminder of how the
flow of money, goods, and people across increasingly fragmented spaces is
transforming social landscapes, making them less bounded, more confus-
ing. Although social worlds have never been as neat and tidy as scholars
have described them, the sometimes dazzling, if not perplexing, juxtaposi-

tions brought on by globalization have compelled social theorists to rethink such fond and comforting concepts as culture and society.

In this book, I attempt to add to our understanding of how globalization is changing contemporary urban worlds in North America. In February 1999, the tragic New York police shooting of Amadou Diallo, an unarmed street vendor from Guinea, brought into brief focus the presence of West Africans in urban America. Although reporters focused most of their attention on the political and racial ramifications of the Diallo tragedy, several sidebar articles considered briefly the social and cultural texture of Diallo's life in New York City.[2] In *Money Has No Smell*, I intend to present a more complete portrait of the lives of West African immigrants like Amadou Diallo. To this end, I relate the experiences of several West Africans who have come to North America in search of economic opportunity, for their rich stories underscore many important themes articulated in ongoing scholarly debates on immigration, the informal economy, and the changing nature of communities in North America.

The text that follows is a montage of social analysis and ethnographic description. Janet MacGaffey and Rémy Bazenguissa-Ganga employ a similar strategy in their admirable multisite ethnography *Congo-Paris*, which describes the lives of Central African transnational traders in Paris. In that work MacGaffey and Bazenguissa-Ganga "combine political economy and interpretive anthropology by situating detailed texts on the lives of individuals in the context of trade between countries and continents in the global capitalist economy."[3] Other urban researchers have also employed this technique in recent works—with noteworthy results.[4] Following their example, I employ social analysis to flesh out the stories of immigrants who have left their lives near the hot and dusty wadis of the West African Sahel to make their way on the bustling and gritty streets of New York City. This book, then, is ultimately about the West African immigrant's struggle to maintain a measure of dignity in America.

Money Has No Smell is based on intermittent fieldwork undertaken in New York City from July 1992 to December 1998. The fieldwork consisted mostly of participant observation in street markets along 125th Street and Lenox Avenue and 116th Street and Lenox Avenue, both in Harlem, and along Canal Street between West Broadway and Broadway in lower Manhattan. Other field sites included 6th Avenue near Rockefeller Center, 14th Street between 6th and 5th Avenues, and 27th Street between 11th and 12th Avenues. During this extended period of fieldwork, I used methods similar to those described by Robert Desjarlais in his award-winning study, *Shelter Blues:*

I spent much of my time hanging about, listening to conversations, and then finding a place to write down the gist of these exchanges. . . . My notes on these conversations, which typically contained quasi-verbatim accounts, lacked the precision that tape or audio recordings could have provided. However, as many anthropologists have found, especially those who have worked among homeless populations, the advantages of unassuming participation in daily activities, during which one can develop lasting, informal ties with people, often outweigh the benefits of information obtained through surveys and more intrusive methods.[5]

Although none of the West African traders I met between 1992 and 1998 were homeless, I thought it best to follow Desjarlais's example and adopt an unassuming research strategy. More invasive methods, including the use of a tape recorder, might have made them uneasy. Many of the vendors, after all, were publicly selling wares that violated trademark and copyright statutes. What's more, many of the traders were undocumented immigrants fearful of publicity or special attention. Given these conditions and the primacy that West Africans place on their privacy, I have given pseudonyms to all the traders in the book. In some cases, the professional and domestic particulars of their lives have been altered. All of these matters were discussed and agreed upon prior to publication of this book. It was also agreed that a percentage of the royalty proceeds would be deposited annually in the Samariya Fund, which I have established to give financial assistance to Nigerien immigrants facing legal or medical problems.

Funds for this research were generously provided by the following institutions: the Wenner-Gren Foundation for Anthropological Research, the National Science Foundation (Law and Social Science Program), and West Chester University. The manuscript could not have been completed without sabbatical leave granted to me by West Chester University in the spring of 1998.

No book of any magnitude is the product of a solitary scholar. I have many people to acknowledge. Rosemary J. Coombe, my coinvestor on the National Science Foundation Grant and a specialist in intellectual property law and cultural studies, provided much of the intellectual framework and inspiration for the project. For hospitality and friendship in New York City, I thank Robert Rosenberg and Lisa Ruggeri. For friendship, methodological guidance, and intellectual inspiration, I thank Allen Feldman. For his part, T. David Brent, executive editor at the University of Chicago Press, has been a continuous source of existential encouragement. The copyediting of Carlisle

Rex-Waller saved me from many infelicities. Several friends and colleagues have read some or all of the manuscript and have provided constructive criticisms. They include Rosemary J. Coombe, John Chernoff, Alma Gottlieb, Edith Turner, Neil Lazarus, Linda d'Amico, JoAnn D'Alisera, John Homiak, Allen Feldman, and David Napier as well as two readers for the University of Chicago Press who provided many useful comments. The suggestions of Jasmin Tahmaseb McConatha have been especially important to the development of this book. Feedback from audiences at Brown University, Columbia University, and the University of Illinois, Champaign-Urbana, has also been instrumental in shaping the book. I thank Sarah Castle (then of Brown), Rosalind Morris (Columbia), and Alma Gottlieb (UICU) for inviting me to present lectures.

On Canal Street near Broadway, El Hadj Harouna Souley, a trader from the Republic of Niger in West Africa, sells T-shirts, sweatshirts, and baseball caps from sidewalk shelves wedged between the fronts of two car stereo shops. Whenever I have visited the pious forty-three-year-old, who is called El Hadj because he has already made his pilgrimage to Mecca, he has preached to me about the virtues of Islam. Like his fellow Muslim traders, he tries to pray five times a day. During the month of Ramadan, he fasts during the daylight hours. Whenever he can, he gives to the poor. He also avoids alcohol and pork products. Unlike some of the West African traders, he has remained faithful to his wife, whom he has not seen in more than four years. During our various conversations, he has consistently stressed the morality of pious Muslims and unfailingly decried what he considers the immorality of Americans. "It is accepted here that some men have sex with one another. Men and women think nothing of adultery. Children have babies. People use foul language and show no respect to one another—especially their elders."

During one of these discussions, I pointed to one of the baseball caps he was selling. On the cap's front, bold silver letters spelled out, "Fuck Off." I asked El Hadj Harouna if he knew what that meant.

He said he didn't.

I explained and then asked how a self-proclaimed pious Muslim could sell an item featuring such foul language.

Seeing no dissonance between his views on Islamic morality and his business practices, he said: "We are here in America, trying to make a living. We have to do this to look after our families. Money has no smell."[6]

Merchants at the Malcolm Shabazz Harlem Market dread January. No one likes to be outside on cold, bleak days. Braving plunging January temperatures, the merchants stand stiffly at their market stalls at 116th Street and Lenox Avenue resisting the biting north wind and hoping that shoppers, already jaded by the Christmas holidays, will step out into the frosty air and buy a scarf, a sweater, a wool hat, or a piece of cloth. Even though January is the slowest, most difficult month, the merchants, mostly West Africans from Niger, Mali, Senegal, and the Gambia, show up every day, arrange their product displays, and pray to Allah for a trickle of business.

Issifi Mayaki is no exception. Like some of the other West African traders at the market, he grew up in Niger and Côte d'Ivoire. He came to New York City in 1992 and has traded in Harlem since 1993. Issifi is a Hausa, and the Hausa, a West African ethnic group from Niger and northern Nigeria, are known for their skill in commerce. Issifi's brothers, his father, and his grandfather are all, like him, itinerant merchants.

I went to see Issifi, whom I had known for three years, on the first Saturday in 1997, an unusually warm day for January. Saturdays and Sundays are the most productive days at the Malcolm Shabazz Harlem Market—even in winter. Taking advantage of an uncharacteristically warm day, Issifi had started earlier than usual to set up his display of African print cloth. By the time I arrived at noon, he had already arranged his bolts of cloth on two card tables covered with black felt.

The flair of the display revealed Issifi's sense of style. The table to the left featured assorted bolts of brightly patterned African cloth. Issifi had

THE MALCOLM SHABAZZ HARLEM MARKET, SUMMER 1997. (PHOTO BY JASMIN TAHMASEB MCCONATHA)

placed the prints with bright blue and red backgrounds at the far end of the table. Next to them, midway in his display, he'd arranged more muted colors in descending order of brightness. The effect of this color spectrum was striking. On the table to the right, Issifi had bolts of cloth imported from Mali. At the front he offered mud cloth, also known as *bokolanfani,* created by applying mud in geometric designs to a rectangle of homespun white cloth, which is then dyed black. The process leaves white symbolic patterns on the dark background. Toward the back of this table, he had placed bolts of homespun cloth fashioned in brightly colored stripes. Larger pieces of mud cloth hung like flags from the walls, giving the stall the feel of a salon. A canvas tarpaulin stretched over aluminum poles served as a tent, protecting Issifi—and the other merchants—from sun, rain, and snow but not from the cold wind.

Issifi and I hugged one another and exchanged New Year's greetings. As usual we spoke in French mixed with a smattering of English. Issifi is an attractive man of average height with a fine-featured oval face. He wore a shiny black leather jacket, black corduroy pants, and a black and white cap fashioned from mud cloth. With wire-rimmed glasses framing his soft brown eyes, Issifi cut quite a sophisticated figure. He proudly pointed to a sign hanging at the back of his stall:

IME African Cloth
Booth #185
116th St. & Lenox Ave.
Harlem
7 Days A Week

"I understand what the 'I' is on the sign," I said. "But why the 'M' and the 'E'?"

Issifi smiled with some embarrassment. "The 'M' is for Monique. The 'E' is for enterprises."

Monique was his African American girlfriend, whom I had met on previous visits to the market. "Is she your partner?" I wondered.

"No," he said resolutely. "She isn't. She wanted me to put her initial on the sign and on business cards so that other women would know that I'm taken." He paused a few moments and added. "She gives me a hard time. She doesn't trust me. She wants me all for herself. When I travel she wants other women to know about her."

Meanwhile two African American shoppers perused Issifi's offerings. They seemed more interested in our conversation, some of which had been in English, than in purchasing cloth. Issifi knew both the man and woman—regular customers.

"You're listening to our conversation," he said lightly, but with some embarrassment.

The man smiled and said nothing—a quiet affirmation. He finished looking around and said, "Catch ya later, brother," as he moved away.

"So," I said, resuming the conversation, which I found interesting. "You said Monique gives you trouble?"

"You know how it is," Issifi said. "There are many differences between African and American women. Two different cultures. You lived in Africa. You know how it is."

Issifi was in a confiding mood. He went on to explain his personal situation in great detail. He said that in Africa men could pretty much do as they please. African women, he stated, make few demands of their husbands. A wife usually does not question her husband's decisions or behavior. "I respect my wife and she respects me," he said, "but she doesn't consume me."

"And here?"

"Here," said Issifi shaking his head, "they want to own you, to control your life. And they're jealous."

He described the evolution of his relationship with Monique. When they met on 125th Street in 1994, Issifi told her that he was married and had children. He explained to her that his first allegiance had to be to his family in Africa, meaning his wife and children, his mother and father, and his five brothers. Monique said she understood Issifi's situation and appreciated his candor. As time went on, however, she began to fall in love with him and became more possessive, especially when Issifi told her how much he missed Africa (see chap. 8).

Not having seen his family for five years, Issifi had begun to long for them. "I miss Africa so much that I've become a nasty person, giving everybody a hard time. I really want to go back to see my family."

Issifi's mother is in her mid-fifties and lives near Maradi, Niger, a hot, dusty, windswept region of the West African Sahel. His father and three of his brothers are merchants who live in Abidjan, a major West African commercial center in Côte d'Ivoire. At the time of our conversation, a fourth brother, who had trained as a primary school teacher in Niger, had been living for several years in Melbourne, Australia, where he worked in a boutique specializing in African art.

Talk of his family compelled Issifi to think of his mother. "For me," Issifi said, "there is no more important person than my mother. You know how it is between sons and mothers. I really miss my mother. But when I tell this to Monique, she thinks that I really miss my wife. I care very much for Monique and I respect my wife, but my mother is more important. We are of the same blood."

This longing, according to Issifi, had made him irritable. He reiterated how Americans couldn't understand why family is so important to Africans. "You understand," he said to me, "because you lived there for seven years. But Monique?" He shook his head. "Maybe next year, I'll go back," he went on. "One of my brothers will come here. After I train him, I'll go back to Abidjan and he'll stay here."

"Maybe your brother in Australia could come?"

"I already asked him, but he won't come. He doesn't like Australia. He says that there aren't enough black people there."

"Did you tell him that New York is different?"

"Yeah, but he doesn't believe me. He thinks New York and Australia are the same. One of my other brothers will come."

For some reason the unusual warmth of the day hadn't drawn customers to the market. Merchants passed by offering their greetings to us. A young African American woman asked if Issifi had Dutch Wax cloth. Issifi searched through the bolts and found some. The woman didn't like the color scheme and sauntered away. Issifi faced me squarely and continued our conversation.

"There are two important things in my life: family and the things that stir my heart. I sell my products to any person, Christian or Muslim, pastors or drug dealers, for if I am honest, money has no smell. If God grants me money in exchange for hard honest work, I must first make sure that my family is okay, that they're well fed, well clothed, well housed, and in good health. Then, if there is something left, I buy things that stir my heart."

Issifi pointed to his black leather jacket and said that he bought it at the Gap on Broadway and 75th Street. He touched his corduroy trousers. "The Gap. I bought three pair." He unzipped his jacket to reveal his rust-colored linen shirt. "The Gap, also," he said, smiling.[1]

Issifi's new purchases resulted from economic opportunities sparked by Kwaanza, a recently established African American holiday celebrated between Christmas and the New Year (see chap. 5). During Kwaanza, which commemorates the cultural and historic linkages of Africa and Africa America, Issifi rented space at the Jacob Javits Convention Center, the site of the Metropolitan New York Kwaanza Exposition. He sold a great deal of cloth to African Americans who came to celebrate African values, African culture, and to buy, Issifi added, "African" products. Flush with cash from his Kwaanza success, Issifi sent money orders to his family. Then he followed his heart to the Gap.

But the New Year, as always, brings a shift in economic fortunes. It brings many days when merchants outnumber shoppers at the Malcolm Shabazz Harlem Market. On slow January days, merchants like Issifi welcome the chance to talk to friends, shoppers, and fellow traders. In mixtures of English, French, Hausa, Songhay, Bamana, Malinke, and Wolof, they express their frustrations about living in New York City or work out deals with visiting suppliers or compatriot colleagues. They might travel downtown to Canal Street to buy inventory. As practicing Muslims, they invariably pray at midafternoon, late afternoon, and sunset. Some of them, like Issifi, sit behind their tables quietly studying the Qur'an. And sometimes, when the market lull seems to stop time itself, they stare dreamily out into space and watch the gray sky darken.

Two days after my visit uptown, I ran into Issifi at the Chase Manhattan Bank ATM machine at 73rd Street and Broadway. It was still early in the evening, and after we greeted one another, we walked north together along the west side of Broadway. Issifi was on his way to see a fellow trader and dealer in African art, Hamani Gado, who lived at the Hotel Belleclaire on 77th and Broadway. But since he had some time to kill before his rendezvous, we wandered over to the Gap. His eyes sparkled. I invited him to have dinner with me and some friends. He declined. "I need to see my friend," he stated. "Another time." Smiling, he slipped inside the Gap to browse and perhaps to buy.

•••

In 1996, Issifi had his ups and downs. Like all peddlers, he lives in seasonal limbo. Summers are usually good; winters are usually bad. Like many immigrants in New York City, Issifi has also been in a kind of existential limbo, for in 1996 he was an unregistered alien. Although it was unlikely he would be caught, he lived with the possibility of being detained and deported. His unregistered status also meant that he had some difficulty finding health care, obtaining licenses, and finding wage-paying work with benefits. As is true of most immigrants in New York City, the variegated texture of his life remained unknown to others. Most people who talked to him at the market knew little about his family, his past, his culture, his values, aspirations, or dreams. Although he worked daily on the streets of New York City, he remained, like Ralph Ellison's *Invisible Man*, an unseen person. Like his brother traders, he walked among the shadows, earning money but maintaining a judicious distance from a society whose values he found both fascinating and disturbing.

Issifi and his colleagues from West Africa inhabit one small, virtually unknown niche of urban immigrant America. Their arrival is symptomatic of the groundswell of economic and social change that has profoundly affected North American cities over the past fifteen years.[2] Most writers who have discussed "the new immigration" stress how it has resulted from the economic and social dislocations brought on by globalization.[3] Their analyses are illuminating but seldom do justice to the stories of the real men and women who have left their families to come to places like New York City to earn a living.

This selective inattention is not all that surprising given the invisibility of West African immigrants like Issifi. Indeed, Issifi has multiple invisibilities. He is one of thousands of black men who blend into the background of Harlem. He is a pious Muslim. He is a cosmopolitan African merchant who earns money from African Americans, most of whom have only a partial understanding of his culture or his economic sophistication. In 1996, he was torn by contested allegiances—to his wife and children, to his girlfriend and her child, to his mother, father, and brothers, and to his own desires.

There are thousands of Issifis along the East Coast of the United States. For more than fifteen years, West Africans have steadily poured into New York City. Most of these immigrants, most of them men, have not been formally educated. They are traders or unskilled wage laborers, not diplomats. Many of them make a living as street vendors in Harlem, Brooklyn, and lower Manhattan, where they share informal vending space with African

Americans, Jamaicans, Koreans, Chinese, Vietnamese, Ecuadorians, Mexicans, Pakistanis, and Afghanis. Those who are literate and have work permits may drive Medallion cabs, which are licensed; others, perhaps without documentation, drive the so-called gypsy cabs, which are not always regulated by city hall. The more successful West African traders have used their profits to open restaurants or boutiques like Karta Textiles, a shop on West 125th Street in Harlem that sells cloth and clothing from West Africa. Other merchants operate thriving import-export businesses. From April through October, Issifi sometimes joins the groups of West Africans who pack vans with exotic leather goods, cloth, and jewelry made in Africa, as well as baseball caps and T-shirts—with the logos of American sports teams—made in China and Korea. They tour through what they call the bush—Indianapolis, Kansas City, Detroit—following the African American trade show and convention circuit.[4]

Not all the West Africans living in New York City, however, are merchants. Many of them work as stock clerks, security guards, and grocery store delivery people. On the Upper West Side of Manhattan, for example, many of the stock clerks in Price Wise Discount Drug Stores speak to one another in Wolof, the major Senegalese language, as they take inventory. From 1994 to 1997, their boss, the manager, was also Senegalese. At Lexington and 92nd Street on the Upper East Side of Manhattan, sidewalk conversations sometimes take place in Songhay, a major language in the Republic of Niger, as several Nigeriens take a break from delivering groceries. Larger groups of West African deliverymen can be found in front of Fairway, a large grocery store on Broadway between 74th and 75th Streets. On 110th Street and Lenox, a community of West Africans live in a "vertical village," which they call "Le Cent Dix" (the 110th), a rundown, rat- and drug-infested hotel.[5] Some apartments function as communal kitchens; others operate as "neighborhood" boutiques (see chap. 8).

Deteriorating urban conditions have made the American "bush" more appealing to many West Africans, luring them away from New York City—especially if they have what they call "papers," namely, an employment authorization permit from the U.S. Immigration and Naturalization Service (INS). This card not only enables them to drive registered cabs, but also allows them, unlike Issifi, to work for wages in factories and stores.

Several years ago a toy factory in Providence, Rhode Island, attracted a small group of Guineans and Senegalese to that community.[6] When the toy factory closed, workers dispersed to Boston and New York City. A woman from Côte d'Ivoire who chose to remain opened the Restaurant Benkady, featuring West African cuisine. On Saturday nights, she transforms the restaurant into a West African club—food, music, dance, and an occasional fashion show. In Philadelphia, Senegalese have sold Africana at the Reading Terminal Market in Center City; Malians, Nigeriens, and Senegalese sell T-shirts, sunglasses, incense, and handbags on 40th street near the University of Pennsylvania. Like some of their brothers in New York City, West Africans drive cabs in the City of Brotherly Love. When asked why he had come to Philadelphia, one cabby from Ghana told a colleague of mine: "Because there is no room in New York."

In Washington, D.C., Muslim men from Sierra Leone also drive taxis. Muslim women from the same country sell hot dogs along Connecticut Avenue and K Street, competing directly with Ethiopian women in the kosher

FLYER FOR RESTAURANT BENKADY. (PHOTO BY AUTHOR)

hot dog street trade.[7] On Columbia Road in Washington's Adams Morgan neighborhood, a Malian street vendor has been selling African leather goods from Mali and Niger for more than twelve years. He routinely houses his many cousins and "little brothers" who come as tourists to the nation's capital. In Greensboro, North Carolina, a growing community of West Africans (Ghanaians, Nigerians, Malians, Senegalese, and Nigeriens) has taken root and grown. In 2000, Nigerien traders estimated that nine thousand of their compatriots lived in Greensboro. Most of these new immigrants work in factories and restaurants. Many of them hold two jobs, work seven days a week, and sleep only three to four hours a day.

Immigration to the United States has intensified during the past fifteen years. The United States is, in fact, "experiencing the largest wave of immigration in the country's history. The 1990s saw more new immigrants enter the United States than in any decade in American history." According to the 2000 census, one in every ten Americans is foreign born.[8] But recent immigration is different from that of the past. The majority of recent immigrants are poorly educated people of color from third world nations. Like previous generations of newcomers, many of these immigrants—both registered and unregistered—have no intention of remaining in the United States. They come to exploit what often turn out to be disappointing economic opportunities. Most of them send much of their meager earnings back home to their families. Most of them want to return one day to their country of origin.

As the waves of new immigrants come and go, culturally distinct immigrant communities have taken root in many urban, suburban, and rural areas of the United States. The presence of these neighborhoods within neighborhoods has threatened the myth of the American melting pot, making the new immigration a bitter political issue of national scope. By the same token, the proximity of peoples with conflicting social practices has sparked controversy in local contexts. In 1994, there was great debate in Harlem, for example, about the expanding presence of vendors, mostly West Africans, along the sidewalks of 125th Street (see chap. 7). The Harlem business establishment eventually convinced Mayor Rudolph Giuliani that illegal vendors had to be dispersed from Harlem's major commercial thoroughfare.[9]

Men like Issifi may seem mere pawns in the scheme of global economics, national politics, and local confrontation. But they are quietly redefining the boundaries of urban economic and social practices. Their stories demonstrate the dynamic tensions that make the linkages between the global and the local vibrate with creative energy. They have much to teach us about life in contemporary North America.

This book is mostly the story of the lives of Issifi and several of his compatriots in New York City. It is an attempt to render the invisible visible, to bring into relief Issifi's complex understanding of our world, to listen to the people who live in one of many fragmented sociocultural niches now emerging from the shadows of our complex society. And yet this book is not a life history; rather, it uses Issifi's unique perspective—as well as those of several of his West African friends—on city life in New York as one way of approaching the underside of urban social life in contemporary North America.

The book's chapters explore, layer by layer, the adventure of West African traders to and in the United States. What economic and social forces compelled them to leave West Africa? In the absence of family, why do they choose to remain in New York City? What set of values do the traders bring to the trading enterprise and how do those values affect their social and economic lives in New York City? How is Issifi, for example, able to operate IME African Cloth? Who are his suppliers? What are his marketing strategies? How do he and his colleagues manipulate Afrocentricity to their economic advantage? How have Issifi and his brother traders adjusted to living with the rules and regulations imposed by the federal government and the City of New York? How do global, national, and local politics affect their economic and social life in New York City? What is the quality of their life there, their personal struggles and triumphs? Finally, what can the unique perspective of Issifi teach us about the nature of social life in contemporary America?

In the pages that follow, I explore the personal and theoretical issues that these questions implicate. I hope to demonstrate that West African traders in New York City are a savvy group of entrepreneurs who have built cohesive and effective transnational trading networks. In so doing, they have realized the economic power of simulation. By "selling" a simulated Africa to African Americans, they have substantially expanded their economic pursuits as well as their profits. Even so, the traders must confront the economic and personal constraints of a dizzying array of government regulations. Even though they have managed to deal with these regulations, city life in New York is no simple matter. The traders are, for the most part, culturally alienated from American life. To combat this alienation, they have used their various networks to construct an array of community forms that provide the potential for economic, political, and cultural integration. In the end, their tales of economic agility and cultural dexterity teach us a great deal about the complex textures of social life in contemporary urban worlds.

In October 1994, two men in black suits and bow ties hawked Nation of Islam pamphlets and sold bean pies on the northeast corner of 125th Street and Lenox Avenue, the commercial crossroads of Harlem. It was a sunny and crisp day. The sky was deep blue and the wind was calm. People streamed along the sidewalks. Traffic choked the intersection: buses transported people to appointments uptown and downtown, fleets of large delivery trucks made their rounds, late-model cars blared rap music as they passed through, and older more silent clunkers featured hand-lettered signs that said "livery" or "taxi." These gas-guzzlers were gypsy cabs, the main substitute for taxis in the poorer neighborhoods of New York City; their drivers discharged and picked up fares at 125th and Lenox.[1]

The crowds thickened considerably on the west side of Lenox Avenue at 125th Street, the site of the African market. From a distance, the market was a collage of parked vans, aluminum tables, incense smoke, and brilliantly colored and patterned cloth. People sauntered through this space, pausing here to chat, there to bargain and perhaps buy strips of brightly colored Ghanaian kente cloth, Kenyan baskets, leather bags from Niger, Meccan incense, West African trade beads, or Tuareg silver jewelry. They could also select from assortments of "trademarked" American T-shirts, sunglasses, handbags, and baseball caps, almost all of which were manufactured in export processing zones outside the United States.

At first glance the African market appeared to be pure chaos, sidewalks cluttered with vendors' tables. To an outsider, nothing seemed to govern where or what a vendor might sell. But first impressions were misleading, for the space of the African market had its own organization, albeit an informal one.

Such informal organization is the hallmark of markets throughout West Africa. As in Harlem, the movement of goods and peoples through open market space in West Africa appears chaotic to outsiders—at least initially. It is well known, however, that the space of most West African markets is often, if not always, apportioned and regulated through informal mechanisms.[2] Members of the same ethnic group or small village usually occupy contiguous space and sell the same kind of merchandise. In the larger Songhay/Zarma markets in the Republic of Niger, for example, Fulani herders sell cattle, milk, and butter; Hausa people butcher and sell meat; Yorubas from Nigeria sell pots, pans, and hardware; and Songhay/Zarma people sell grain and spices—all from spaces informally designated for these products.

The story of markets in West Africa is one of great sociological and religious complexity. Since medieval times, the lure of trade and markets has spurred the spread of Islam from North to West Africa. The attraction of centralized urban markets has also sparked urban migration throughout West Africa. The history of migration—long and short term over the past century and more—of Songhay and Hausa from Niger to the Guinea Coast is a case in point.[3] Men like Issifi Mayaki and his compatriots in New York City have extended this long-standing tradition of economic migration to North America.

In the West African political arena, Islam has provided the context for the construction of specific religious identities that have continuously fragmented local, regional, and state social relations in West Africa.[4] The Quadiriyya, Tijaniyya, Hammaliyya, and Muridiyya all represent Sufi brotherhoods in West Africa. The Wahhabiyyas are antimystical and reject Sufi practices. Differences among all of these sects have aroused political schism and turmoil in West Africa. But despite the frictions generated by religious fragmentation, it has not usually interfered with trade. The Muridiyya, for example, are an important political force in Senegal. Their international economic networks have become increasingly important in Europe and North America, especially New York City.[5] As Emmanuel Gregoire wrote in his study of Islam and identity among the Hausa in Niger: "A marabout explained, 'You can do business with anybody; what's important is to earn a profit.' Another went even further: 'Money has no smell, and you can, indeed, do business with non-Muslims, with Christians for example.'"[6]

This rich and complex set of traditions and practices influences the attitudes and behaviors of Issifi and other West African traders in New York City (see chap. 3). The now defunct 125th Street space was organized like many West African markets, though more by country of origin than by ethnic identity. Malians, for example, were the principal cloth merchants. They sold from tables and stalls along both sides of the wide Lenox Avenue sidewalk. Pockets of Malians could also be found along the north sidewalk of 125th Street. Senegalese and Gambians occupied the northwestern corner of 125th and Lenox, where they sold trade beads, incense, leather bracelets decorated with cowry shells, and earrings and rings also decorated with cowry shells. Walking farther west on 125th Street, one passed some African Americans selling religious books, including the Qur'an. One bookseller hawked Afrocentric titles as well as cassettes (see chap. 5). He displayed books on two tables. Videos, including lectures by Ivan Van Sertima, an Afrocentric historian, were projected on a television set on the roof of the vendor's parked car—a complex articulation of multiple ideologies in the space of fifty feet.

Farther west, on the north side of 125th Street, one approached the Carver State Bank and the vendor space occupied by Issifi's compatriots. Some of these Nigerien vendors sold handbags from Korea; others hawked straw hats from China or straw bags from Kenya. One man offered kilim bags from Turkey and leather bags from Niger. Another Nigerien sold sunglasses from Chinatown in the summer and pirated videos in the winter. In order to demonstrate the quality of the videos, he had placed a television and video playback machine on his vending table. These were wired to a car battery under the table. Other Nigeriens offered baseball caps with the insignias of professional and college sports teams. Other caps, T-shirts, and sweatshirts were inscribed with trademarked social messages from film director Spike Lee or with such trademarked names as Hugo Boss, Karl Kani, or Timberland.

Moving ever westward, one came upon the Adam Clayton Powell State Office Building. Here were Senegalese selling sunglasses (including Ray Bans), dolls, and jewelry. A vendor from Uganda sold print reproductions of batiks. Toward the corner of 125th Street and 7th Avenue, Jamaicans sold what West African vendors call "wood"—statues carved in Africa.[7] Much of this "wood" had been carved in the parodic image of West African colonial officials. This type of African art (known as the "colon") has become commercially viable, perhaps because it ironically accords well with mainstream tastes for colonial nostalgia as well as African pride. In Harlem, dreadlocked men from the Caribbean, situated among closely cropped West Africans, sold "authentic" images of African pride, most of which were incomprehensible to the Africans "represented" by the statuettes.

Unlike West African markets, none of these "national" spaces in Harlem was purely national.[8] A few African American vendors could be found among the Malians, Senegalese, and Nigeriens. Several Malians operated from tables among Nigeriens. Small clusters of Senegalese sat next to Jamaicans. No "national" space was inviolable at the African market.

The market's informality gave it an easy, festive air. Double-decker buses from Apple Tours brought camera-packing Europeans to shoot the African market—from a safe distance. Swarms of shoppers moved freely up and down the sidewalks, looking at bags, touching print fabrics, trying on straw hats or jewelry. Their movement was constrained only by the presence of other shoppers and by Senegalese women selling African food from shopping carts.

The vendors talked freely to shoppers in American English of varying degrees of sophistication, a lingo influenced by local African American idioms. The traders conversed among themselves in English, French, and a variety of West African languages, enjoying the banter that comes with periodic lulls in trading. During their afternoon prayers, the vendors looked after one another's merchandise—informal protection against the ever-present threat of theft.

The easy, festive openness of the 125th Street African market, however, came to an abrupt end on October 17, 1994, when Mayor Rudolph Giuliani, responding to political pressures, ordered it closed (see chap. 7). Most of the African traders, including Issifi, relocated to the Masjid Malcolm Shabazz Harlem Market on 116th Street and Lenox Avenue. Others set up operations on Canal Street in lower Manhattan. Still others left New York and sought wage-labor jobs.

Throughout 1994, Issifi Mayaki worked the 125th Street African market, but not by choice. He had come to the United States in 1992 as a cloth merchant, not a street vendor. For most of his adult life, in fact, Issifi had surrounded himself with cloth. He learned the business from his father, who had lived for many years in Côte d'Ivoire, establishing contacts with indigenous cloth producers in southern Mali, Ghana, and Nigeria. In time, Issifi had created his own network of indigenous producers in Mali (for mud cloth), Côte d'Ivoire (for Senufo cloth), and Ghana (for kente cloth). While his father bought and sold a wide variety of goods, Issifi soon realized that Europeans would pay handsome sums for prized pieces of cloth. Patiently, he traveled to the hinterlands to create profitable economic relationships. He bought cloth of varying quality. Eventually Issifi set up a stall in Abidjan's Treichville market.

Like most African markets, the one in Abidjan is divided by product and ethnic group. Hausa merchants sell the great majority of African art and textiles in Abidjan. Like Issifi, they come from Niger and northern Nigeria. The economic challenge in such market circumstances is to distinguish one's business from that of others. There are two ways to accomplish this business goal: (a) purchase superior merchandise and (b) attract loyal customers through the force of one's personality. Issifi would purchase a few quality antique pieces, but he also counted on his charm to drive his business.

He realized that he could improve sales if he cultivated clients in the considerable and well-healed expatriate community of Abidjan. With his impeccable French, he could visit the homes of French expatriates and give them private showings. By studying English, he began to court diplomats from England, Australia, and the United States. "The difference between me and some of my compatriots," Issifi told me, "is that I realized that English was a route to success. Many of my colleagues never learned English, let alone French. What kind of business could they do in Abidjan or New York?"

As Issifi's English improved so did his business fortunes. He became an African textile resource for the American diplomatic community. He sold cloth to officials of the State Department, USAID contractors, Peace Corps volunteers, officials from nonprofit voluntary organizations like CARE, as well as to the American ambassador himself. His renown soon attracted visitors to his stall, which meant that the sale of cloth to tourists increased—especially African Americans who seemed eager to buy his antique cloth. "They wanted some concrete memento of their trip to Africa, which, I'm sure had great meaning for them. They were happy to give me my price."[9]

Issifi's path to New York City resembles the one taken by Gaabe Barré, the central character in Lucien Taylor, Ilisa Barbarsh, and Christopher Steiner's award-winning documentary film *In and Out of Africa* (1992). Like Issifi, Gaabe Barré is a Hausa from Niger. Through diligence, knowledge, and skill, Barré has become a successful international art broker. The film follows Barré as he packs and ships "wood" in Abidjan and unloads, doctors, and sells it in New York City and East Hampton. In 1992, Issifi followed Barré's path to the lucrative New York market. Taking a gamble, he airfreighted much of his inventory of cloth from Abidjan to New York. Upon his arrival, he quickly found lodging with brother traders in the Hotel Belleclaire, a rundown single-room occupancy (SRO) hotel at Broadway and 77th Street on the Upper West Side (see chap. 8). From his cramped room—despite its SRO designation shared with as many as four other traders—he set out to make his killing in New York and beyond.

Issifi's introduction to the realities of the international trade in New York City proved brutal. Several weeks into his sojourn, a trading partner refused to pay him for a large shipment of kente cloth. His telephone calls and faxes to the partner went unanswered. What had taken Issifi years to collect in Africa had been lost in a matter of weeks—without a trace.

The loss of Issifi's inventory left him completely stranded. In order to obtain a six-month business visa to the United States, most African art traders are required to buy round-trip airfares between West Africa and New York City. They often sell the return portion of their tickets to raise more operating capital. When the time comes to return, they use the proceeds of their sales to finance their flight home. By the time of the theft, Issifi had already sold the return portion of his ticket and had already spent most of his money.

Issifi looked to his compatriots for assistance. Informal credit associations are common among West African traders in New York City. When a trader suffers a theft, his compatriots use pooled money to offer him a loan to buy new inventory. Issifi received such a loan, bought rap, rhythm and blues, and jazz cassettes and set up a table on 125th Street west of 7th Avenue, just opposite the Apollo Theater. Since he planned to sell the cassettes to African Americans, it seemed reasonable to position his table near the great hallmark of African American music. He sold cassettes steadily and remained at the Hotel Belleclaire. In 1994 he moved in with another Hausa trader, Sala Fari, who lived in a tenement on Lenox Avenue near 126th Street. When the police dispersed the 125th Street market, Issifi relocated to the Malcolm Shabazz Harlem Market, where he rented a stall for seven dollars a day and began to sell cloth along with cassettes and a few CDs. In 1995 he increased his investment in cloth, buying large supplies from West African wholesalers. In time, Issifi once again became cloth merchant. "The margin of profit," he told me one day, "is much higher on cloth. You don't make enough money selling cassettes and CDs." He smiled. "I make more money now."

And so a business trip from Abidjan to New York City compelled Issifi to adjust his business—and his life. This Nigerien who once lived in Treichville, Abidjan, now lived in Harlem, New York City. Once surrounded by a majority of Hausa, Songhay, Bamana, Baulé, Dan, and Abron, he now found himself an invisible black immigrant living among thousands of African Americans.

"Was it difficult to negotiate the crossroads of New York City?" I once asked him.

"Life in New York," he answered, "is filled with uncertainties. If I fall sick, will I be able to get help? Will immigration detain and deport me? Will I make enough money to send to my family in Niger and Côte d'Ivoire? Will I make enough to pay my bills? So far, God has blessed me. The only certainty is that I have always been a trader and will always be a trader. That will see me through every crossroads that I come upon."[10]

•••

Before 1980, it would have been unthinkable for men like Issifi to travel to New York City in search of economic opportunity. In the past, the great majority of West African traders went to France in search of European profits. West Africans who ventured to New York City came as students or diplomats. What forces brought Issifi and his compatriots to North America?

Although it could be argued that more repressive French immigration policies triggered increased West African immigration to North America, most scholars seek a broader explanation. They believe that the increased migration of third world peoples—including West Africans—to North America devolves directly from what economists call global restructuring. As a complex of economic, political, geographic, and sociocultural phenomena, global restructuring has spurred the growth of multinational corporations and imploded notions of space and time. Its changes have encouraged the outplacement of manufacturing from the first to the third world, the outsourcing of industrial parts, and the downsizing of corporate payrolls.[11] The emergence of globalized financial markets has contributed to the feminization of the workforce in rapidly proliferating export processing zones, eroded large sectors of the American middle classes, and induced the exponential growth of informal economies.[12]

This complex of relations has thus led less to the global integration of human and economic resources than to the polarization of rich and poor. This polarization is particularly evident in sub-Saharan Africa, a region of the world in which "the number of poor will rise by 85 million to 265 million by the year 2000."[13] Economic problems in West Africa, for example, have recently been exacerbated by the World Bank's insistence that credit-hungry West African governments live within their means, no matter the volatility of international currency markets.[14] The resulting devaluation of the West African franc in 1994, which in one day lowered the region's standard of living by 50 percent, affected the lives of millions of people, including traders, who liquidated their inventories and headed to New York City.[15]

New York City, which most arriving West African traders considered a garden of economic opportunity, is of course no stranger to social and economic polarization. Manufacturing in New York, once a center of the industrial economy, has declined substantially during the past thirty years, resulting in the loss of hundreds of thousands of stable factory jobs. Financial service industries, the key component of the postindustrial economy, have replaced the manufacturing sector, attracting to New York a managerial elite in advertising, finance, real estate, and information technology. This service industry requires a legion of clerical workers, most of them women work-ing for low wages, with little security and limited health insurance.[16] The forces that have made New York what Saskia Sassen has called a "global city" have also provoked massive economic and spatial dislocations, creating what John Mollenkopf calls a "dual city." In the dual city, a "core" group of highly trained professionals wired into the global economy are set apart from an increasingly transnational "periphery," whose members are more and more powerless to influence the elite group from whom they derive limited forms of security.[17]

The expansion of the gulf between rich and poor in New York City has cre-ated space for the rapid growth of an informal economy. As leading scholars suggest, the worldwide growth of informal entrepreneurial activities, which are unregulated, devolved from global restructuring.

> The term informal sector has come to replace more pejorative terms like the black market and the underground economy, for what makes an activity in-formal is not its substance, the validity of the goods or services produced, the character of the labor force or the site of production, but the fact that "it is unregulated by the institutions of society, in a legal and social environ-ment in which similar activities are regulated" (Castells and Portes 1989, 12). The parent who purchases day care service without filling out social security forms, the unlicensed gypsy cab driver who serves poor neighborhoods, the craftsperson building furniture in an area not zoned for manufacturing ac-tivity, the immigrant woman reading pap smears or sewing teddy bears in a poorly lit suburban garage, and the unlicensed African street vendor are all participating in the burgeoning informal economy that characterizes a global city like New York.[18]

From West African villages, New York City glitters with economic opportu-nity. Ironically, this view is shared by the elite managers of the service indus-try that dominates the formal sector. From the perspective of people living in the Bronx, East New York, or Harlem, however, New York City is too often a place of despair, disenfranchisement, drugs, and crime—a place dominated by the informal sector. And it is in this New York that West African traders like Issifi live.

At first many of the West Africans attracted by the global lights naively expected to earn decent wages in the formal sector. They did not come to New York, according to many of them, to settle, but to make as much money as possible and then return home. After arriving, they soon found out that their lack of English, limited technological skills, and murky immigration status made working in the regulated economy a difficult prospect at best. Facing this hard reality, West Africans entered the informal economy, many of them becoming street vendors. West Africans who have arrived in New York City more recently harbor no illusions about economic life in contemporary New York; most of them expect to work in the informal sector.

Prior to 1990, the primary West African traders were Senegalese men, vending from tables set up along midtown Manhattan sidewalks. Given the difficulties of obtaining a vending license from New York City, the majority of the Senegalese conducted unlicensed operations.[19] By 1985 scores of Senegalese had set up tables in front of some of Manhattan's most expensive retail space along 5th Avenue. This cluttered third world place in a first world space soon proved intolerable to the 5th Avenue Merchants Association. Headed by Donald Trump, the association urged city hall to crack down on the unlicensed vendors. Mayor Koch granted the association its wish.

Following the cleanup, Senegalese vendors relocated to less precious spaces in Midtown: Lexington Avenue, 42nd Street near Grand Central Station, and 34th Street near Times Square, to name several locations. They worked in teams to protect themselves from the authorities and petty criminals. One person would sell goods at a table. His partners would post themselves on corners as lookouts. Another compatriot would serve as the bank, holding money safely away from the trade. In this way, Midtown side streets became Senegalese turf.

As more and more Senegalese arrived in New York City, the vending territory expanded north to 86th Street on the East Side and south to 14th Street in Greenwich Village and Canal Street in lower Manhattan. In some areas, the Senegalese replaced vending tables with attaché cases filled with "Rolex" and other "high end" watches.

By 1990, the Senegalese had a lock on informal vending space in most of Manhattan. Backed by the considerable financial power of the Mourids, a Muslim Sufi brotherhood in Senegal to which many of the vendors belonged, the Senegalese soon became the aristocracy of West African merchants in New York City.[20] When merchants from Mali and Niger immigrated to New York City in 1989 and 1990, the Senegalese had already saturated the lucrative Midtown markets, compelling the latecomers to set up their tables along 125th Street, the major commercial thoroughfare in Harlem.

Although African Americans have a long history of vending on the streets of Harlem,[21] the informal 125th Street market gradually took on more and more of an African character. Between 1990 and 1992, the so-called African market grew substantially. Although vendors reported that business along

AFRICANA ON SALE AT THE 125TH STREET MARKET, HARLEM, SUMMER 1994. (PHOTO BY AUTHOR)

125th Street was fair during the week, on weekends the market swelled with shoppers. By 1992 the African market had become one of New York City's tourist attractions—one of the photo opportunities for tourists on double-decker tour buses following uptown routes.

The success of the market provoked a spate of political problems (see chap. 7). Harlem's business and political leaders lobbied the Dinkins administration to disperse the "illegal" market. Mayor Dinkins attempted to disband it, but he backed down when confronted with a raucous demonstration. The beginning of the Giuliani administration, however, meant the end of the African market on 125th Street. On October 17, 1994, Mayor Giuliani declared street vending illegal on 125th Street. Although the 125th Street Vendors Association staged a protest, the vendors did, indeed, disperse. Many of the West African vendors moved their operations to the new Harlem market on 116th Street and Lenox Avenue. Owned and managed by the Masjid Malcolm Shabazz (the religious organization founded by Malcolm X), the majority of this market's vendors are, like Issifi, from West Africa. Other West African vendors set up shop along Canal Street. Still others who had obtained employment authorization permits found work as security guards, or low-skill workers in factories, restaurants, liquor stores, and drugstores. Some of the traders moved away from New York, seeking wage labor in more rural areas where the cost of living is more reasonable. Several vendors returned to West Africa.

The majority of vendors from Niger and Mali live in apartments with one or two of their compatriots. Vendors who work the 116th Street market usually live in Harlem or the South Bronx. Traders who work in lower Manhattan often live in Brooklyn in buildings where the occupants are almost exclusively West Africans. None of the vendors I've met live outside the New York City limits.

The population of West African street vendors is predominantly male. Most traders, young and middle-aged alike, leave their wives and children in West Africa and wire home as much money as they can. Several of the vendors, though, have married American women and have started North American families, which usually means that they support families on two continents.

In Islam, these transnational family practices present no moral or legal problems, although they sometimes increase the instability of marriages. In fact, the practice of settling and starting a family in another country, even if only for a limited period of years, extends the long-standing West African tradition of long-distance trading in foreign lands.[22] A generation ago, for example, large numbers of Nigeriens, like Issifi's father, settled in Côte d'Ivoire or Ghana. Some of them married Ghanaian or Ivorien women and raised families. Most of them eventually returned to their first families in Niger, leaving their Ghanaian or Ivorien families behind. From Niger, they would try to send money regularly to Ghana or Côte d'Ivoire and would periodically visit their coastal families.

The vast majority of traders, however, do not marry American women. Even if they have wives in West Africa, they sometimes present themselves to local women as single men in search of companionship. There are also traders who remain resolutely faithful to their wives in West Africa, but they are usually older men who tend to be rather strict Muslims.

Between 1992 and 1998, there were also a few female traders at the Harlem markets, mostly middle-aged Wolof women from Senegal, who sold dolls, jewelry, and cooked food. Some of these women are single entrepreneurs who divide their time between Senegal and New York City; others have accompanied their husbands to New York. Senegalese women have also opened thriving hair salons in Harlem and Brooklyn.

Almost all the West African traders are practicing Muslims. If they are able, most of them pray five times a day and follow Muslim dietary restrictions, avoiding pork products and buying lamb and beef from Muslim butchers. Traders at the 116th Street market attend Friday Sabbath services at the Malcolm Shabazz mosque on 116th and Lenox Avenue. They also observe the Ramadan rituals, fasting from sun up to sun down. Indeed, during the month of Ramadan in 1996 and 1997, the Masjid Malcolm Shabazz, the managers of the 116th Street market, prohibited the daytime sale of cooked foods in their market space. Muslim clerics from West Africa, many of whom are Islamic healers, routinely visit New York City to treat the traders' physical disorders with herbal medicines. Traders also seek their advice about social and psychological problems.

The traders face a host of social and economic problems. Like Issifi, they usually live in outrageously expensive substandard housing located in crime-infested neighborhoods, which, as the tragic killing of Amadou Diallo demonstrated, are too vigorously patrolled by special police units. Like all peddlers, their fortunes rise and fall with the seasons. In summer they may have plenty of money in their pockets; in winter they often suffer from financial as well as meteorological freezes. They have limited access to medical care, let alone medical insurance. Many of the traders don't like going to public hospitals where medical staffers often have difficulty understanding their English, let alone their French, Wolof, Bamana, Songhay, or Hausa.

For most of the traders, however, the defining social problem is their immigration status. Traders with green cards (permanent residence card), a very small minority indeed, are free to travel and work as they please (see chap. 6). Traders with employment authorization permits, which are issued to immigrants who have married American women or who have been granted political asylum, are also free to work in either the formal or informal sector. They must renew their authorizations every year. Sometimes the INS restricts travel to the work permit holder's country of origin.[23]

Many West African traders in New York City are like Issifi—undocumented immigrants. This status makes it risky for them to travel outside the city limits, where many say they feel more vulnerable to American law enforcement. Lack of documentation means they may avoid going to physicians, postpone English instruction at night schools, keep their proceeds in cash rather than bank accounts, and fail to report the theft of inventory. Although

I don't know of any West Africans who have been deported, many of them fear being placed in detention or sent home—in disgrace (see chap. 8). Many undocumented traders spend much of their time trying to obtain what they call "papers." They hire immigration brokers to fill out forms and immigration lawyers to represent them at the INS.

In short, this community of documented and undocumented West African traders is profoundly transnational. Only a small percentage of traders have married American women and started families. These men, who are among the most successful traders, still hope to raise their children in West Africa as well as in New York. The vast majority of traders, however, remain single and have no plans to marry in America. As they almost invariably put it, they've come to exploit an economic situation and return to West Africa as soon as they possibly can. In other words, they will leave New York when they've made enough money to return home with dignity and start a new enterprise.

Few of the traders aspire to American citizenship and they feel little connection to the communities in which they live. As a result, they contribute little to community life in places like Harlem, where I've often heard local shoppers grumbling about how the African traders have exploited them. This attitude, expressed all too frequently, has kept a low-grade fever of mutual resentment simmering between West African traders and African American shoppers. The sociocultural, legal, and political tensions of living in New York City have also hardened the negative impressions of many West Africans about America as a violent, insensitive, rushed society where morally depleted people (non-Muslims) haven't enough time to take care of one another. To counter these alienating qualities, West African traders have created formal voluntary associations for mutual protection (for example, the Association de Nigeriens de New York and the Club des Femmes d'Affairs Africaines), as well as informal associations for purposes of emergency credit. It was from an informal credit association that Issifi received the loan that enabled him to start a vending business at the commercial crossroads of Harlem, the cultural crossroads of Africa America.

In West African cosmology, crossroads are points of danger and trickery. Among the Yoruba people of southern Nigeria, for example, crossroads are the domain of Eshu, the trickster deity. Accordingly, crossroads must be approached carefully and negotiated with the greatest of care. It is easy, after all, to lose one's way. For the Songhay people of the Republics of Niger and Mali, crossroads are points of existential danger where decisions of depth and consequence are deliberated and made. Even carefully made decisions can have ramifications that threaten a person's very existence.

From a West African vantage, one should never underestimate the difficulty of negotiating a crossroads; it requires courage, daring, and imagination. Courage is necessary to resist the very real temptation to turn around and embrace the comforts of the past. Daring is required to fight off the pull of false consciousness. It is easy to take the most direct—and painless—path into the unknown. Imagination is needed to avoid the pitfalls of new terrain.

Issifi has been well aware of the perils of negotiating crossroads in West Africa, let alone in North America. He demonstrated considerable courage by taking the economic and social risks to ship his inventory of cloth from Abidjan to New York City. When betrayal brought his cloth enterprise to a full stop, he dared to change course and begin a new enterprise in Harlem. His imagination compelled him to adjust his business practices to changing local conditions. In time, he was able to stabilize his economic position and begin to reestablish his cloth enterprise.

But Issifi's ongoing negotiations of crossroads did not end with his changing economic circumstances. In the space of just a few months, he left the culturally familiar and comfortable confines of being an African among Africans at the Treichville market in Abidjan where he sold African cloth to Europeans. He arrived in New York City and immediately found himself in the culturally unfamiliar and uncomfortable confines of being an African among African Americans on 125th Street in Harlem where he sold African American music to African Americans. To his credit, he quickly adapted to the cultural and economic ground rules of informal vending on 125th Street, the most significant thoroughfare in the cultural capital of Africa America.

Anthropologists, too, must face the delicate and humbling task of negotiating crossroads. Prior to beginning ethnographic fieldwork in New York City in 1992, my research experience had been in the rural western region of the Republic of Niger, where I conducted fieldwork in ethnically diverse villages. Despite the multiethnicity of these villages, I focused my attention on the majority population, the Songhay people, who had been in residence for almost a thousand years. In addition to their glorious history of empire and conquest, the Songhay regularly practiced such profoundly interesting religious rituals as spirit possession and sorcery. Since the solitary ethnographer cannot describe everything in the field, I concentrated on Songhay religious practices. This decision meant that I backgrounded many significant topics: the political economy of multiethnic diversity in western Niger, the social importance of Islam, and the impact of modernization on cultural identity and production.

Between 1977 and 1990, I periodically lived in rural Nigerien villages like Tillaberi, Mehanna, and Wanzerbé, where I listened to the stories of sorcerers, spirit possession priests, and spirit mediums. As I returned to the field year after year, these practitioners asked me to participate in Songhay religious ceremonies. Through this participation I came to understand that, in Niger at least, it was best to conduct research in a slow-paced and open-ended manner. In this way, the longer the period of research, the more involved one became in a network of social relationships, all of which bore personal as well as professional consequences.

During the time of my fieldwork in Niger, I nevertheless felt economically, socially, and politically autonomous. The government of Niger had officially sanctioned my presence; indeed, I carried a research authorization letter signed by the president of the Republic. This autonomy also resulted from Niger's colonial legacy. Although Niger became independent seventeen years before I began my research, the cultural reality of colonialism seemed very much intact.[24] Peasants used categories of race to resent and revere the French, to admire modern technology, and to denigrate African backwardness.

My whiteness in spaces of colonized blackness made aspects of my research frustrating, for most people categorized me as a rich white tourist seeking adventure in Africa. Accordingly, typical interactions took on mercenary dimensions. When people heard me speak the Songhay language, however, they smiled and wondered where I had learned it. Perhaps their attitude toward my whiteness had softened a bit, but it hadn't changed, as I was to learn later on. In only a handful of relationships, in fact, did Songhay friends and I cross the racial divide defined by Nigerien colonial culture.

The contours of the racial terrain in which I found myself had other repercussions for my work. Racial and cultural difference may have made me by definition untrustworthy, but it also identified me as someone who had to be accommodated. Many of the people who listened to my endless questions probably felt that they had no choice but to answer—no matter how much charm I attempted to call upon. Several spirit possession priests did not like the fact that I attended ceremonies and had been given a minor position in the Tillaberi spirit possession troupe. And yet, between 1977 and 1990, they did little to block my research. I had, after all, a government authorization and the backing of the region's most senior spirit possession priests and sorcerers, who for their own reasons thought highly of my research. As for the dissenters, they probably concluded that I was too close to power to be ignored and too far away from their social experience to be trusted. This sociological context made me morally but not politically accountable.

The cultural and political realities of working among West African street vendors in Harlem compelled me to change my research practices. Soon after my initial confrontation with street traders in Harlem in 1992, I realized that I would grasp little of the trader's ethnographic present if I didn't understand the global forces that had compelled them to leave West Africa. I also needed to understand more fully the political, economic, and racial contexts in which they found themselves. I no longer had the luxury of focusing on one narrowly defined cultural element, but had to embrace sociocultural complexity. This shift meant that I needed to be more thoroughly grounded in urban and immigration studies—economics, geography, law, political science, and urban sociology.

Working on 125th Street in Harlem also meant that I had to learn how to do North American street ethnography among a mix of people, many of whom were in violation of city regulations, trademark and copyright statutes, and immigration laws. The precarious situation of the traders, of course, made them suspicious of *any* newcomer, even one who spoke an African language. Rather than plunging into the field with a barrage of demographic surveys or intensive participant observation, I decided to start hanging out at the 125th Street market. I told the traders from the start that I was an anthropologist who had spent a lot of time in Niger, and I gave them examples of my work. I told them that I wanted to continue my visits and eventually write a book about their experiences in New York City. They encouraged me to come and talk and bring my friends. From that point on, we sat together behind their tables, ate lunch, traded stories, and interacted with shoppers. The traders gradually invited me into their lives, sharing with me their frustrations, loneliness, insecurities, triumphs, and disappointments. After two years of low-key interactions, one of the traders invited me to his apartment. After three years of intermittent fieldwork, an older trader told me how he had treated his compatriots with herbal medicines. Another man revealed that he headed a thriving import-export enterprise that required monthly trips between Abidjan and New York. Several traders asked me to find them lawyers and doctors or to accompany them to immigration hearings. Others asked me to write letters to the INS or fill out job applications. One man introduced me to his Asian supplier. These, of course, are far from extraordinary field activities. I am convinced, however, that had I adopted a less open-ended and more intensive field approach, the results would have been far more limited.

This slow, periodic approach to fieldwork also suited the political context in which I worked. Undocumented West African traders did not want to draw attention to themselves because that might engage the attention of local authorities. I hoped that by limiting my field stays and keeping our encounters informal, I would remain an unobtrusive presence in the traders' world. The sense of autonomy I felt in Niger, however, never materialized in New York City. On 125th Street and Lenox, the central crossroads of African American culture, my whiteness sometimes aroused suspicion and distrust. Unlike the Nigerien context, however, my accountability in New York was legal and political as well as moral. African Americans might find it easy to perceive me as a transient white tourist seeking an afternoon's adventure in Harlem. When some of the market regulars heard me speaking Songhay, however, they wondered how I came to learn the language. When I came to the market on two or three consecutive days, people sometimes asked the traders about me. "Who is this white man? Why is he here? What is he up to?" "Is he okay?" In these rare circumstances, which were uncomfortable for the traders as well as myself, they constructed me as their friend who had spent many years in Niger and who visited occasionally to talk "African" and eat good African food. Given the frenetic swirl of social and economic activity on 125th Street, most people either paid little attention to me or kept their distance. The traders told me that some people thought that I might be an undercover cop.[25]

Ethnographers in complex spaces like Harlem are compelled, I think, to work within the limited scope of their sociologically determined situation, which, in turn, limits their access to certain information and experience. Put another way, my experiences in and knowledge of West Africa have given me access to the dynamic but rather unstable community of West African traders in Harlem. By the same token, my whiteness and cultural difference have also limited my access to that community.

Any kind of ethnographic research endeavor is constrained by myriad factors—personal, social, cultural, political, legal—that construct a series of crossroads. The dynamics of these constraints, in turn, shape the contours of the ethnographic text. In this book the ever-present constraints have prompted a text that details how an unstable mix of cultural, social, economic, legal, and political forces have affected the lives of Issifi and his brother traders in North America. In the next chapter, we examine how Islam and West African cultural beliefs have influenced the social and economic practices of Issifi and his comrades in New York City.

28   The jaguar is sleek and moves silently through the forest. Its power stems not only from its brute strength, but also from its physical adaptability. The jaguar blends in with its surroundings. Other animals know little of its clandestine habits or isolated habitats. It doesn't disturb the calm of the forest, which enables it to make its kill more easily. Once the jaguar makes its kill, it does not linger over it; it takes from the kill what it needs and moves on.

During the 1940s and 1950s, the jaguar became the icon of young itinerant traders who had migrated from Nigeria, Mali, and Niger to Accra and Kumasi, the colonial Gold Coast. Like the jaguar, the young traders blended into their adopted surroundings. They quickly learned the idioms of local languages and established themselves in various Ghanaian markets. Despite their public presence in Ghana, Ghanaians learned little of them. Typically, the young men from the north traded for quick returns. Anticipating new product trends, they bought their inventories cheaply and sold them for handsome profits. These quick turnarounds enabled them to go home to distant villages, where, like returning heroes, they distributed the fruits of their labors. After the Sahelian planting season, they would set out once again for Accra or Kumasi in search of new economic prey. The young travelers dreamed of economic adventure and fashioned themselves as jaguars— young, solitary, sleek, adaptable, knowledgeable, and daring.[1]

Issifi's father, Hamidou, had been a jaguar, though he cut his teeth on the economic quarry of Abidjan rather than Accra or Kumasi, the two principal destinations of Hausa migration during the colonial period. When Hamidou migrated to Côte d'Ivoire in 1960s, Abidjan was a more popular jaguar destination owing to incessant problems with Ghanaian currency exchange. By the 1960s, Abidjan had also become the economic capital of West Africa, outpacing such bustling centers as Lagos, Lomé, Accra, and Kumasi. Hamidou, who hailed from Maradi in central Niger, soon established a dry goods shop in the Treichville market.

Like his brothers, Issifi grew up in the dust-swept Sahel near Maradi. When he reached adolescence, however, his father sent for him. In time Hamidou brought his three remaining sons to Côte d'Ivoire—to learn how to be traders. Little did the four brothers know that in the early 1990s one of them would set out for New York City.

"The words Hausa and trader," Issifi said one afternoon at the Malcolm Shabazz Harlem Market, "they're the same thing. Hausas have always been traders. Everyone knows that."[2] It is well known that the Hausa-speaking peoples have for centuries practiced long-distance trading. Hausa trading networks today extend from Kano, perhaps the epicenter of Hausa culture in northern Nigeria, to Lomé, Abidjan, Dakar, Paris, and now New York City.

Togo Côte d'Ivoire

> Aloof and distinct in his white robes, proud of his customs, Islamic beliefs and practices, and of his "Arabic learning," [the Hausa trader] is often regarded by the host peoples among whom he lives or moves as an exploiter, a monopolist, rogue and trouble-maker. When his business fortunes are at an ebb, he may pose as an Islamic teacher, diviner, barber, butcher, commission agent, porter or beggar. His high degree of mobility, skill and shrewdness in business are widely acknowledged and have earned him the reputation of having a certain "genius" for trade.[3]

The "genius" of the Hausa trader, Abner Cohen argues, springs not from a particular intellectual trait, but from time-tested economic and political organization. In West Africa, this organization consists of a patchwork of Hausa enclaves, little colonies in foreign towns. In Abidjan, Côte d'Ivoire, Hausa traders live in the Treichville neighborhood. In Lomé, Togo, they live in Zongo. In Ibadan, Nigeria, Hausa occupy Sabo.[4] Each of the Hausa enclaves has a chief who is recognized as such by municipal or village leaders. The chief is the political intermediary between his people and the local power holders. According to Cohen, no matter where the Hausa settle, their enclaves abroad are culturally distinct. Their customs, however, are not replicas of the cultural mores of their communities in Hausa country, but have developed over the years to facilitate the movement of people and goods—to grease the wheels of trade and enable the establishment of further communities along important trade routes.

In West Africa, the Hausa have long monopolized the kola trade. Among other commodities, Issifi's father traded in kola, a rain forest nut that West Africans chew as a stimulant. Kola grows in the forest belt of the western regions of Nigeria as well as in densely wooded areas of the Guinea Coast. Once harvested, the nuts must be shipped, usually from south to north. Because of shipping distances and difficulties of transport, most of the kola consumed has been stored, usually in baskets fashioned from banana leaves, and protected by dampened burlap sacks. "According to men in the business, stored kola greatly improves the flavor; and, because of the scarcity of supplies, the expense of storage, of the cost of expert care, and of the risks of speculation, off-season stored kola fetches nearly twice the price of fresh kola."[5]

There are three technical problems prompted by the kola trade: (a) the need for up-to-date market information; (b) the need for speedy transactions of a perishable good; (c) the need for credit and trust. Kola prices fluctuate widely depending on local conditions, the length of storage, the costs of transport, and local preferences for the nut. Traders must have good market information to make profitable decisions. Kola is perishable and must be packed properly for transport to market. Transactions must be quick to avoid spoilage and to repay credit. Without credit and trust, the kola trade, like trade in other commodities, would not exist. Large shipments of kola are entrusted to truck drivers, loaders, and unloaders. Kola traders living in the forest belt of West Africa send thousands of pounds of the nut to agents in the north, who will sell or send on the product and recompense their suppliers in the south.

In other regions of West Africa, merchants solved the problems of long-distance trading by using caravans to transport their goods. With the advent of railroads and automobiles, transport became cheaper and speedier, if no less risky. And so Hausa traders, some of whom used caravans themselves, established Hausa communities along the trade routes—a veritable diaspora not only in Nigeria, ably described by Cohen, but also in Togo, Benin, Côte d'Ivoire, Ghana, and Burkina Faso. Once the Hausa had established trading enclaves in larger towns, they began to settle in smaller towns, creating a far-reaching trading network along which goods and money flowed without obstruction.[6] The reach of the network now extends to Paris and New York City.

Hausa traders have long manipulated ethnic distinctiveness to their commercial advantage. The power of the widely spoken Hausa language, according to Abner Cohen, has facilitated the Hausa diaspora. Through the medium of the Hausa language, traders exchange market information on trade conditions. In Ibadan, Nigeria, for example, Hausa is used to circulate messages and coordinate information. "The importance of having one language in the trade is equally crucial in facilitating speedy communication and interaction between men of different occupational specializations who should co-operate at many stages in the business. Thus kola traders, landlords, commission buyers, packers, measurers, carriers, transport agents, lorry drivers or railway porters, and various other occupational categories must co-operate and interact in the purchase, packing and dispatching of goods."[7] The importance that Cohen attaches to the Hausa language may be somewhat overblown. Hausa has long been a principal trade language in West Africa, which means that many non-Hausa speak it. More important is Cohen's suggestion that ethnicity facilitates economic interactions. No matter their location, Hausa traders tend to live near one another, engage in similar social pursuits, share similar cultural beliefs, and practice the same religion: Islam. This is also the case among Hausa traders in New York City. These similarities create economic and social comfort—and trust, perhaps the key factor in establishing credit relationships and maintaining long-distance trading networks. They also create a ready-made set of procedures for adjudicating business disputes—all of which, Cohen argues, promotes ethnic specialization in long-distance trade.[8]

The Hausa diaspora model that Cohen describes has not been completely replicated in New York City. West African traders, including Hausa from Nigeria, Niger, and Ghana, have created some degree of ethnic specialization, but it appears to be based as much on country of origin as on strict ethnicity.[9] Hausa-speaking traders in New York City sell T-shirts, scarves, gloves, hats, but so do people from other West African ethnic groups. A considerable contingent of Hausa traders buy and sell African art, but so do Bamana from Mali and Soninke from the Gambia.

The historical foundation and importance of West African trade is clear. The glitter of gold has long triggered the wanderlust of traders. Well before the arrival of the camel in the second century A.D., gold compelled Gharmantes traders to trudge their horse and oxen carts through the Libyan Desert. The presence of gold south of the Sahara prompted trade before the tenth century and led, after the year 1000, to the emergence in the south of coherent and spectacular states in the loop of the Niger, and in the north, the Maghreb, to the founding of new towns like Algiers and Oran.[10] The establishment of trans-Saharan trade networks not only brought power to the medieval empires of Ghana, Mali, and Songhay, but enormous wealth to North Africa and

Muslim Spain. In exchange for sub-Saharan gold, such European merchandise as textiles, hardware, and trinkets crossed the Sahara (see fig. 1).

Gold dust, slaves, textiles, copper, and salt were the commodities that fueled early long-distance trading in West Africa. Black Africans controlled the first two commodities, which traders shipped north; North Africans and Europeans controlled the copper, salt, and textiles, which traders shipped south. "Long distance trade wove a network of commercial relations among merchant communities and drew into alliance the leaders of pastoral groups involved in guaranteeing the wide-ranging caravan traffic."[11] Eventually the strategic points in the trade, entrepôts between the gold mines of the West African forest and the salt mines of the West African desert, came under the control of "politico-military elites, usually composed of the slave soldiery, a paramount sultan who taxed and ruled in conflict or accommodation with members of regional elites."[12]

From an early time, then, the economic complexities and sociocultural logistics of long-distance trading bore political consequences. In West Africa, at least, trading networks wielded great economic power but had little direct political power, which was usually marshaled by the region's military elites. Through alliances with these elites, West African and Saharan traders reaped considerable profits. From a political perspective, long-distance traders enabled the military elites to maintain their armies, thereby increasing their wealth and power.

In West Africa, the need for long-distance trading arose from the limitations of local commerce, which consisted primarily of household economies.

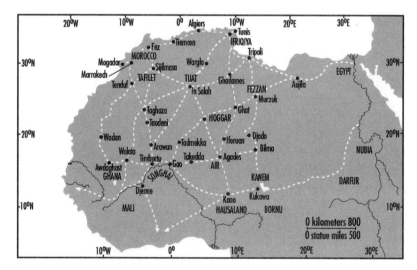

FIGURE 1. PRECOLONIAL LONG-DISTANCE TRADE ROUTES IN WEST AFRICA

Women dominated this trade of foodstuffs, locally woven textiles, livestock, and locally manufactured pots, soap, and yarn. Although it was just as expensive to supply locally produced goods for long-distance shipment, "long distance trade presented an opportunity of connecting dispersed islands of purchasing power, those consumers who, though only a small proportion of the population, had sufficient wealth between them to support a market which was greater than that available to local traders in any one area."[13] In this way, long-distance trade usually catered only to wealthier consumers who could afford imported items.

To connect what A. G. Hopkins called "geographically dispersed islands of relatively wealthy consumers," West African traders established an extensive network of trade routes. Most of these ran north to south. Considering that in West Africa ecological zones run parallel east to west, this array of north-south routes made great sense. Pastoralists from the Sahel traded cattle, milk, cheese, and salt with savanna farmers, who supplied the herders with millet. Peoples in the savanna regions, for their part, traded cattle, salt, dried fish, potash, and cloth with forest peoples in exchange for slaves, kola, ivory, iron, and cloth. To complete the north-south circuit, the forest peoples received sea salt and fish in exchange for foodstuffs and household manufactures. All of which suggests that from early on, long-distance trade in West Africa involved generalized rather than reciprocal exchanges.[14]

Hopkins identifies four groups of people who engaged in this trade. First, there were occasional traders who might make dry-season trips, trading cloth, kola, or perhaps salt to obtain money for specific purposes. Hopkins calls them "target traders." They usually financed themselves and traded their own goods. The second group were traders whose commerce developed from their specific productive activities: smiths, for example, and tobacco or cotton farmers. These traders would stockpile their product until its scarcity caused the price to rise. At the right moment, they would bring their product to regional markets where they would use their profits to buy commodities like cloth, livestock, or foodstuffs. Third, there were specialized, professional traders who, through kinship or professional patron-client relations, established large corporate networks. The Dyula and Hausa have been the most notable of these professional traders. Like Issifi, many of the West African traders in New York City trace their economic, if not their social, origins to one of these two groups. Official traders make up the fourth group. Employed by the region's politico-military elites, these traders represented the interests of states. "Directly or indirectly, trade seems to have been an important source of state income, particularly since 'feudal' rents derived from land were far less common in Africa than they were in medieval Europe. All West African states had a keen interest in encouraging trade. Prudent rulers kept in close touch with leading traders and mercantile organizations, and commercial policy formed a large part of state policy as a whole."[15] West African traders, therefore, have a long history of political sensitivity, a skill they employ daily in their dealings in New York City (see chaps. 6, 7, and 8).

Despite the value of trust between trading partners, the security of goods has always been a primary concern in the West African trade. No matter their historical circumstances, long-distance traders, whether in New York City or Bamako, Mali, have needed a secure means to transport their goods. In precolonial West Africa, the armed caravan provided, however ponderously, that transport. In postcolonial times, the camel and donkey have given way to transatlantic shipping and cargo jets to carry goods between West Africa and North America with varying amounts of efficiency and safety. As ever, long-distance traders must rely on credit and capital. Like merchants of the past in the Mediterranean or West Africa, West African traders in New York City have established procedures and organizations for obtaining informal credit and raising capital. Like the traders of the past, the values and practices of people like Issifi have been shaped profoundly by Islam, which has a strict set of rules concerning commercial transactions. Although today money may have no smell in New York City, Islam has always constructed the moral framework for West African trading transactions.

Through repetition, Issifi internalized the practices that embody a culture of trading in West Africa. Through honesty, he engendered trust in his trading partners and clients. To him, one's word is solemn and sacred. If he shipped goods to a trading partner, he could be almost certain that his goods would arrive intact and that he would receive the correct sum in exchange for them. If he extended credit to a partner in his trade network, he knew he would get his money back. These values set the economic parameters for Issifi's foray into the international market. And why not? Like him, many of the African art and cloth brokers were Hausa from Niger, Nigeria, or Ghana. Other art and cloth merchants, Muslim traders all, hailed from Mali, Burkina Faso, Guinea, and Senegal.

When Issifi came to New York City in 1992, trust formed the firm foundation of his image and practice of trading. Imagine, then, his existential shock when a non-Hausa trading partner stole his inventory. "I never expected this to happen. My whole life disappeared, snatched away from me by bad people. I trusted my trading partners. I shipped goods to them and they did not pay me. New York is not Africa. Bad things happen to people here. People here

Islam

betray their trusts. They lie and cheat. They misrepresent themselves. A bad business."

"How did you go on?" I asked.

Issifi smiled. "What happened to me is part of fate—God's plan. It was terrible, but I came out okay. Now, I make more money than before, and perhaps my own brothers can come here and sell cloth. I will never betray my trust to others. It is not our way."[16]

Issifi's path is not only to follow the commercial traffic along North American highways, but also to honor the dictates of Islam. From its inception, Islam has been inextricably linked with commerce. More specifically, commerce has been central to the development and diffusion of Islam since the time of Muhammad. The political importance of merchant capital, capital generated exclusively through exchange, is widely recognized as having been a major factor in Arab power relations prior to Islam. Mecca's long history as a powerful pilgrimage center triggered the growth of merchant capital in the city. The growth of merchant capital prompted the rise of Mecca's power and influence generations before Muhammad's birth. "Merchant capital in the Meccan context also meant power—political power in the sense that merchants harnessed their wealth in the mobilization of force to influence the course of events and social relations in a manner to suit their interests."[17]

Meccan wealth devolved from the institution of the *haram*, "the sacred area and the sacred time, where and when individuals enjoyed security of life and property and thus were provided the opportunity to trade."[18] Mecca's *haram*, of course, was—and continues to be—the sacred Kaba, the holiest site in Islam and the destination of pagan pilgrims centuries before Muhammad's epoch. Given the Kaba's sacredness, pre-Islamic Meccans created institutions that made it easy for people to undertake pilgrimages to the site. Merchants supplied water to pilgrims and created alliances to provide widespread access to markets. Through these institutions, Meccan merchants became wealthy—and entrenched.

As long as the Meccan economy remained substantially localized, rich merchants could manipulate tribal alliances to protect their interests. As time passed, however, these tribal leaders—principally the Quraish, found it increasingly difficult to control their social and political affairs. The influx of merchant capital and settlers attracted to a center of wealth had transformed Mecca's traditional society, making it more heterogeneous. Control of capital soon outstripped tribal blood as the Meccan resource of power. This structural schism provoked much conflict in sixth- and seventh-century Mecca.

This disequilibrium manifested itself in continuous social conflict, which posed several threats to society, especially to the merchant-clan leaders, who had most to lose from social violence or from a total breakdown of the social order. It is in this milieu that Muhammad appeared as a man singularly inspired, a prophet who articulated the problems of his society and in the process founded a new religion with an institutional framework relevant to the solution of the social, political and economic problems that impeded the progress of Mecca's merchants.[19]

Muhammad's new social structure, defined by the Ummah, transformed the authority of clan-based merchant capital to the power of those who followed the Prophet. For Muhammad, the Ummah, as spelled out in the Constitution of Medina, is a collection of beings protected by Allah. Allegiance to the Ummah transcended all ethnic identification. Muhammad deemed trade an honorable and essential activity in the Ummah, for with economic expansion, the Ummah would grow, prosper, and expand its power and influence. The Prophet stressed that traders should interact in cooperative ways that would increase commerce. In his sayings on commerce and trade, Muhammad stressed "a high standard of straightforwardness, reliability, and honesty." In various passages of the Qur'an and the Sunnah, there are many statements about giving false oaths, correct weight, and goodwill in transactions. With regard to commercial goodwill, the Qur'an articulates the need for merchants to write clear and comprehensive contracts regarding transactions. "The writing should set out the terms agreed upon fairly, and as a further precaution, it is laid down that the terms of the contract shall be dictated by the person who undertakes the liability."[20]

More specifically, Muhammad stood firm against monopolistic practices that could undermine cooperative relations. Accordingly, he spoke out against the following kinds of transactions:

1. land rental for gold;
2. speculating in green wheat in exchange for harvested wheat;
3. all forms of crop speculation;
4. the sale of grapes in exchange for raisins or wheat for prepared foods;
5. the sale of uninspected goods of any kind;
6. the sale of idols (statuettes, non-Muslim amulets) and forbidden foods (wine, swine, any kind of carrion), though Muslims could profit from the sale of dead animal skins.[21]

In essence, Muhammad rigidly rejected all forms of speculation, monopoly, and usury. Because monopoly and speculation undermine commercial and social relations, they are violations of Islamic intent and are therefore condemned.

By the same token, the Prophet promoted trade to the exclusion of usury, which at first seems contradictory, for usury amounts to trade, but in capital rather than tangible commodities. In Islam, trade is seen to involve risk, which means that profits fluctuate. Interest is fixed. The profits produced by trade result from hard work and personal initiative, which is not the case in usury. In trade, commodity exchange marks the end of the transaction. In usury, interest continues to be collected as long as the principal remains unpaid. Trade gives rise to employment and economic growth; usury has the opposite effect. In the end "trade may act as one of the dominant factors in the process of the building of civilization through cooperation and the mutual exchange of ideas. But interest creates in man the undesirable weakness of miserliness, selfishness and lack of sympathy"[22]—the very antithesis of Muhammad's notion of Ummah. And so when Issifi, who studies the Qur'an and the Prophet's Hadiths regularly, speaks of hard work, honest commercial relations, and trust, his beliefs devolve directly from Islam.

Boubé Mounkaila, whose enterprise is several stalls away from Issifi's at the Malcolm Shabazz Harlem Market, provides a contemporary example of the trading principles first articulated by the Prophet Muhammad. Boubé has sold wristwatches, as well as leather sacks and handbags from Niger. He is a Songhay, rather than Hausa, and came to New York City from Nemega, Niger, by way of Abidjan in November of 1990. Boubé makes no secret that the watches he has are "copies," for their style and trademark mimic the original: DKNY, Gucci, Rolex, and Swiss Army.

"I must be honest in my dealings. I let everyone know that what I sell are copies, not originals."

"They probably know anyway," I interject, "from the price. I mean it's hard to get a real Rolex for $25.00."

"It doesn't matter," says Boubé. "I must tell them anyway. That is our way. I am a merchant, and I try to establish trust with my clients. That way, they will, Inshallah, come back."

Boubé also spoke about the Islamic subtext to his trading. "I try to be a good Muslim. I say my prayers five times a day, avoid alcohol and pork, and give to the unfortunate. I try to be honest in trade. That is our way, and it makes me a better trader."

In many instances, Boubé has practiced what he preaches. In 1993, he bought a mountain bike that he loved to ride through Central Park at night. Two years later, he gave it away to a young boy. He regularly gives small amounts of money to destitute African Americans who pass by his market stall. He appears to be scrupulously honest in his commercial dealings.

"If you are honest," says Boubé, "clients know exactly what they're getting. If suppliers know that I'm African, they have no problem extending me credit. I always pay them back, and I keep my word. We have trust. That's what my father taught me. That's what my brother traders taught me in Abidjan. It is difficult to follow the rules of Islam, especially here in New York, but it is my great strength as a person and a trader. People around here may not like me, but they respect me for my beliefs, and my ability to work—honestly."[23]

Listening to Boubé, it is not difficult to understand why trade was the fuel that propelled the spread of Islam from Arabia westward across North Africa and southward into sub-Saharan Africa. Much has been written about the early trans-Saharan trade and how the flow of goods and commodities prompted state formation in medieval West Africa. The military-political elites of Ghana, Mali, and Songhay manipulated their economically strategic positions—lying midway between gold fields and salt mines—to create armies and bureaucracies. These states attracted Muslim merchants from North Africa, some of whom settled in entrepôts like Gao, Djenné, Mopti, and Timbuktu, which in time became the commercial centers of the medieval West African states. Islamic scholars arrived soon thereafter to teach the merchant children the religion of the Prophet and to convert the Africans. From the fifteenth to the end of the nineteenth century, millions of West Africans converted to Islam, which continued to expand through commerce.[24]

Traders and their networks, according to Claude Meillassoux, held considerable power in West African cities. They took every opportunity to free themselves from imperial power. "In this way the power of merchants, backed up by Islam, was established everywhere beneath the surface of the power of the warrior aristocracies, and ready to take over at any time."[25] While states like Ghana, Mali, and Songhay rose and fell, the merchant enclaves endured and trade prospered and proliferated. In the wake of the medieval Sahelian empires, there arose decentralized constellations of fortified merchant cities. These cities became important centers of economic and social power.

Among these merchant enclaves, matters of trade transcended ethnic loyalties. According to Meillassoux, long-distance trade was well established throughout the Sahel by the sixteenth century. And by the seventeenth century, there existed clusters of powerful and wealthy towns, called *maraka* villages. In short order, they became more prestigious entities than the villages of emergent Bamana warriors. Indeed, the emergence of the Bamana state in the mid-seventeenth century was the result of armed conflict with surrounding merchant towns.[26] The key factor in the growth of a merchant economy in West Africa was the trader's ability to conduct commerce relatively free from the interference of warrior states.

> History shows that in the interstices of these aristocratic areas, spaces were formed which were managed by the merchant class and subjected to its rules—the marketplace and their dependencies—and that links were established between these spaces to form a business network which backed up a sort of reticulated merchant "State," with neither territory nor central government. Among themselves the merchants maintained mercantile relations which necessitated ethics, means of payment and arbitration. The preservation of patrimony, which at this stage was much the same as merchant capital, was backed up by a re-interpretation of kinship relations in a form which was neither that of domestic agriculture society nor that of the aristocratic family.[27]

From the merchant class emerged a group of men specialized in science, jurisprudence, and morality to reinforce ideologically the social transformation brought on by nascent merchant "states."

Two of the most noteworthy of these states were El Hadj 'Umar's Tukulor state, and Samory's state of Wasalu. El Hadj 'Umar was a learned Muslim from the Futa Toro in what is now Senegal. After many years of travel and learning, he returned to his homeland in 1840 and, having been converted from a Quadiri to a Tijani Muslim, used Tijanism, a form of Sufism, to attract numerous followers, whom he used as trading agents. The mission of the Tukulor Empire was twofold: to spread Tijanism and to reap profits through expanded trade. Like El Hadj 'Umar, Samory Touré, a brilliant military tactician and economic administrator, expanded his Muslim state through trade. Referring to the Wasalu state, Yves Person called it a *dyula* revolution—a revolution of traders.[28]

Of direct relevance to West Africans in New York City is the Mourid Sufi order, founded in 1898 by Ahamadu Bamba. Bamba preached that hard work—and profits—brought adherents closer to heaven's gate. Based in Touba City, Senegal, the Mourids quickly became a fabulously wealthy merchant cartel, wielding considerable political power in both colonial and independent Senegal. In search of greater profits, the Mourid *cheiks*, the sons and grandsons of Ahamadu Bamba, sent their adherents to exploit international markets. Mourids worked throughout Europe and eventually established themselves in New York City in the early 1980s.[29]

No matter the site or era, there are common themes in the culture of West African trade. For Claude Meillassoux, "the common interest of the traders in the maintenance of moral and cultural conditions favorable to their business, and their desire to keep business at a distance from greedy princes or states which dispensed justice, led them to accept the immanent and inhibiting policy of Islam."[30] Islam triggered an expansion of trade in West Africa; it corresponded well to traders' need to stress mercantile relations above and beyond ethnic solidarity. The ethnic origin of the professional traders, in Meillassoux's view, is less important than how they manipulated kinship, jurisprudence, and political relations to expand their economic base considerably. This history has direct bearing on how West African traders confront the regulatory and political regimes of New York City today (see chaps. 6 and 7). In the past, West African traders knew how to manipulate local politics—its policies and laws—in order to trade more freely. Contemporary West African traders in New York face similar, if not more complex, challenges. The passage of time may have altered West African merchant spaces and the kinds of people and goods traders work with, but modern traders are confronted with many of the same social and economic issues that their forebears confronted in previous centuries.

In the past, Islam reaffirmed the solidarity of West African trading families. Just as Muhammad's religion triggered the expansion of trade from Arabia to North and West Africa, so it promoted the expansion of kinship—both fictive and real—through extended trade networks. As in any kinship system, the rites and obligations in West African trading cartels depend on three principal factors: age, gender, and generation. Among Kooroko trading families in southern Mali, according to Jean-Loup Amselle, the head of household provides food, clothing, and tax money for the people in his extended household, who, in turn, give him whatever they produce. Sometimes the head of household is also a great trader, a *jula-ba,* who directs a long-distance trading cartel from the comforts of his compound. In southern Mali, such trade involves the exchange of cattle and dried fish for kola nuts from Côte d'Ivoire. The kinspeople, affines, and friends of the great trader keep him informed of fluctuating market conditions. When conditions are favorable, the great trader sends his *jula-ben* (lit., trader children)—who may be younger brothers, sons, and brother's sons—to Côte d'Ivoire to sell cattle and buy kola. In Côte d'Ivoire, the "children" are welcomed and housed by

THE NEW MALCOLM SHABAZZ HARLEM MARKET, SUMMER 1999. (PHOTO BY JASMIN TAHMASEB MCCONATHA)

hosts who usually have blood or marriage ties to the great trader. Following their transactions, the "children" of the trader return home and report on the outcome of their efforts, for which they receive no remuneration. In time, however, these young kinsmen of the great trader may ask for economic independence, which will be granted along with a payment that will be used to start a new enterprise.

Great traders may sometimes face situations in which there aren't a sufficient number of paternal male kin to run their long-distance cartels. In such cases, they will engage maternal kin, their sister's sons, or even the male children of associates outside their kindreds. Like the great trader's paternal kin, these "children" receive no remuneration for their initial services. After several successful missions, however, trader children in this category can ask their "father" for a loan to invest in their own inventory. The "children" continue to perform services for the great trader but have entered into a contractual partnership—albeit an unequal one—with their "father."

In the early stages of the contractual relationship, the "child" must give his "father" two-thirds of earned profits. If the "child" manages to squeeze profits continuously from his loan, the great trader may offer him another. If profits fail to materialize, the great trader will continue to employ him but will never grant him another loan. Successful "children" eventually split the profits equally with their trading "father." If the "child" becomes truly prosperous, he takes his leave of the great trader and becomes a *jula-ba* himself.[31]

This pattern of kinship-based economic networks has been central to the formation of Hausa cartels. In the Hausa system, there are *uban-gida* (father of the house) and *bara* (dependent in the house). Dependents or "children" put themselves in service to the "father" and perform many services without pay. "Fathers" by contrast, must give gifts to their dependents. According to Emmanuel Gregoire, "The distinctive quality of this relationship is that the economic ties linking the two are less important than social or affective ties. The *bara* often obtains a certain prestige because of his link to the *uban-gida* and may even have numerous *baraori* dependents himself."

> The *bara* to *urban-gida* relationship assured cohesiveness in its networks and, by reason of its successive hierarchical levels, made it possible to link the commercial houses with farmers. An important person (trader, buyer) would have numerous dependents who themselves would go out to buy groundnuts from the farmers, or who would do so through an intermediary of their own dependents. The economic weight of a given individual was thus related to social importance, to "richness in men" (*arzikin mutane*). The maintenance of the social network created even more economic power, which in turn made it necessary for patrons to redistribute part of their own wealth among their dependents.[32]

The prestige of a Hausa trader, then, is not only determined by material wealth, but by the extensiveness of his network of dependents—his "wealth in men." Among the merchants Gregoire studied in Maradi, Niger, most *uban-gida* headed regional cartels. A small number of traders, however, directed networks of global proportions. In a wealthy urban center like Abidjan, there are unquestionably dozens of *uban-gida* who watch over their "children" in faraway places. Men like Issifi may be the "children" of these kin and fictive kin–based trading relationships that currently exist in New York City.

Trust and confidence and rights and obligations in West African trading networks derive from patterns of kinship—patterns that are themselves reinforced by the commercial dictates of Islam. The past and present practices that have made long-distance trade possible in West Africa hold today in New York City. There are several economic networks of Hausa and Songhay traders that regularly sponsor "trade children" in New York City. In West Africa, the established elder traders, or "fathers," pay airfare, secure visas, and provide investment capital for their "children," the recipients of their investments. Unlike the West African case described by Amselle, however, many international *jula-ba* do not remain in their West African compounds; they travel periodically between Abidjan to New York City to receive accountings from their North American "children."

El Hadj Soumana Tondi of Niamey, Niger, and Abidjan, Côte d'Ivoire, is one of the international *jula-ba*. Between 1994 and 1998, El Hadj Tondi, a man of about sixty, traveled from Abidjan to New York City every six weeks to, as he put it, "check up on his 'children' " at the Malcolm Shabazz Harlem Market. Unlike Issifi, who is linked only to his paternal kin in Abidjan— Hausas all—El Hadj's "children" were all Songhay men in their thirties who used to work for him in Abidjan. Only two of his New York City "children" were his paternal kin. The others had contractual arrangements with him.

In the summer of 1995, El Hadj Tondi wanted to send more of his "children" to New York City, but had trouble getting them tourist or business visas from American embassies in West Africa. In one of our 1995 discussions, he asked me about my work.

"I'm an anthropologist. I teach students about life in Africa and about Africa's history."

"That's very good," he told me. "But you should be a diplomat," he told me.

"Why?"

"It is getting hard to bring my 'children' to New York. Before, it was easy. I knew some good people and we got visas, no problem. I'd go and see people and vouch for the good character of my people. Trusting my judgment, they'd give them visas, no problem. You see, I'd stake my reputation on their good behavior, and the embassy people had confidence in me. But those people left Niamey and with the new people I couldn't get visas for the 'children.' Then we got them visas in Abidjan. I'd go in there and stake my reputation as an honest businessman on their good behavior. For some time, we had no trouble there. Now there are new people there and things are difficult—no visas are forthcoming. I will have to start going to Cotonou [in Benin]. Maybe I'll find visas there."

"I wish you luck," I said.

"Why aren't you a diplomat?" he asked once again. "You could help me."

"It's not done easily, El Hadj. You have to take exams and do much training. Besides, it's not my work. I very much like what I do."

El Hadj wasn't listening. "You know, you should come to Côte d'Ivoire or better yet, Niger, and give out visas. With someone who understands our ways as well as you do, it would be very good for business."[33]

In New York City, the notion of family is extended to other traders of the same ethnicity. For Issifi, then, family also refers—in descending order of importance—to "brother" traders who are Hausa, Songhay, Malian, Senegalese, and Gambian. His most important transactions and dealings are with other Nigerien Hausa traders whom he knows from Abidjan. He engages in less important transactions with Songhay traders, also from Niger by way of Abidjan. He can expect to give and receive a small amount of credit from any of his brother traders, no matter their actual proximity to his informal personal trade network (see chap. 4 for a more detailed analysis). These "kin" relations, according to Issifi, are extensions of West African kinship as applied to the inner workings of economic networks. Ties of rights and obligations, bolstered by a mutuality of trust, are reinforced by Islamic morality, which as we have seen, applies directly to commercial practices. "Islam," Issifi says, "makes us strong, resilient, and disciplined. It encourages our creativity in new lands. It creates a climate of trust."[34] Like most of the West African traders in New York City, Issifi is part of an economic network. In his case, the network consists of his paternal kin to whom he incurs obligations (to send money to the family head—his father—and to look after his mother and his brothers). Issifi's first social and economic priority, as he has put it, is his family.

Despite the climate of trust and Islamic morality among the traders, they, like the jaguar, must be flexible. In the jaguar's world, changing conditions call for adaptation: exploring new areas, seeking new opportunities—all in the effort to maintain its way of life among the shadows of the forest. Traders are also affected by changing economic and political conditions to which they must adapt if they are to maintain their way of life. They, however, cannot hide in the forest; rather they have derived economic strength from kinship, time-tested business practices, and religion.

These outlines allow us to see more clearly how the values and practices of the West African culture of trade play in the hardball arenas of New York City's informal economy. It is a culture of trade in which kin-based social obligations and a climate of trust based on time-honored Muslim principles are paramount. It is also a culture of trade in which cooperation as well as competition plays a central role in economic transactions. In chapter 4, we shall see how Issifi and his brother traders have used their culture of trade to create multiethnic networks of suppliers and buyers in New York City.

In 1993 Moussa Diallo, a Malian, sold a variety of African crafts from his
table on 125th Street in Harlem. In August of that year, he draped his aluminum card table with a brightly colored African print cloth—a deep blue
background with clusters of variously sized red, yellow, and green circles
that looked like sand dollars. On the left side of the table he displayed dolls
clothed from head to toe in African print cloth. Behind them, he arranged
Woodaabe Fulan jewelry from Niger—black leather necklaces and bracelets
into which were sewn cowry shells and round copper ornaments. Varieties
of silver Agadez crosses, which are fashioned by Tuareg smiths in Niger and
symbolize the Southern Cross constellation, glistened in the center of the
table. They were flanked on the right by reproductions of Ghanaian gold
weights and an assortment of tooled Akan earrings and necklaces also fashioned from "gold." At the far end of the table, Moussa arranged a collection
of kente cloth caps.

On a sun-splashed weekday afternoon in 1994, I went to 125th Street to
find a slow market day. After greeting the traders in the Nigerien section of
the sidewalk on the north side of 125th Street, I said hello to Moussa Diallo.
Although he came from Mali, he had lived many years in Niger and spoke
fluent Songhay. I admired his display of West African crafts and jewelry, and
wondered about the kente caps.

"Do they make those caps in Ghana?" I asked Moussa, thinking that
caps made from traditional Ghanaian cloth would have been imported from
Ghana.

"No," he answered. "I buy them downtown. You know, on Canal Street."

"Who do you buy them from?"

"I buy them from Asians, who give me a good price," he answered. "Most times I go downtown to buy. Sometimes, they bring them uptown. The American blacks," he added, "like these caps. They sell very well in Harlem."

"Why do they come from Asians?" I asked, wanting to know about the circuitous history of these objects.

"It's a long story," Moussa replied.[1]

Kente is the name of a colorful, intricate, handwoven silk cloth traditionally worn by Asante nobles on ceremonial occasions. The antique cloths are colored with vegetable dyes of deep blue, yellow, green, and red hues and are stitched in subtle and elegant patterns.[2] Large pieces of kente consist of many strips of cloth attached to one another. Kente has always been expensive—the province of members of the Asante nobility, who commissioned their wardrobes. As time has passed, however, old kente has become increasingly hard to find. Newer kente, moreover, pales in comparison to the antique cloth, for "the repertoire of patterns together with the technical skill needed has decreased."[3] In addition, the decline in the quality of yarn and the increase in price have limited the production of newer kente, which is often sold as individual strips. Silk and rayon kente strips—handwoven but admittedly inferior to the original cloths—gradually became popular in the United States. Many icons of African American cultural life began to wear these kente strips as scarves—colorful material badges of African identity, a notion that is discussed at length in chapter 5.[4]

Sometime in the early 1990s, according to Moussa and his compatriot, Sidi Maiga, who in 1993 was a cloth merchant on 125th Street, enterprising Korean entrepreneurs saw an opportunity. Working from photographs of handwoven Ghanaian silk kente, they designed a cotton print cloth version—for a fraction of the original's cost. Soon their small textile factories in New Jersey began to spit out bolts of economical cotton print "kente," which were shipped to warehouses in and around Canal Street in lower Manhattan. The Asians contacted several West African buyers in Harlem who traveled downtown to inspect the new merchandise. The quality of the "kente" pleased them; the wholesale price per bolt made the cloth a fine business opportunity. Ever cautious with their investment dollars, they tried out samples on 125th Street. Patrons bought up the reasonably priced "kente" in short order, and soon West African cloth merchants in Harlem, boutique owners and street vendors alike, ordered many bolts of what Sidi Maiga called "New Jersey kente."

The reasonably priced New Jersey "kente," which in 1993 sold for five dollars per yard (four dollars per yard for "special friends," large orders, or on slow days) sold well along 125th Street. When African Americans bought the cloth on the street, they'd take it to an African tailor, like Issa Trouré, who worked at Karta Textiles, located at 121 West 125th Street. For a reasonable fee, Issa, following the suggestions of his clients, would transform the New Jersey reproduction of traditional Ghanaian cloth into contemporary African American fashion—including "kente" cloth caps, sport jackets with "kente" cloth lapels, as well as dresses, skirts, and trousers. By 1994, a rather ironic symbolic reversal had presented itself on 125th Street: many African Americans—especially on Saturdays and Sundays during the summer months—would stroll along the sidewalk dressed in clothing fashioned from African print fabrics, including, of course, New Jersey "kente"; many West African vendors, by contrast, would sport the uniform of young urban African American males—baggy jeans or fatigue pants, T-shirts, baseball shoes, and leather hats worn backward or sideways.

Given the rapid transnational flow of people, information, and ideas in 1993, it is not surprising that the success of New Jersey "kente" shocked the African textile industry into action. Ghanaian textile factories, according to Sidi Maiga, had already reproduced the more popular West African cloth designs, undercutting the costs, but not exceeding the quality of their

KARTA TEXTILES ON 125TH STREET IN HARLEM. (PHOTO BY AUTHOR)

regional competitors. Now they reproduced, he suggested, one of their own traditional designs—kente cloth—and shipped it to New York City as well as to other West African markets. In his magisterial book, *Wrapped in Pride: Ghanaian Kente and African American Identity*, Doran Ross traces the machine reproduction of kente to the early 1960s. "Both Asante and Ewe weavers have serious problems with calling . . . these factory-made cloths 'kente' and view their industrial appropriation something of a copyright infringement. It is significant that these cloths are not produced by the textile mills in Ghana but are turned out in large quantities by mills in Benin, Togo, Côte d'Ivoire and Senegal among other countries (some of which are outside of Africa)."[5]

The "Ghanaian" reproduction of kente, whatever its origin, surpassed the New Jersey version in quality at a cheaper price. Small-time Asian factories, in the end, could not compete with state-sponsored industries. The New Jersey "kente" quickly lost its appeal, and following sound business instincts, West African cloth merchants in Harlem invested in bolts of what they called "Ghanaian kente." Sales of "kente" continued to be strong; profits increased. One Malian cloth merchant, Samba Soumana, claimed that his increased profits, part of which derived from the sale of "Ghanaian kente," enabled him to feed his entire village in Mali.[6]

Korean merchants in lower Manhattan, however, did not want to bow out of a lucrative market. And so they traveled uptown to invest in bolts of wholesale "Ghanaian kente," which they brought to their sweatshops in lower Manhattan, producing hundreds of "kente" caps at a price cheaper than one could get by buying cloth on 125th Street and commissioning an African tailor. Seeing samples of these new caps, West African street vendors traveled downtown to buy "African" merchandise, most likely sewed by indentured Asian immigrants using an African reproduction of an Asian reproduction of traditional African cloth. When these new caps appeared on 125th Street, they sold well and provided substantial profits.

"We told the people," Moussa Diallo said, "that they were kente caps. That's all. The African Americans were happy to buy them."

"Did your clients ever wonder if the cloth was 'true' kente or where they were produced?"

"Some think the caps come from Africa; others don't care where they come from. We don't talk about any of it. They just wanted to wear those caps, which make them feel more connected to the African tradition."[7]

On 125th Street in Harlem, African Americans bought "African kente" caps from West African street vendors who purchased the caps from Asian suppliers. The Asian suppliers manufactured the caps in downtown sweatshops in which mostly Asian immigrants, who were mostly undocumented, quickly produced large amounts cheap clothing. They produced "kente" caps, however, from "Ghanaian kente" cloth, a cheaper and higher-quality reproduction of New Jersey "kente" cloth, which Asian entrepreneurs had previously reproduced from the original handwoven kente. They manufactured this reproduction to sell to West African cloth merchants and African American boutiques.[8]

The convoluted story of the production and reproduction of "kente" caps is a gripping example of the central role of simulacra in contemporary economic social contexts; it is also a concrete case that demonstrates how economic and social networks work in transnational settings. In chapter 5, I employ the Baudrillardian notion of simulacrum to unpack West African strategies of marketing Afrocentricity. Here, more briefly, we can compare what anthropologists have written about market behaviors and structures to the experience of contemporary West African street vendors in a global city like New York.

Economic anthropology has a long history in the discipline. Economic anthropologists have written a great deal about many subjects, including, of course, descriptions and analyses of individual market behaviors and the economic dynamics of urban and regional market systems. For example, Malinowski's classic work of the 1920s, *Argonauts of the Western Pacific*, describes and analyzes the mesh of economic and social relationships that made up the Melanesian kula ring, a striking instance of a regional economic network. Since Malinowski's time, economic anthropologists have focused on such varied topics as exchange, money, the economic behavior of hunters and gatherers, pastoralists, and subsistence horticulturists, markets, industrial agriculture, Marxism, and the informal economy.[9]

What conceptual insights can this literature provide a study of market relationships in a contemporary transnational setting? What can the literature tell us about the multidimensional relationships, among African American patrons on 125th Street, Harlem street vendors like Moussa Diallo, Sidi Maiga, Issifi Mayaki, and Asian suppliers in lower Manhattan?

This rich literature highlights some key concepts that underscore social relations in markets—transnational or otherwise. The transaction, for example, is the cement that binds economic relationships in markets. The transaction is "any change of status between a good or service between persons, such as a sale." There are two kinds of transactions: impersonal and personal. Impersonal transactions, like buying clothing from a salesperson in a shopping mall, present few or no social contours outside the context of exchange. Personal transactions, by contrast, are conducted among people, like peddlers and their suppliers, whose personal relationship extends beyond the transaction context; "they are embedded in networks of social relations."[10]

Most economic anthropologists agree that long-term personal economic relationships are superior in many situations. This assumption would most certainly apply to such informal economies as New York City street vending, in which transactions develop almost exclusively from the traders' various social networks. "The most important attribute of long-run exchanges is that they tend to be personalized, meaning that knowledge of the other's personality, family, history, church, and so on is relevant to the trust one has that the exchange will be satisfactorily completed. The riskier the economic environment, the more traders need additional information about a partner over and above the specific facts of the proposed deal."[11] The business connections among the buyers, sellers, and suppliers of New York "kente" cloth and "kente" products, for example, are based on a degree of trust that can only arise from ongoing personal relationships. West African cloth vendors, mostly Malians and Gambians, buy much of their inventory from Asian merchants in lower Manhattan, which means that the two parties have ongoing business relationships. These relationships, which transcend linguistic, religious, and cultural barriers, tend to be limited to economic contexts. Most West African traders know little of the personal or social lives of their Asian suppliers. Most Asian suppliers know little about the history and culture of West Africa. Asians offer the West Africans cheap merchandise—often counterfeits of designer clothing or bolts of New Jersey "kente" cloth. The West Africans usually pay cash for their merchandise, though some Asian suppliers extend them credit. As one West African street vendor put it. "The Asians like doing business with us Africans. We pay them cash, or if they extend us credit, we pay them back quickly. No funny business."[12]

Transactions, of course, involve goods and actors. Goods possess several attributes. Among the most important are the "search" and the "experience" quality of goods. The search aspect of goods includes such attributes as style, dimension, or color. The buyer's problem is to locate the right combinations in the marketplace. "Experience quality refers to those attributes revealed through use such as durability in clothing."[13] Here the buyer must have information about product quality before purchase. Buyers need more information from and more confidence in sellers who deal in riskier merchandise.

An example from the Malcolm Shabazz Harlem Market exemplifies these fundamental concepts. Several Senegalese traders used to sell pirated videocassettes at the market. They received their videocassettes from groups of Arab and Israeli traders who reproduced the cassettes illegally.[14] Cassettes from first-run films typically appeared at the market one to two days following the film's premiere. The cartels made their illegal copies from a stolen or bought original or by using a camcorder to video the film at the opening. Knowing that their Arab and Israeli suppliers had made thousands of copies of the videotaped films, the Senegalese traders knew that a cassette's quality could be somewhat off—a bit snowy.[15] They also knew that their clients would assume the worst about the quality of pirated videos. To bolster buyer confidence, the Senegalese allowed their clients to sample the quality of the videos on televisions that were hooked up in market stalls. As one Senegalese video merchant said: "With the TV my clients can see what they are buying. If they like what they see, they buy."[16]

We have already seen how Moussa Diallo and Sidi Maiga inserted themselves in African/Asian/uptown/downtown networks. Moussa Diallo bought "kente" caps from downtown Asian suppliers. Sidi Maiga bought New Jersey "kente" cloth from Asian suppliers, but eventually received cheaper and lower-priced cotton print "kente" directly from Africa. Issifi Mayaki, like all West African traders in Harlem, has also participated in several transnational economic networks in New York City. As we know, when he first came to New York City, Issifi sold African textiles that he had shipped from Côte d'Ivoire. He lived with fellow Hausa traders in a room at the Hotel Belleclaire and participated in an extended network comprised of his suppliers in the major textile-producing areas of West Africa (Mali, Ghana, and Nigeria), fellow Hausa traders in Abidjan, and fellow traders (Hausa, Songhay, Bamana, Malinke, and Wolof) in New York City.[17] After his financial difficulties when someone refused to pay him for a shipment of goods, Issifi lost all transaction confidence—a prime component in maintaining relationships in economic networks—and he temporarily severed most of the ties in his network of suppliers, transporters, fellow traders, and North American wholesalers.

Facing this loss of inventory, Issifi followed a time-honored practice and sought out members of his own ethnic group from his country of origin. These were people with whom he shared language and tradition—people he could trust. These men sold T-shirts, Africana (cheap crafts like dolls, jewelry, and "kente" strips), handbags, and hats at the informally organized 125th Street African market. Issifi, in fact, had met many of them when they shared space at the Treichville market in Abidjan, Côte d'Ivoire. Ever vigilant to the threat of theft, these traders maintained an informal fund from which compatriot traders who had suffered a loss, like that of Issifi's, might be extended credit to get started again. After hearing of Issifi's loss, his compatriots quickly provided him with a loan. One compatriot, Sala Fari, invited him to share an apartment on 126th Street. Loan in hand, Issifi decided to sell cassettes and CDs. Accordingly, another compatriot trader introduced him to downtown Asians who sold these items cheaply in their stores on and around Canal Street. Issifi paid cash for an inventory of cassettes and CDs—mostly rap, reggae, and rhythm and blues—and set up a table on 125th Street, where he sold his wares to local African Americans and Hispanics and to African American and European tourists.

When Issifi moved to the Malcolm Shabazz Harlem Market, he continued to sell cassettes and CDs, but the nature of his economic network shifted. He now established a formal relationship with the Masjid Malcolm Shabazz, administrators of the new market, which collected stall rents, policed the premises, and resolved disputes among traders. Dissatisfied with the profit margins obtained from selling cassettes and CDs, Issifi decided to return to trading West African textiles, but as a sedentary trader in Harlem. Besides, he didn't much care for rap music or rhythm and blues, preferring the music of Hausa musicians. Issifi also admitted that selling African cloth had brought him much pleasure. He had liked being surrounded by the bright colors and elaborate patterns and looked forward to hanging them again in his market stall. He especially appreciated the aesthetic contours of antique cloth, a few pieces of which he hoped to buy.

His Hausa compatriots and newfound Malian colleagues, the principal African cloth sellers in Harlem, introduced him to Malian, Nigerien, and Senegalese middlemen who wholesaled West African print fabrics in New York City. He also reestablished contacts with itinerant textile traders, whom he knew from his days in Abidjan, who specialized in antique cloth.

When he had firmly established IME African Cloth, I noticed that Issifi displayed a large piece of machine-made "kente" cloth. As an immediately recognizable symbol of Africa, the item attracted much interest in Harlem where the discourse of Afrocentricity has had significant commercial ramifications.

I asked Issifi where he had found the kente.

"I bought it in Midtown from Senegalese."

"Did they get it from Ghana?" I asked naively.

"No," he answered, "it comes from Tunisia. They're doing a lot of African cloth reproductions."

"Is it good for business?" I continued with interest.

"Very good," Issifi replied with considerable satisfaction.[18]

...

It is clear that the myriad economic relationships of Issifi Mayaki and his fellow traders are shaped through participation in a shifting array of socioeconomic networks. These networks respond with sophistication to the nuances of the global economy, which itself is affected by highly politicized regimes of supply, demand, assessment of profit, and state regulation.

The idea of the social network, pioneered by British social anthropologists, emerged from the analysis of social structure. Pioneers in social network analysis like James Clyde Mitchell and John Barnes had become increasingly frustrated with the inadequacy of British structural functionalism. They claimed that structural functionalism lacked the sophistication to probe the density of social relations in urban research sites.[19] From this perspective, a social network "refers to a set of points (individuals) defined in relation to an initial point of focus (ego) and linked by lines (relationships) either directly or indirectly to this initial point of focus."[20]

Anthropologists, according to Jeffrey Johnson, have considered social networks with one of two models: metaphorical and formal. Many anthropologists who are bent against formal models in sociocultural analysis see networks simply as a heuristic device.[21] They usually consider the network as a social "given." The great thrust of anthropological writing about networks, however, has been concerned with the formal analysis of social network data gathered primarily in complex societies.

There are many debates between culturally oriented cognitive anthropologists, who do network analysis of kinship, semantic fields, and self-report data, and the more sociologically oriented analysts who employ network analysis to generate more powerful explanations of social activities. Much of this formal literature has examined mathematical applications, schemes for sampling, tests for reliability of self-report data, and the nature of intracultural variation. Although this literature is inherently interesting, especially for anthropologists with formal training in mathematics, it is of only partial relevance to a study of the dynamics of New York's West African trading networks.

Of greater relevance are those studies that link ethnographic practice to social network analysis.

There is no doubt that networks were an important element in the earlier work of social anthropologists in urban settings . . . , but it was more than the complexity of urban life that led these researchers to rely on these concepts so centrally in their work. Had they been survey researchers, it is doubtful that the notion of a social network would have had such a prominent place in their studies. Because they were ethnographers, engaged in the web of everyday life, an understanding of social networks was critical for obtaining the latest gossip, seeking information on hard-to-see events (e.g., rituals, drug use), and establishing friendships that would ultimately lead to the development of key informant relationships. It was the ethnographic context itself, that, explicitly or implicitly, made understanding network relations so important.[22]

As Mary Noble stated more than a generation ago: "A network approach then appears to offer a deeper understanding of human behavior."[23]

This innovative analytic technique has resulted in several important studies of urban networks. Scholars have studied the personal networks of former mental patients and delimited urban structures by isolating overlapping cliques. Others have applied the same technique further afield. Thomas Weisner, for example, has focused on the dynamics of urban-rural networks in East Africa, discovering that network entanglements vary with clan, social rank, and location.[24]

There are two kinds of social networks that anthropologists have considered: personal and whole. The great thrust of anthropological writing has focused on personal, or ego-centered, social networks. Within these networks, according to Mitchell, social behavior is interpreted in terms of three orders of social relations: structural, categorical, and personal. The structural order concerns the relation of the individual to some kind of institution (family, association, or trade union). The categorical order refers to how behavior is considered in terms of such broad social constructs as class, race, or ethnicity. The personal order, by contrast, is a framework for behavioral interpretation held in place by the mesh of the individual's personal relationships in a social network.[25]

When people in social networks interpret behavior from one of the three frameworks, they generate, in Mitchell's language, information, transactions, and expectations. Information that is exchanged between members of a social network is extremely important in economic contexts, for information about goods is central to ongoing transactions. After the theft of his cloth inventory, Issifi Mayaki integrated himself in the network of compatriot street vendors in New York City through which he acquired an informal loan. Issifi also received information from compatriot traders that enabled him to find reliable suppliers of cassettes and, later on, textiles, both original and reproduced.

Transactions define a key activity in the social networks of West African traders in New York City. People in these multiplex networks, which transcend ethnic and national categories, engage in continuous transactions.

There are, of course, countless exchanges between West African merchants, with many permutations. Thus, it is possible to find

1. exchanges between compatriots of the same ethnicity (e.g., Nigeriens who are both Hausa);
2. exchanges between compatriots of differing ethnicity (e.g., a Songhay and a Hausa Nigerien);
3. exchanges between noncompatriots of the same ethnicity (e.g., a Malian and a Nigerien Songhay); and
4. exchanges between noncompatriots of differing ethnicity (a Malian Fulan and Senegalese Wolof).

The greater the degree of proximity between national identity, the greater the density of transaction. Compatriots of the same ethnicity exchange inventory and extend one another informal loans. Sometimes they combine resources to travel to what they call the American bush. In the summer of 1995, Soumana Harouna, Issifi Mayaki, Amadou Bita, Moussa Boureima, and Sala Fari, Nigerien Hausas all, frequently traveled in the American bush. These travels usually excluded non-Hausa and non-Nigeriens (see chaps. 5 and 8). Transactions in the informal economy of New York City, of course, are not limited to exclusive West African networks. As we have seen, West African street vendors are supplied by a variety of wholesale traders—Asians, Arabs, and Israelis. In Harlem, many traders enter informal agreements with African American, Korean, and Jewish store owners, who rent them storage space. In lower Manhattan, West African traders rent store and shelf space from Jewish and Arab store owners.

One must also consider to whom West African vendors sell their merchandise. Issifi Mayaki, for example, sells almost exclusively to patrons at the Malcolm Shabazz Harlem Market, which means that most of his clients are local African Americans. In addition, he sometimes sells items to tourists: Europeans, Japanese, and Americans, both African Americans and whites curious about Harlem, which, it should be added, has become a favorite tourist stop in Giuliani's New York. At the Malcolm Shabazz Harlem Market, entrepreneurs like Boubé Mounkaila, who has sold both leather goods from Niger and wristwatches from Korea and China, routinely ask tour group leaders to bring tourists to their booths—for a fee, of course.

Some of the traders at the market have engaged in both retail and wholesale activities. Issifi Mayaki has sold colorful African cloth to individual buyers at the market, but has also supplied cloth to various African American boutiques up and down the East Coast of North America.

Information and transactions result in varying amounts of economic satisfaction, which in turn generates multiple sets of expectations. In Mitchell's language, the normative content of social networks "refers to that aspect of the relationship between two individuals which can be referred to the expectations each may have of the other because of some social characteristic or social attribute the other may possess. . . . These perceptual categories exist as frameworks for evaluating the behaviour of people in the appropriate situations."[26] Prior to the theft of his inventory, Issifi participated in the wide-ranging social networks associated with the African art and textile trade in the United States. The theft obliterated his trust in international textile traders, and as a result, his expectations of them, which had been based on Islamic precepts, shifted. Asian traders say they like to do business with West Africans because men like Boubé Mounkaila and Issifi Mayaki usually pay in cash. If they are extended credit, according to the Asians, they repay their informal loans quickly. Based on their transaction experience, Asians expect West Africans to be good trading partners. By the same token, they tend to be suspicious of African American informal traders, expecting them to be devious or dishonest. Such a belief may well be the result of their transaction experience or of what Mitchell calls the categorical order in which behavior—actual or expected—is judged in terms of a person's social category. In the latter case, the Asian assessment of African American traders seems to spring from a combination of actual experience and racist stereotyping, all of which affects how information and transactions course through the maze of socioeconomic networks.

With this focus on the personal, anthropologists have been less concerned with what Johnson calls "whole networks," more abstract structures that can be represented in matrix form. Studies of "whole networks" have considered "studies of relations, studies of structures, and statistical approaches to the study of networks."[27] More specifically, scholars working on whole networks are concerned with such issues as the dynamics of network formation, network density and clustering, formal treatments of how people communicate through networks and how network structures affect decision making.[28] Working specifically with economic networks, Borje Johansson constructs a variety of mathematical models that describe the dynamics of economic organizations that have "composite internal networks for resource flows and for communication and coordination of production and other activities. The links of such networks function as channels for information exchange and flow of resources. Attached to internal networks one can identify links which extend beyond the boundaries of each organization. Those links connect the organization with other economic units." After presenting a dizzying array of equations that construct models to predict market behavior, Johansson states that his work "suggests how and under which conditions the economic links remain, develop or disappear. The links form networks and these we claim to be an important ingredient in many types of markets."[29]

Although Johansson's equations are of questionable relevance to an ethnographic study of economic networks in transnational spaces, his framework is quite useful. The personal networks of individual West African traders do indeed consist of a series of what Johansson calls links across which information and goods flow. In New York City, moreover, the network of West African informal traders is linked to other networks that constitute other kinds of economic organizations: Asians in lower Manhattan; Arabs and Israelis in midtown Manhattan; Arabs, Jews, and Pakistanis along Canal Street; cloth and leather goods suppliers in Ghana, Cameroon and Mali.

To render these networks a bit more precisely, let us reconsider the economic links of Issifi Mayaki in terms of network analysis. Consider figure 2, a schematic of Issifi's personal economic network in New York City. First and foremost, Issifi is part of a large network of West African traders in New York who are connected through ties of fictive kinship, ethnicity, and national identity. This network has varying degrees of density, determined by the frequency and nature of interaction between Issifi and his trading partners. The space closest to Issifi, noted as area 1, is reserved for people who like Issifi are Hausa and Nigerien. These men are Issifi's intimates, with whom he shares a wealth of information and resources that constitute a foundation of sociocultural, emotional, and economic support. Compatriots who do not share Issifi's ethnicity are linked in area 2. Issifi has frequent contact with these Nigerien Songhay and Fulan men, but he doesn't share an African language with them, and because of historical and sociocultural differences, the level of economic trust and social intimacy doesn't match that of his contacts in area 1.[30] Moving further from Issifi's center, we encounter traders from Mali, proximate to Niger, who share with Issifi neither ethnicity nor national identity. These men are Bamana, Fulan, and Soninke, ethnic groups with whom Issifi has had extensive economic and social contact in Niger and Côte d'Ivoire. They are middlemen in Issifi's cloth dealings and occupy a more distant space in Issifi's network, area 3. Issifi has less extensive contact with Senegalese traders, mostly Wolof. Many of them are Mourids, who owe allegiance not so much to other West Africans in New York City as to their *cheik* in Touba City, Senegal.[31] In our depiction of Issifi's network, they are located in area 4. As we move farther out into the space of Issifi's West African trading network, the frequency of contact and degree of trust diminishes.

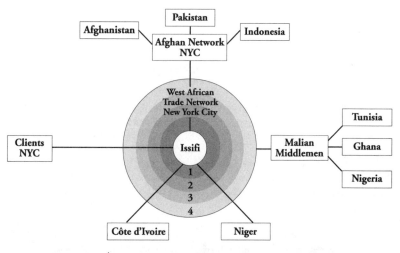

FIGURE 2. ISSIFI MAYAKI'S PERSONAL ECONOMIC NETWORK

Issifi's economic network in New York, of course, is not limited to West Africans. He receives some reproduced cloth from Asians (Indians, Pakistanis, and Afghanis) who are, in turn, linked not only to Issifi but to their own Asian contacts in New York as well as to suppliers in India, Pakistan, and Indonesia. In Issifi's network, these non-African links are both literally and figuratively more distant than his West African connections. His interactions with the former are purely economic and short-lived. There is a lack of shared culture, although trust has built up over time through mutually satisfactory transactions.

Issifi's links to clients extend the space in his personal economic network. He has a few regular clients to whom he sells cloth. Most of his clients are either local African Americans or tourists—Americans of all backgrounds, Europeans, and Japanese. The social contours of specific transactions frame these socially distant, but economically productive interactions.

Issifi's personal economic network among West Africans is not limited, of course, to New York City. He has economic and social ties to both Côte d'Ivoire, where his father and brothers reside, and to Niger, where his mother and her kin live. Like many West African long-distance traders, his kinship and economic networks are inextricably linked. This linkage, a process of using kinship idioms and ideology to shift social dislocation into culturally productive categories, transforms urban social instability and uncertainty into economically productive social continuity.[32] The linkage of kinship and long-distance trading, as we saw in chapter 3, has been common among African merchants. There are many traders in New York City, however, who are part of international networks that are not kin-based. Even so, as we have seen, the social continuity of these networks is ensured by the mutually binding system of rights and obligations characterized by West African systems of kinship.

The depiction of Issifi's transnational and transcultural interactions in figure 2, despite its complexity, is nonetheless incomplete, for it primarily plots Issifi's economic interactions. It says little about how political and legal regimes—and their representatives—affect his economic well-being. It reveals even less about how people in his personal network provide him social and emotional support. These topics will be considered in chapters 6, 7, and 8.

Boubé Mounkaila refers to himself as a leather specialist. He has been selling African leather goods—purses, wallets, satchels, traveling bags, and attaché cases—since his arrival in the United States in 1990. Boubé says that he likes to sell African leather goods. He likes the ingenuity of their various designs as well as the opportunity they give him to meet a wide assortment of people—mostly women. Since 1996, he has complemented his African bag inventory with wristwatches. Between 1990 and 1992, Boubé sold from makeshift tables on 34th Street near Times Square. Although that spot in midtown Manhattan provided him substantial returns on his investment, he found it difficult to deal with continuous police pressure. "The police would come and ask if I had a permit. I didn't. But they liked me and didn't give me a fine and didn't ask me for my papers. They just told me to move on."[33]

After Boubé had some of his leather inventory confiscated, he decided, based on information gleaned from links in his personal economic network, to try to sell his wares on 125th Street in Harlem. His contacts told him that the police would not bother him uptown and that 125th Street, Harlem's main thoroughfare, attracted legions of shoppers. He set up his table with Sala Fari, on the north side of 125th Street between Lenox and 7th Avenues, where a cluster of Nigerien traders, Hausa and Songhay, had established themselves. The information he had received through his network proved to be correct. Even though he had no permit to sell his goods, Boubé operated his business openly without any interference from the police. At that time, New York's finest seemed more interested in ticketing illegally parked cars than enforcing city regulations, licensing agreements, or trademark statutes.

As promised, legions of shoppers filled the streets during the week and especially on weekends.

Boubé's personal network, however, is far different from that of Issifi (see fig. 3). Although both of them share links in a West African trading network, Boubé, who is a Songhay, gathers his economic information from a wider array of sources, many of whom are non-Songhay and non-Nigerien. Unlike the Hausa, who have a long history of relying on one another in long-distance trading situations, Songhay are more widely known for their warrior past than for their prowess as long-distance traders. Boubé, for example, has rarely traveled in the American bush with his compatriots. He routinely receives information on market and other economic conditions from Senegalese traders and from African American clients and suppliers—people who are more culturally and experientially distant from him.

He also has ongoing and productive economic relationships with Taiwanese and Korean watch wholesalers. Since both the Taiwanese and Koreans supply Boubé with knockoff goods (watches with "trademarked" logos), trust is a major component of their relationships. Boubé says he has always paid his Taiwanese and Korean suppliers in cash, which, he says, instills confidence and ensures continuity. He also says that his Asian suppliers have never complained to him about police harassment, or citations, meaning, from Boubé's perspective, that they trust him with their "unregulated" merchandise.[34]

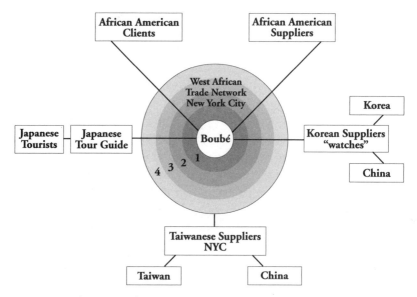

FIGURE 3. BOUBÉ MOUNKAILA'S PERSONAL ECONOMIC NETWORK

In August of 1994 this trust was momentarily compromised—unwittingly so. Boubé had invited me to meet his Taiwanese wristwatch supplier, who has a showroom near Broadway and 28th Street, a section in Manhattan called the Gift District. This neighborhood, which is mostly Asian, is well known for its wholesale business in hats, caps, handbags, beads, and costume jewelry. Before entering the shop, Boubé pointed out other Asian wholesalers—Broadway Bags and Ronette Hats—major suppliers of West African traders. Accordingly, it was not surprising to see many West African traders, mostly Senegalese, walking along streets with bags filled with newly purchased inventory. We entered the showroom.

Two young Taiwanese greeted Boubé by name.

"This is my friend, Paul," Boubé said introducing me.

The Taiwanese men frowned and seemed visibly upset.

Sensing their discomfort, Boubé said: "He's been to my country and to my village and he speaks my language. He's really an African," he said.

One of the young men said he didn't believe Boubé.

"Listen," Boubé said turning to me. In Songhay he said: "Speak Songhay to me. These people think you're a cop who has come here to arrest them."

"Why do they think I'm a cop?" I responded in Songhay.

"They wonder why else would a white man wearing jeans accompany an African trader on a visit to his supplier of knockoff watches?"

"I see," I said to him. I turned toward the two young Taiwanese and spoke to them in English. "I lived in Boubé's country for seven years. Now I live near Philadelphia where I work as a teacher. When I come to New York, I like to visit him and speak his language. He invited me here to meet you."

With that explanation, some of the tension drained from their bodies and they smiled a bit as they extended their hands to me.

"Boubé," one of the men said to me, "is a good customer. Always pays his bills."

The Taiwanese still seemed nervous. Boubé inspected the new inventory and ordered 150 watches. One of the young men calculated the bill for the wholesale goods; it came to $450.00.

"I'll come back tomorrow with cash and pick up the order," Boubé said.

"But, Boubé," one of the young men said, "you take the order now. We trust you."

"No thank you. You know that I'd rather pay and then pick up the order tomorrow."

One of the Taiwanese smiled at me. "Boubé is a good customer."

After we left the showroom, Boubé said that the Taiwanese's nervousness hadn't surprised him. "They think that a bearded white man wearing jeans," he said in French, "is going to be the police or an undercover agent for the City [the Bureau of Consumer Affairs, which enforces trademark statutes]. These Chinese," he said, "are often suspicious of whites and African Americans, but usually get on well with African traders."[35]

I was pleased that my visit had not compromised Boubé's relationship with his wristwatch supplier, but it underscored the legal fragility of unregistered operations that are major links in the transnational networks that constitute much of New York City's informal economy. This fragility requires a bond of unflagging trust between economic partners, a trust that, given the conditions of informality in New York City trading, frequently transcends sociocultural and national boundaries.

Boubé's network has also been linked to African Americans in Harlem. Prior to 1997, he stored his inventory of leather goods in a battered black Econoline van. Although Boubé was at the time an undocumented alien who had no driving license in Niger or New York, he managed to buy the van from another West African—no questions asked. Enlisting the aid of compatriots, he procured liability insurance. In 1996, Boubé painted the address "1 Fifth Avenue," on one of the van's side panels, an address, he said jokingly, that gave his van an aura of economic authenticity. He proudly showed me his inspection stickers. Even with its 145,000 miles, the vehicle had easily passed.

The van became central to Boubé's operation. At the end of each business day, Boubé packed the van with his inventory and took it to a fenced-in "security" parking lot at 123rd Street and Park Avenue—just under the Metro North railroad tracks. He paid $150 a month to the African American attendants, which enabled him to park his vehicle there. After thieves broke into his "secured" van, Boubé found another parking/storage facility at Lexington Avenue and 125th Street. Because of his then undocumented status, he didn't report the theft to the police. Frustrated by the expense and time he had to devote to storage, Boubé eventually built and secured his own storage bins at the Malcolm Shabazz Harlem Market. "No more parking garages. No more dealings with the parking garage people."[36] By tapping into his network, Boubé had been able surmount a variety of economic challenges. By the winter of 1998, an improving economic climate combined with Boubé's commercial skills brought a flood of profits to his enterprise, enabling him to buy a Lexus.

So far, we have sampled a slice of life at the Malcolm Shabazz Harlem Market and have seen the broader economic and social context within which West African traders in New York City operate. We have also considered how Islam and the history of long-distance trade in West Africa have influenced the trading practices of West Africans in New York City. Through those time-honored practices, West African traders have created complex and highly flexible transnational networks from which they derive valuable information, generate trust, and receive economic support.

I have tried to present an overview, then, of a community whose economic values are profoundly influenced by their faith and by their cultural and family histories. We also have a sense of how they have employed tradition to meet the economic challenges of a global city's informal economy. In short, we have seen how and why West Africans have established their informal enterprises in New York City. In the next chapter, we shall consider how these traders market their wares in New York City. More specifically, we look at how West Africans have commodified Afrocentric ideology, transforming it into profits.

64   One morning in July 1993, Boubé Mounkaila and Sala Fari parked their
Econoline van on 125th street just opposite the Carver State Bank, which
is perhaps a hundred meters from the cultural crossroads of Harlem: 125th
Street and Lenox Avenue. They hadn't put much mileage on the van because
they used it almost exclusively to store inventory. Each morning they un-
loaded their wares and set up their display on rickety aluminum tables; each
evening they folded their tables packed up the van and parked it in a 125th
Street garage. That morning Sala, dressed in baggy blue jeans, black tennis
shoes, a plain white T-shirt, a denim vest, and a New York Yankees baseball cap, arranged on his table a variety of men's and women's straw hats,
which he sold for between five and ten dollars each. Boubé wore black jeans
and a black T-shirt that had an image of a homeboy on it—a young African
American male dressed in baggy jeans, tennis shoes, and a baseball cap worn
sideways. The shirt listed seven major African American universities and
spelled out in large red letters, "It's a Black Thang." Put together much like
the homeboy depicted on his shirt, Boubé arranged sets of Nigerien leather
wallets and bags, his primary product. At that time he was also selling baseball caps, many of which carried the logos of sports teams.

"Georgetown Hoyas sells well," he said. "So do the Chicago Bulls and the
New York Yankees."

I noticed that he had several caps that spelled out "Harlem," another
several with two men shaking hands under the words "Brother to Brother."
Finally, I noticed a new item: black baseball caps inscribed with a large silver
"X," which, of course, represented Malcolm X.

I asked Boubé about the Malcolm X caps.

"They sell well," he said. "They have put 'X' on everything." He pointed to another table close by that featured "X" T-shirts and sweatshirts. Boubé admitted that he didn't know too much about Malcolm X. He had heard that Malcolm X had preached on the streets of Harlem and that he founded the mosque on 116th Street and Lenox and that he had been assassinated.

"They have a good *halal* [Muslim] butcher," he said, "at his 116th Street mosque. That's where I buy my meat. I also go to that mosque for Jummah [Friday/Sabbath] prayers."

"Where do you get the caps?" I asked him.

"I have two kinds of caps: original and copy. Originals come from Spike Lee. Copies come from Koreans off Broadway." Boubé continued to arrange his baseball caps. "Right now many *frères* ['brothers,' that is, fellow Africans] are selling 'X,' and many people here are buying and wearing it."[1]

Malcolm X is one of the principal icons of Afrocentrism. For Molefi Asante, a central figure of the Afrocentric movement, Malcolm X is a powerful symbol of African culture.

> Malcolm's view of culture was centered principally on an Afrocentric founda-
> tion. He did not assert the development of national culture as a result of eco-
> nomic necessity. He neither tried to prove nor would he have been so inclined
> to prove that historical events were always caused by economic necessity. In
> reality, Malcolm was an astute observer of the historical conditions of African
> Americans and he saw that in the serious reconstruction of African culture,
> the struggle for power and the ability to create categories which are accepted
> by others frequently played a much more important role than economic neces-
> sity. Beyond this, however, was his insistence on African cultural autonomy by
> which he meant all things considered cosmological, axiological, epistemolog-
> ical and aesthetical. Given such autonomy it was possible to imagine a culture
> of resistance as well as a reconstructive culture.[2]

For Boubé Mounkaila, the significance of Malcolm X is more mercenary than political. In fact "X," which stood for Malcolm Little's lost African iden-tity, is for Boubé and his friends a polysemous symbol of major cultural con-sequence. As already stated, Boubé is Songhay. Among the Songhay people of Niger, "X" marks a particular spot in Songhay ritual: it is one sign for a crossroads and considered a point of power in the Songhay cosmos. It marks the spot of sacrifice during spirit possession and is articulated as a target for power in sorcerers' rites. In these ceremonies, a deity acting through a human medium draws an "X" in the sand of the dance grounds, designating where the priest is to slit a chicken's or goat's throat. Blood soaks into the earth where "X" marks the spot; it nourishes the land and makes it fertile for planting. In sorcerers' rites, "X" also serves as a point of articulation. When sorcerers prepare *kusu,* the food of power, they mark an "X" on the dirt floor of their huts where a clay pot will sit. Only then will power infuse the millet paste and enable it to do its work—to make one impervious to sorcerous attack and to reinforce the sorcerer's embodied integrity.[3] In North America, however, the significant religious contours of "X" are eclipsed by the symbols' economic potential.

In fact, "X" marks one of the largest merchandising agreements and most controversial marketing campaigns in twentieth-century North America. As a consequence, the image, likeness, name, and meaning of Malcolm X has been an ongoing focus of political and legal controversy. The choice of Spike Lee to direct a film about the martyred black nationalist sparked disputes about Malcolm X's legacy; it also marshaled forces that promoted the "commodification" of his persona. The late Dr. Betty Shabazz, Malcolm X's widow, fought the first round of legal battles with a copyright infringement suit against publishers of the book, *Malcolm X for Beginners.* Opponents accused Shabazz of violating her late husband's code of ethics by prohibiting wider access to Malcolm X's progressive ideas. For her part, Shabazz downplayed her financial interest and stressed her copyright as the proper guardian of Malcolm X's legacy. When publicity for Spike Lee's Warner Brothers film increased the value of Malcolm's persona, she began to assert her proprietary rights.[4] In 1992, *Forbes* magazine claimed that "retail sales of licensed Malcolm X products, all emblazoned with a large 'X' could reach $100 million this year. (The estate would then collect $3 million in royalties.)"[5] A licensing manager was hired when various assortments of unlicensed X merchandise—even Malcolm X potato chips—began to appear on the streets of New York and other North American cities. By October of 1992, thirty-five licensees had signed contracts, and seventy more were negotiating contracts.[6] Of these negotiations, those of Spike Lee's corporation, Forty Acres and a Mule, which had initiated the retail trade, proved to be the most drawn out. Lawyers for the Malcolm X estate described his use of X as a blatant trademark infringement. This charge, triggered perhaps by a 1992 estimate of some $20 million in sales of unlicensed X merchandise, complicated the negotiations and set the stage for a settlement. The negotiations entailed dozens of interested parties and a legion of attorneys, who worked out the details of copyright, trademark, publicity, and merchandising rights to the iconographic presence of Malcolm X. Eventually these rights were multiplied, divided up, and licensed out.[7] This licensing, of course, did not prevent trade in counterfeit Malcolm X goods. Indeed, West African merchants like Boubé Mounkaila bought and sold "originals and copies" of X. Most of his customers, Boubé admitted, couldn't tell the difference between the two—"except in the price."[8]

The buying and selling of Malcolm X's persona is but one example of how the marketplace has transformed powerful elements of Afrocentrism. Regardless of whether we are talking about African American or West African marketing, for Asante and other scholars it is a disturbing trend. It undermines the reconstruction of a historically profound Afrocentric culture among African Americans and dilutes powerful Afrocentric symbols in the commercial mainstream of North American social life. As a consequence, the essential components of Afrocentrism are sometimes lost amid commodification's hype and hoopla.

Afrocentrism is a specific philosophical orientation to African and African American sociocultural life. It is a serious attempt to construct an epistemology based on principles of African philosophy, principles that, according to Molefi Asante, protect scholars from making interpretive errors that devolve from Eurocentric categorizations. Asante says that Afrocentrism is primarily a set of guidelines one can use to interpret a wide variety of data. Afrocentrists work in two domains, the cultural/aesthetic and the social/behavioral, which cut across traditional disciplinary boundaries. In essence, "Afrocentricity is a perspective which allows Africans to be subjects

AFROCENTRIC SIGNS DISPLAYED IN WILMINGTON, DELAWARE. (PHOTO BY AUTHOR)

of historical experiences rather than objects on the fringes of Europe. This means that the Afrocentrist is concerned with discovering in every case the centered place of the African."[9]

More specifically, Afrocentrism is a sustained critique of Eurocentric philosophy, which in Asante's universe means the various constructive philosophies—beginning with Kant and Hegel—that constitute the universalizing modernist project, in which elegantly simple principles explain a diverse array of data. Asante's orientation is not so much to condemn Eurocentric philosophy as to suggest alternative explanations. Alternative epistemological sets are needed, he claims, to fully understand culturally specific sets of data. Put another way, Asante suggests that one needs to assume an African perspective, shaped by African ideas, to interpret data on African or African American social life and culture.[10] According to Asante's "Diopian" (or diffusionist) view, the fundamental tenets of African systems of thought, which he describes in both *The Afrocentric Idea* (1987) and *Kemet, Afrocentricity, and Knowledge* (1990), devolve from Kemet, or the civilization of ancient Egypt.[11] Asante argues that all African societies, including those found in the New World, trace their fundamental philosophical concepts to ancient Egypt. Take, for example, ideas about harmony in the world associated with the ancient Egyptian goddess Ma'at. These concepts include

1. *tep* (beginning), associated with the adornment of children, late weaning, age-grading, and the cultural importance of fertility;
2. *pet* (extensions), in which the group is more valued than the individual in a society of extended families that honor their ancestors;
3. *heb* (festival), in which the group emphasizes ritual in social life;
4. *sen* (circle), in which the group celebrates in a cyclical rather than a linear cycle of life; and
5. *meh* (crowning glory), belief in a supreme deity, a quest for harmoniousness as well as a pride in one's life.

Asante believes that these core social concepts are embedded in the expressive culture of all African peoples—including African Americans. "The transformation of these concepts throughout Africa and the African world has meant that the influence of Kemet continues unabated even in the language and behavior of African Americans. We are essentially a people of Ma'at, we cannot escape it because it is based upon thousands of years of history."[12]

There are by now many works written by Afrocentric scholars like Asante that focus on questions of history, the arts, culture, psychology, and education. But Afrocentrism is more than the exercise of employing these core principles to the scholarly analysis of things African and African American; it is also the attempt to extend them to African Americans through ritual.

The most important and widely practiced Afrocentric ritual is Kwanzaa, a seven-day African American holiday celebrated between Christmas and the New Year. Kwanzaa was first celebrated by Maulena Karenga on December 26, 1966, in Los Angeles. Karenga shaped the festival to celebrate a set of core African values, what Dorothy Winbush Riley calls "ancient wisdom." This wisdom is more or less what Molefi Asante attributes to Kemet. For Karenga, these values are best articulated in Swahili, one of the most widely spoken languages in Africa. The seven core principles (*nguzo saba*) are *umoja*, unity; *kujichagulia*, self-determination; *ujima*, collective work and responsibility; *ujamaa*, cooperative economics; *nia*, purpose; *kuumba*, creativity; and *imani*, faith.[13] Each day of the seven-day festival is associated with one of the seven sacred principles. On day one, for example, which celebrates the *umoja* principle, people are urged to celebrate in some fashion the principle of unity. On day seven, *imani*, people express their faith through the exchange of gifts, preferably homemade. Just as Kwanzaa features seven principles, it also features seven symbols that underscore its Afrocentric foundation.[14] In her book, *The Complete Kwanzaa: Celebrating Our Cultural Harvest*, Dorothy Winbush Riley produces something akin to a Kwanzaa handbook, replete with poems and literary passages reflecting the themes of the seven sacred principles. The book also describes in great detail the rituals encompassed by the Kwanzaa feast and includes menus and recipes from Riley's own Kwanzaa celebrations. Mirroring the Afrocentric discourse of Molefi Asante, Riley writes: "Kwanzaa unites nuclear families and extended families, reaffirming that we must live in reciprocal dependence, while seeking dignity, justice and equality. It is system that welcomes change, celebrating the present while planning for tomorrow. This modern holiday allows Africa's children, scattered on every continent, a way to preserve the details of the motherland and to enjoy prosperity by using ancient wisdom to solve today's problems."[15]

Just as the serious and complex persona of Malcolm X has been commodified on T-shirts, sweatshirts, baseball caps, and bags of potato chips, so the rich symbolism and meaning of Kwanzaa has been marketed to the North American mainstream. According to Malauna Karenga, Kwanzaa originated as an attempt "to reaffirm African culture. . . . It was at the same time a political act of self-determination. The question is how to make our own unique culture. We were talking about Africanization."[16] At first Kwanzaa drew only about two hundred celebrants. In 1995 an estimated ten million African

Americans celebrated Kwanzaa. In some sense Kwaanza "is rapidly winning a place on the nation's holiday calendar alongside Chanukah and Christmas. But like all things that succeed in America, Kwanzaa . . . has become big business. What was conceived . . . as a low-key, low-cost ritual centered on table and hearth is now beginning to look a lot like, well . . . Christmas."[17]

Kwaanza has become, in other words, a mainstream American holiday. This fact has two social ramifications: Kwanzaa is increasingly celebrated by middle-class African Americans who have a great deal of money to spend and the holiday has become increasingly commercial. "The changing celebration patterns of Kwanzaa reflect national patterns in America, notably the rise of the black middle class and the simultaneous popularization in the 1980s and 1990s of a 'multicultural' ideal in which people assert themselves as members of ethnic minorities instead of integration into the 'majority culture.' In the late 1960s, Kwanzaa was a manifestation of the black separatism of that decade, a backlash by 'revolutionaries' against what was seen as the failed integration of 'black bourgeoisie.' "[18]

Henry Louis Gates Jr., who is among the most widely respected African American intellectuals in the United States, also links the mainstreaming of Kwanzaa to the rise of a black middle class that feels alienated from white society. "We were the first large-scale number of black people to come to historically white institutions. . . . There is a resulting cultural alienation." Gates goes on to suggest that middle-class African Americans often feel "the guilt of the survivor" and buy Afrocentric items as a way of maintaining cultural fidelity with blackness.[19] Kwame Anthony Appiah, author of the much celebrated *In My Father's House* (1992), has a similar take on Kwanzaa: "African American culture is so strongly identified with a culture of poverty and degradation . . . you have a greater investment, as it were, more to prove [if you are middle class], so Kwanzaa and kente cloth are part of proving you're not running away from being black, which is what you're likely to be accused of by other blacks."[20] For his part, Gerald Early, a professor of African American studies at Washington University in St. Louis, sees the mass appeal of Kwanzaa somewhat differently from Gates and Appiah: "Racial piety also permeates the Kwanzaa principles. Such simple maxims are the sort of earnest ideals that are difficult to oppose or argue with. No one questions whether they really have any connection to the complexity of modern African-American life. The genius of Kwanzaa—the reason it has taken on the air of a mass movement—is that these rather innocuous principles are joined with an historical complaint, one that blacks have long harbored, against the cultural celebration of Christmas." In other words, the success of Kwanzaa is an expression of African American alienation from the whiteness of Christmas. But Early argues further that the rituals of Kwanzaa operate on both a more profound and a more superficial level:

> In Kwanzaa, African Americans seek nothing less than redemption from their status as second-class Americans and incomplete Africans. It is the culmination of a century-long project to create a civic religion that will be able to contain their American and African selves. But the danger with this sort of therapy is that it trivializes the profundity of the very heritage it is attempting to make sacred. With Kwanzaa the African American reduces the complexity of his ancestry to the salve of cure. All that we get from millennia of history and profound cultural experience is to feel good about ourselves.[21]

Whatever reason one suggests for the mainstreaming of Kwaanza, few people—including, of course, West African entrepreneurs in Harlem—can doubt its vast commercial power. During Kwanzaa, Afrocentric symbols—strips of "kente" cloth, Hallmark Kwanzaa greeting cards, gift wraps, and Nia Umoja (a white-bearded doll symbolizing the wisdom of African story-tellers)—are easily found in giftshops, bookstores, drugstores, and supermarkets, as well as in such stalwart American stores as Sears, J. C. Penney, and Montgomery Ward. Afrocentric products are also highly visible at various Kwanzaa Expos. Among the most firmly established of these is the Kwanzaa Expo in St. Louis, established in 1987. It typically draws some 220 merchants and perhaps 35,000 people during its two-day run.[22] The largest Kwaanza Expo takes place in New York City. Held first in 1981 at a public school in Harlem, the New York Kwanzaa Expo moved to the Jacob Javits Center in 1993. What had been a small commercial gathering needed a larger venue to make space for more than 300 vendors and 50,000 shoppers. Booths representing such mainstream American corporations as Anheuser-Busch, Pepsi, Revlon, Chemical Bank, AT&T, and Time-Life Books had been set up. And no wonder, "for the middle-class black community supports a national market for Kwaanza goods estimated to be worth as much as $100 million."[23] In 1995, the New York Kwanzaa Expo featured elaborate arrays of Afrocentric books, cloth, and crafts—all meant to symbolize in some fashion the seven principles of Kwanzaa. In 1995 the Expo also drew African American entertainers, savvy politicians, and a good number of West African street vendors, including Boubé Mounkaila and Issifi Mayaki, both of whom "sold out" at the exposition. In December 1997, however, they chose not to attend the event at the Jacob Javits Center. "The fees for booths have become far too high," Issifi lamented. "We can no longer make a profit."[24]

The commodification of Kwanzaa is defended by many of the celebration's boosters. Speaking on behalf of Hallmark Cards, Rashena Lindsay stated in 1995: "If we want to embrace all cultures of the world, we need companies marketing to all people. What Hallmark tries to do is make cards for people regardless of color."[25] Taking a less capitalistic stance, Malik Ahmed, founder of the Kwanzaa Expo in St. Louis, called his creation an example of *ujamaa,* the Kwanzaa principle of cooperative economics. Cedric McLester, the spokesperson for the New York Kwanzaa Expo and creator of Nia Umoja, the African storyteller doll, agrees with Ahmed but also worries about the increasing corporatization of the celebration. "There is no problem with commercializing it, but who will be the benefactors of the commercialization . . . it should be people of African descent, not just corporate America."[26]

Many African American entrepreneurs share McLester's concern. In December 1997, the International Black Buyers and Manufacturer's Expo and Conference (IBBMEC), an association based in Washington, D.C., that represents more than a thousand black businesses, asked African Americans to boycott Kwanzaa goods not made or distributed by black companies. They suggested that "the sale of Kwanzaa products by companies 'not of African descent' is arrogantly exploitative of the culture of the African people.'" The boycott intended to cover Hallmark and other greeting cards reproduced by non–African American companies, as well as items manufactured by African American businesses but sold at white-owned supermarkets and drugstores. Sala Damali, one of the founders of IBBMEC, explained to the *Washington Post:* "Many companies look at it as a normal exercise of commerce. We find it insulting and disrespectful to the actual spirit of Kwanzaa." Understandably, "the association's campaign . . . sparked a debate among retailers, celebrants of Kwanzaa, and scholars over the holiday's growing commercialization and who should benefit from it. Kwanzaa devotees say buying holiday goods from nonblack businesses violates the very spirit of a celebration commemorating black culture. But the merchants say they are simply responding to the demands of the marketplace and showing respect for the holiday."[27]

Some of the West African merchants in New York City simply dismissed this debate: "It's just politics," Boubé Mounkaila said in 1994. "We are here for business, not politics."[28] Indeed, West Africans were among those merchants who routinely violated the principles of the proposed boycott. They sold Afrocentric products that are usually not produced or distributed by African American concerns. For them, the meaning of Kwanzaa has little cultural resonance; it is not so much a sacred celebration as a simulation of Africa that is good for business.

•••

As savvy entrepreneurs, Boubé Mounkaila, Issifi Mayaki, and their West African colleagues have realized that Africa sells very well indeed in North America. They are, of course, not alone in this realization. Many African American entrepreneurs are seeking profits by marketing Afrocentricity.

Five years ago, brightly colored hand-woven Kente cloth, brimless Kufi hats, earthy mud cloths from Ghana and Senegal and bone-toned cowrie shell jewelry appeared to be a nostalgic way of dressing among African Americans. Instead of a short-term fad, these elements have formed an exciting new trend— the Afrocentric lifestyle.

African Americans have placed ethnic products high on their shopping lists. No longer a form of "alternate" dressing or decorating, Afrocentric merchandise is among the hottest selling retail products on the market, with a growing crossover appeal to mainstream consumers.

Many African Americans are cashing in on this market. For these new black-owned businesses, the key to retailing success lies in selling ethnic products in large volume. But while the spirit is willing, their pockets are not always as deep. To take their message and products to market, many black-owned companies are forming joint-ventures with majority-owned corporations, from manufacturing to retail, to underwrite their production, marketing and distribution efforts.[29]

A case in point is Blackberry, an African American–owned retail company that sells Afrocentric products ranging from figurines to linens. Blackberry first opened a boutique in suburban Washington, D.C. Brisk sales compelled owners Dorothy and Diane White, mother and daughter, to open stores in leased spaces in major department stores (Woodward and Lothrop in Washington, D.C., and Wanamakers in Philadelphia). Before these two stores closed, however, the Whites had established a joint venture with Federated Department Stores, which runs Macy's and is the largest retailer in the United States. As a result Blackberry was, in 1996, one of eight shops at the Arcade at Macy's Herald Square store in New York City. Diane White says that 85 percent of her customers were African Americans, who mostly buy candleholders, pillows, ceramics, picture frames, and greeting cards. Blackberry also sealed a deal with Spiegel, which featured the store's merchandise in the fall and holiday issues of its catalog. "Looking ahead, White wants to make sure her deal with Macy's is so successful that more Blackberry shops can be opened in other locations. She envisions Blackberry becoming a national chain of boutique stores over the next five years. 'I'd like to be the next

Museum Store. Or to have an operation like the $100 million MOMA stores. I didn't leave a job at the World Bank for just one or two stores.' "[30]

As a report in *Black Enterprise* magazine makes clear, Afrocentric products have great commercial potential and are beginning to appeal to mainstream American consumers. Many Afrocentric products are sold through catalogs. Tonia Rawls, one of the organizers of the IBBMEC, told *Black Enterprise* in 1996 that African Americans, like any other segment of the American population, are mass consumers. They have also become, she stressed, retailers and manufacturers. She went on to say that Afrocentric products are "hot." Thus, the appeal of Afrocentric products has spread to the fash-

THE SPREAD AND APPEAL OF AFROCENTRIC PRODUCTS: MALIAN MUD CLOTH HAT IN MADRID, NEW MEXICO, WINTER 1997. (PHOTO BY JASMIN TAHMASEB MCCONATHA)

ion industry. African American jewelry designer Coreen Simpson, who runs Cameo Designs Ltd., has signed a joint venture agreement with Avon Products. "It's great being successful in the African American market. But to become successful, an African American designer must become popular and cross over. I always design with crossover appeal and never limit myself to my ethnic group. It's a matter of economics." Through Avon, Simpson established the Coreen Simpson Regal Beauty Collection, a budget line of jewelry. By 1996 Avon had created joint ventures with six additional African American designers.[31]

Prior to her association with Avon, Therez Fleetwood designed Afrocentric clothing for Mickey and Minnie Mouse in Disneyland. She began her association with Avon in 1994 as the main designer for Avon Boutique, a quarterly catalog of beauty and gift items geared to the African American market. "I always design with African American consumers in mind. I select elements from authentic African products I want to use, then water them down slightly to fit the lifestyles of African Americans." The Avon Boutique, according to Black Enterprise, produces twelve million catalogs each year. The catalogs generate multimillion dollar sales. Some 60 percent of its customers are African Americans, which signals, it seems, the crossover appeal of Avon's Afrocentric products.[32]

The tendency to "water down" African objects for contemporary African American tastes worries some commentators in the African American community. Timothy L. Jenkins, writing in a 1995 issue of American Visions, is concerned about dilution of African symbolism in Africa America:

> Accordingly, as kente-related products have soared into a major market, those who kept their fingers on the pulse of the African-American consumers soon learned that they neither understood nor seemed to care much that the hats, wraps, handbags and now umbrellas ostensibly worn to boast African roots had labels reading "Made in Taiwan."
>
> Not only was pricing more important than quality and authenticity for such enthusiasts, but the age-old sacred meanings and symbolisms of indigenous culture reflected in such products were oftentimes both figuratively and literally stood on their heads.

Jenkins goes on to suggest that this diluted comprehension of things African is widespread. He laments the fact that African American consumers of Afrocentric products have more desire for commodities than a comprehension of heritage: "And they virtually never questioned the fact that most of their fraternal and organization paraphernalia were mass produced from sweatshops generating no relevant employment along the pipeline of their production. Gone was any concern for the indigenous technical genius, unique social significance or residual economic benefits. Rather theirs was an appetite for mere commodities at the expense of heritage."[33]

Jenkins's commentary may be somewhat narrow and bit snobbish, but what he describes is part and parcel of a global phenomenon, the commodification of culture, which is not constrained by class, gender, or ethnicity. African Americans are not the only consumers attracted to diluted symbols or products—Afrocentric or otherwise. Throughout the world, people are increasingly drawn to the copy of the original, to the simulation of the real.[34] Much of this fascination with the copy can be traced to the emergence in the twentieth century of mechanical reproduction, the cinematic image in the theater. The allure of the copy has been further intensified through electronic reproduction, the computer image on the information superhighway. The power of the dynamic electronic image has eclipsed that of the static printed word. These issues have been explored in depth in Michael Taussig's *Mimesis and Alterity* (1993) in which the author documents powerfully the contemporary fascination with and power of the copy.[35] Drawing on the work of Walter Benjamin, Taussig identifies the human predilection to copy originals as the "mimetic faculty." He says that mimicry is about power. To copy something is to master it. But once it is made, the copy influences the original. As Rosemary Coombe puts it, the representation gains or shares in the power of the represented, and the image affects what it is an image of.[36]

As we have seen in the marketing of Afrocentric merchandise, the predilection to make copies and copies of copies significantly affects commercial relations as well as margins of profit and loss. In her work on the cultural and political signification of trademarks and copyrights, Coombe has focused on how the mimetic faculty affects the political and economic impact of trademarks. Focusing on contemporary commercial arenas like a Kwanzaa Expo or the Malcolm Shabazz Harlem Market, Coombe demonstrates how the trademark, which is an image, links the copy with its originator.

> A mark must attract the consumer to a particular source that, in mass markets, is often unknown and distant. A logo registers fidelity in at least two senses. It operates as a signature of authenticity, indicating that the good that bears it is true to its origins—that is, that the good is a true or accurate copy. It is exactly the same as another good bearing the same mark, and different from other goods carrying other marks (these are both fictions, of course, but ones that are legally recognized and maintained). The mark also configures fidelity in a

second sense; it registers a real contact, a making, a moment of imprinting by one for whom it acts as a kind of fingerprint-branding. But if the mark figures a fidelity, it also inspires fidelity in the form of brand loyalty. The consumer seeks it out, domesticates it, and provides it with protective shelter; he makes a form of bodily contact with it. The mark distinguishes the copy by connecting it to an originator and connecting the originator with a moment of consumption.[37]

Given this framework, we can see that Afrocentric marketing is one increasingly important example of the mimetic faculty. The original meaning of Malcolm Little's "X," which refers to African Americans' brutal disconnection from Africa, is often eclipsed by more contemporary significations. It also refers to the powerful and proud Black Nationalist discourse of Malcolm X, which can sometimes be heard on loudspeakers at the Malcolm Shabazz Harlem Market. It can be associated as well with the hype that surrounded Spike Lee's film *Malcolm X,* the publicity for which sparked the sales of "X" products. The marketing of this central Afrocentric symbol transformed it into a commodity that bears the considerable weight of current political, cultural, economic, and legal machinations. The same can be said of Kwanzaa, which like all celebrations is, in paraphrase of Eric Hobsbawn and Terrance Ranger, an invented holiday. Celebrants of Kwanzaa have borrowed ideas from Christmas and Chanukah to create a uniquely African American simulation, to use Jean Baudrillard's language, of an African harvest ritual. The stylized symbols and transcendent themes of Kwanzaa, which fit perfectly into the informational contours of what Manuel Castells calls the network society, have propelled the efflorescence of the celebration.[38] It now takes its rightful place along with Christmas and Chanukah as an end-of-the-year American holiday. A similar process is at work in the generalized marketing of Afrocentric products, which are often, as we have seen, "watered down" to fit the lifestyles of contemporary African Americans. African American designers, like the celebrants of Kwanzaa, have borrowed motifs from African material culture and have fashioned them into greeting cards, figurines, jewelry, clothing, bed linens, and tablecloths. Recognizing along with Homi Bhabha that the mimetic faculty is "the subject of difference that is almost the same, but not quite," African American entrepreneurs have captured the economic force of the copy.[39] By marketing Afrocentricity, they have sparked an expansion in the numbers of black-owned companies and the exponential growth of their sales.

African Americans, of course, are not the only entrepreneurs who have realized the considerable economic potential of Afrocentricity. As we have seen, such major mainstream corporations as Hallmark Cards, Avon, and Federated Department Stores routinely sell Afrocentric products. What's more, they have entered into joint ventures with African American design companies specializing in Afrocentric products to increase their market share in an expanding market.

Soon after they began to arrive in New York City in the late 1980s, West African street vendors also grasped the economic significance of marketing Afrocentricity. From their rickety card tables along the sidewalks of 125th Street, they began to sell such Afrocentric products as "kente cloth" strips and caps, Malian mud cloth, Tuareg silver jewelry. They also offered products, like "X" baseball caps and certain "trademarked" products, some original, some counterfeit, that had become fashionable among urban African Americans.[40] These products became part and parcel of a simulated African market on 125th Street.

Even though Afrocentric products have been "hot," there are economic ebbs and flows depending on the season. To maximize their economic opportunities, West African traders in New York have constructed long-distance trade networks throughout the United States. These networks enable the traders to follow the cycle of African American professional and cultural festivals. In 1994, Bandele Publications delighted West African traders by bringing out the first volume of its *Annual Small Business Guide to African-American and Multicultural Events: Conferences, Festivals, Shows.* Enterprising West African entrepreneurs have used this resource, which lists the dates, locales, contact people, and booth fees for more than seven hundred vending opportunities, to help chart their long-distance trading itineraries.

In the spring, summer, and fall of 1994, for example, a crew of four Nigerien traders, Hausas all, spent much of their time circulating among African American festivals in the East, South, and Midwest of the United States. That year the lure of profits propelled them to South Carolina to sell at the Spring Fling in Spartanburg, the Gullah Festival in Beaufort, and the Moja Arts Festival in Charleston. They traveled to Chicago, one of their best markets, to attend the Twentieth Annual Third World Conference and the African Festival of the Arts. In Atlanta, they displayed wares at the Marché Africain/African Market. In Philadelphia, they set up booths at the Africaamerica Festival, the Parade and Market. In New Orleans, they showed up at the African Heritage Festival International, and in Norfolk, Virginia, at the AFR'AM Festival. In Detroit, they presented themselves at the International Freedom Festival and the African World Festival. They also followed the Black Expo USA circuit, a traveling exposition that attracts large crowds of African Americans to regionally organized trade shows that feature and celebrate African American businesses. In 1994, Hausa traders from Harlem attended Black Expo trade shows in Atlanta, Washington, D.C., New York City, Chicago, Indianapolis, Detroit, Milwaukee, Richmond, and New Orleans.

Idé Younoussa, a thirty-five-year-old Songhay man from Niger, is known among Harlem's West African street vendors as "the Chauffeur." Although he has resided in Harlem and on the Upper West Side since 1989, he spends most of his time on the road. "I have been to more than twenty states in

AFRICANA ON DISPLAY AT TRADER JACK'S FLEA MARKET, SANTA FE, NEW NEXICO, SUMMER 1997. (PHOTO BY AUTHOR)

America: Florida, Indiana, Illinois, Texas, Missouri, Tennessee, Oklahoma, even New Mexico. Very beautiful, New Mexico. It's like Niger." In 1996, Idé transported his clients in a white Ford Econoline van with well over a hundred thousand miles on its odometer. When he travels, he helps his clients load their wares, drives them to their destination, and helps to unload the cargo. He expects his clients to pay him a fee for his services; he also insists that they pay for gas, tolls, potential repairs, and lodging. These costs are usually evenly split by Idé's charges.

Idé's van is registered in New York State. He has an international driver's permit as well as a New York license. When Idé transports his clients to distant locations, he usually drives through the night until the destination is reached. It takes Idé about twelve hours to travel from New York to Chicago and about sixteen hours to go from New York to Orlando, Florida. "I don't get tired on the road. Driving is my life; it gives me strength. I like the feeling I get on the road. It makes me feel free. I'm hardly ever in New York. Just for one or two days when I come back and then I'm off again. When I went to New Mexico, I made the round trip in only three days."[41]

Idé's clientele is not limited to West African street vendors from New York. He also transports itinerant West African art merchants. These merchants do not reside in the United States. They come to North America on bona fide business visas for three to six months, during which they sell African art to North American distributors, to galleries of African art, to boutiques or to private clients. Like the West African street vendors, the West African art merchants pay Idé a fee and provide him funds for repairs, gas, tolls, food, and lodging.

Idé is not the only chauffeur in the community of West African traders in New York. In the summer of 1995, Soumana Harouna, a Hausa from Dogondoutché in Niger whom we have met previously, bought a relatively new Econoline van. Soumana, who had been driving a Medallion cab, decided to invest in the van to transport West African merchants to festivals throughout the eastern half of the United States. He did so with great success. In 1996, however, he decided to give up his chauffeuring business. Through overuse, the van had fallen into disrepair. "Too many problems with the van. It was good last summer," he said in the winter of 1996. "But it will cost too much to repair. This summer I'll stay here and drive my cab."[42]

Idé, "the Chauffeur," is a major player in a West African long-distance trading network that has been established in North America. The center of the North American trading network is New York City, which is where one finds the greatest concentration of West African traders and the goods they import, buy, sell, or export back to West Africa. Since 1989, *frères* have routinely left New York. In short order, they have established outposts in Atlanta, Boston, Washington, D.C., Philadelphia, New Orleans, Houston, Chicago, Albuquerque, and Los Angeles, where they sell African crafts at local markets and festivals, form wholesale enterprises, or establish small boutiques. When *frères* from New York travel to one of these outposts, they expect, like their trading ancestors in West Africa, a local host to receive them. As we saw in chapter 3, the reception of traveling traders by their local hosts may entail temporary storage of goods, extension of credit, facilitation of sales in local markets, as well as food and lodging. In turn, when a local host travels to the network center, his trading partners will receive him in a similar manner. These long-distance trading relationships are facilitated by real or fictive ties of kinship, which, as we have seen, encompass a reciprocal set of rights and obligations. In North America, traditional West African trading patterns have been modified with great success.

Some of the traders in New York have blood kin in major markets outside of New York City. Ali Boubakar, another Hausa from Dogondoutché, has two brothers who live in the States. One is in Philadelphia; the other lives in Minneapolis. He also has a cousin who lives in Chicago. When he travels to Philadelphia or Chicago, he relies on his kin. He is his cousin's principal wholesale supplier. Most of the traders, however, do not have blood kin in major markets outside of New York City. They rely on fictive ties born of their shared experience in West Africa and of their expectations as pious Muslims—to create mutually binding commercial ties. In these relationships, hosts who are not blood kin to traveling traders will facilitate the business of their partners but usually do not house or feed them. For this reason, most traveling traders are prepared to spend several nights at cheap hotels, where four or five of them will share a room. When trading partners come to New York City, however, their *frères* not only facilitate their business, but also house and feed them. The reason for these inequities in hospitality is that in New York City there are many traders who have apartments in Harlem, the Bronx, and Brooklyn. Outside of New York, the number of *frères* is as limited as the living space they have to share. Unless visitors have blood kin residing in a place like Chicago, for example, they expect to stay in inexpensive hotels.[43]

So far we have seen that marketing Afrocentricity is a complex—and profitable—process in which the mimetic faculty is centrally involved. As a philosophical doctrine, Afrocentrism is primarily an epistemological stance in contradistinction to Eurocentric philosophy; it is based on long-standing African principles of philosophy—Asante's principles of Ma'at. These principles, borrowed from ancient Egypt, or Kemet, are applied not only to scholarly activities, but have been extended to such public policy issues as the curricula in public schools as well as to such public celebrations as Kwanzaa. Afrocentrism also generates ethnic pride: pride in the past greatness and current wisdom of African civilization. Pride in things African—or quasi-African—also generates economic potential. In 1995, for example, the manufacture and distribution of Afrocentric products produced yearly sales in excess of $100 million. African American entrepreneurs have found their niche in this market and have, accordingly, expanded their Afrocentric-oriented companies as well as their Afrocentric-produced profits.

West African vendors in New York City quickly grasped the appeal of a monolithic Afrocentric "Africa" in the African American imagination and in African American markets. Following a circuit of African American festivals, they extended their trading networks beyond New York City to major markets in the American South, East, and Midwest. Whether they do business at the Malcolm Shabazz Harlem Market or in what they call "the bush," which is any locale outside of New York City, these West Africans sell two forms of goods:

> unmarked goods that represent a reified Africa and counterfeit trademarked goods for an African American market. The African goods, ersatz kente cloth scarves, combs, trade beads, leather goods . . . are unmarked by any authorial signature or point of origin. West African export-importers, who do not reside in New York, order and bring in products specially made for the Harlem and Black Expo, USA, circuit. Knowing what forms Africa must take for an African American market, they produce generic items that are marked neither by artist, village, cultural area or region. Their distinction lies in their being African—a monolithic cultural whole in the Afrocentric imaginary.[44]

To be a real African in an African American economic niche that has constructed ideal Africans living in a largely imagined Africa creates some fundamental ironies for West African street merchants in New York City. West African vendors

> find themselves both catering to and resisting a stereotypical image of themselves (as Africans they say that they are seen as more "primitive" intellectually by some of their clientele) that both benefits them economically and denies their cultural specificity. They, however, may have less at stake in maintaining a . . . cultural identity than we, as scholars whose disciplinary authority still rests upon such distinctions, might presume. Knowing something about the history and plight of African Americans a few . . . migrants accept the fact that

the "Africa" African Americans "need" is not the one they know. In the Harlem market context they are prepared to renounce recognition of the complexities of the Africa from which they come, and make a gift of the more unencumbered significance it has acquired in the local community.[45]

One can consider marketing Afrocentricity an economically astute response to ever-changing local market conditions. African American and African entrepreneurs have exploited the opportunities that Afrocentrism has presented them. Realizing a new niche for considerable profits, corporate America is now producing, marketing, and selling Afrocentic products. Saying that marketing Afrocentricity is simply an economically astute response to the market, of course, does not explain the considerable success of the venture. An Afrocentric reading of this marketing success might suggest that the widespread contemporary appeal of African material culture in North America—however expressed—is generated by the vitality of African social life and the philosophy that it embodies; it also creates a proud link between Africa and Africa America.

Like most readings in the humanities and social sciences, this hypothetical Afrocentric reading is partially true.[46] One cannot deny the appeal of Afrocentric products in North America. And one cannot ignore the expressive vitality of Afrocentric products. And yet the reading does not consider the ironies of real Africans selling products representing an idealized Africa, that are made not only in Africa, but also in Asia and New Jersey. When a West African vendor

dons a hat made in Bangladesh, emblazoned with the slogan "Another Black Man Making Money" while greeting his customers as "Brother" on the streets of Harlem, the cross-cutting significations of this performative add new dimensions to an understanding of the black public sphere. Not only does he echo and refract an ironic African American response to the racism of white America, he also adopts a competitive posture and questions the parameters of Blackness that defines the Man, making his own difference as potentially "Another Young Black Man." He is also complicit with the subtextual tensions of ethnicity, gender and class that reverberate from this phrase. The ironies of its traffic through export processing zones in Asia, factories in New Jersey, wholesalers in Chinatown, West African vendors in Harlem and the African American cultural community do not enable any singular conclusion.[47]

To better comprehend the contemporary ironies of marketing Afrocentricity, we can also attempt to understand it as part and parcel of the global process that Jean Baudrillard calls "simulation." The difference between, say, feigning an illness and simulating one is, for Baudrillard, fundamental. When patients feign an illness, says Baudrillard, they make-believe that they are sick. When patients simulate an illness, they reproduce some of the symptoms. "Thus feigning or dissimulating leaves the reality principle intact: the difference is always clear, it is only masked; whereas simulation threatens the difference between 'true' and 'false,' between 'real' and 'imaginary.' Since the simulator produces 'true' symptoms, is he ill or not?"[48] The presence of simulations therefore confounds objective and subjective, truth and fiction, real and unreal.

The contemporary importance of simulation grew with what Walter Benjamin called mechanical reproduction—the reproduction of phonographic sounds and pictorial images. With the emergence of cybernetic electronic reproduction during the past twenty years, the power of simulation has grown exponentially. In simulatory cyberspace, the distinction between the real and unreal becomes superfluous. In Baudrillard's language, the "very definition of the real becomes: that of which it is possible to give an equivalent reproduction. . . . At the very limit of this process of reproducibility the real is not only what can be reproduced, but that which is always already reproduced. The hyperreal."[49]

For Baudrillard, reality in the contemporary era has disappeared into a game of reality in which signs are joyfully exchanged through a process of endless reduplication. "It is thus that for guilt, anguish and death there can be substituted the total joy of the signs of guilt, despair, violence and death. It is the very euphoria of simulation, that sees itself as the abolition of cause and effect, the beginning and the end, for all of which it substitutes reduplication."[50] The game of reality found in simulations confounds distinctions between truth and fiction, right and wrong; it elevates nostalgia to new heights.

> The transition from signs which dissimulate something to signs which dissimulate that there is nothing, marks a decisive turning point. The first implies a theology of truth and secrecy (to which the notion of ideology still belongs). The second inaugurates the age of simulacra and simulation, in which there is no longer any God to recognize his own, nor any last judgment to separate true from false, real from its artificial resurrection, since everything is already dead and risen in advance.
>
> When the real is no longer what it used to be, nostalgia assumes its full meaning. There is a proliferation of myths of origin and signs of reality; of second-hand truth, objectivity and authenticity. There is an escalation of the

true, of the lived experience; a resurrection of the figurative where the object and substance have disappeared.[51]

Baudrillard sees the escalation of lived experience and figuration as leading inexorably to the "age of simulacra." Using less bombastic language, Manuel Castells positions these collective simulation processes in what he calls the "information age." In the information age, global forces compel the construction of social identities not based on civil society, but on communal principles. In Castells's language, global forces, such as those that brought West African traders to New York City, compel civil societies to "shrink and disarticulate because there is no longer continuity between the logic of power-making in the global network and the logic of association and representation in specific societies and cultures. . . . The search for meaning takes place then in the reconstruction of defensive identities around communal principles."[52]

In this light, the search for cultural meaning and personal meaningfulness in Afrocentrism is centered on the reduplication of a monolithic Africa that, in turn, reinforces communal principles in Africa America. The ideal Africa articulated in Afrocentric signs is one in which, to paraphrase Baudrillard, nostalgia is energized, in which "there is a proliferation of myths of origin and signs of reality."[53] In Afrocentrism, African values, mores, and ideas, do not come from an Africa of the recent past; rather they have their origin in distant times. Thus, Molefi Asante proclaims that African Americans are people of Ma'at.[54]

In the information age, these complex Afrocentric principles are transformed into signs—an "X" on a baseball cap, a "kente cloth" shawl, a greeting card with "African" designs, linens with "African" motifs. From an Afrocentric vantage, these signs embody the communal principles of a proud Africa America; they lend a strong hand to African Americans as they confront the profound difficulty of being a black person in a fundamentally racist society. By the same token, as these signs are commodified in a simulated system of signs, the reduplicatory power of the Afrocentric image overwhelms the referential power of the Afrocentric philosophical principle. "X" may become simply an "in" fashion rather than a symbol for slavery's annihilation of Africa America's connection to Africa. "Kente" may become a casual African American take on Africanness rather than a symbol of Asante nobility.

The ecstasy of the sign, to borrow again from Baudrillard, not only obscures the real and unreal, the simulated and the dissimulated, but also sparks economic engines that today run on the high octane fuel of simulation. Through the circulation of reduplicated signs in the media, marketing

Afrocentricity creates in North America a simulated Africa. There are "watered down" African designs that appeal—quite profitably—to increasingly widespread North American constituencies. There are festivals like Atlanta's Marché Africain/African Market that attempt to recreate African markets in North American urban spaces. There are crews of Hausa, Malinke, and Wolof traders, constructing their economic selves as "real" Africans, who follow the circuit of these festivals, lending to them an "authentic" African presence. And then there are the African markets in Harlem. The 125th Street market, called the African market, was until October 1994 a simulation of an African market. The spatial organization and informal dynamics of the market replicated spatial organization and informal dynamics of markets in West Africa. On 125th Street, the cultural crossroads of Africa America, Hausa, Songhay, Fulan, Malinke, and Wolof merchants, self-constructed as monolithic Africans, sold Africana of no distinct ethnic origin to appeal to the ideological popularity of a monolithic Afrocentric Africa. They sold "trademarked" goods to appeal to the more localized tastes. They burned African incense to evoke the motherland. They addressed shoppers as "brother" or "sister" to appeal to a simulated African/African American solidarity. They have continued these simulated practices at the Malcolm Shabazz Harlem Market at 116th Street and Lenox Avenue. Indeed, the Harlem markets direct a circulation of ecstatic signs in which difference and conflict are diluted to promote economic activity and profits.

By marketing Afrocentricity at outdoor markets, at trade expositions, in mainstream retail stores, on catalog pages, or at the virtual markets found on the Internet, African Americans and Africans have created a simulated Africa. The work of simulation has paid off for African merchants as well as African American entrepreneurs.

As we have seen, West African traders are supremely adaptable. Traders like Issifi's father, Hamidou, left the isolated dunes of Niger in the early 1960s and traveled to Côte d'Ivoire, adapting to the culture of the Benin Coast, to the culture of wage labor and changing fads. He and his compatriots tuned into the ethos of "hot" marketing and constructed themselves as hip young men—jaguars—who exploited the latest trends. They transformed their knowledge into profits. Issifi would probably not call himself a jaguar. He says, after all, that "jaguar" is a dated term. Even so, he claims to have the same adaptability that his father demonstrated a generation earlier. Sitting in his booth at the Malcolm Shabazz Harlem Market, Issifi often burns incense, which makes me think of the Grande Marché in Niamey, Niger. One day I asked him why he burned incense.

"I like it," he said. "It is also good for business. It reminds my clients that I'm an African. I think they like that. And things that remind the African Americans about Africa is good for business."[55] Issifi's practice of contextualizing himself—in economic settings like the market or trade shows—is a central adaptive theme in his marketing Afrocentricity. Capitalizing on his Africanness and the fact that he lives in Harlem, the cultural epicenter of Africa America, he and his compatriots have constructed long-distance trade networks throughout North America to facilitate the sale of their goods at African American festivals. Like the Harlem markets on 125th Street and on 116th Street and Lenox Avenue, these festivals are, in fact, partial simulations of West African markets. Like all simulations in the age of commodified signs, these African simulations energize the sale of goods—in Issifi's case, both Afrocentric and "trademarked" goods.

We have seen how West African merchants in New York City use their familial traditions to construct long-distance trade networks in North America and how they use these networks to facilitate the marketing of Afrocentricity. The picture thus far has been one of relatively unconstrained economic and social activity. This picture is at best partial, for the traders are both informal entrepreneurs and immigrants—categories of social actors very much constrained by state regulation. In chapter 6, we shall consider how the state regulates the economic and social lives of West African traders living in New York City.

88   In 1982, two traders from Senegal arrived in New York City hoping to exploit a new market. Senegalese had been leaving Africa for decades to seek
profits—usually in France and Italy.[1] In New York City, they intended to
sell T-shirts, scarves, sunglasses, and umbrellas in one of the best imagin-
able markets for such goods: midtown Manhattan. Wanting to have their
enterprises completely above board, these two men, the vanguard of Senegalese traders in New York City, applied for and received vending licenses
from the city's Consumer Affairs Board. Soon thereafter, they confronted
the trials and tribulations of having their affairs regulated by the state. Because New York City had licensed their operations, the Consumer Affairs
Board routinely sent inspectors to their sites to see if they were in com-
pliance with local consumer ordinances. At almost every inspection, officials fined them for minor infractions. Their tables were too close to the
street curb. Their tables were too far away from the street curb. In their first
year of operation, they had each been assessed eleven thousand dollars in
fines.[2]

As astute street entrepreneurs, the Senegalese traders let their licenses
expire, but continued their operations outside the regulatory aegis of New
York City. In this way, they and scores of compatriots who followed them
entered the city's informal economy. By not registering with the city as street
vendors, they were technically breaking the law by selling their wares on the
street. And yet they brazenly continued. By 1985, scores of Senegalese had set
up tables in front of some of 5th Avenue's most expensive stores. As we have
seen, an informal third world space in a prestigious first world setting would

not be tolerated by the 5th Avenue Merchants Association, and a crackdown by city hall soon followed.

Following the "cleanup," Senegalese vendors relocated to less precious spaces in midtown Manhattan—Lexington Avenue, 42nd Street near Grand Central Station, and 34th Street near Times Square. They also began to work in teams to protect themselves from the police and from petty thieves. In midtown Manhattan, for example, a vendor positions himself near the curb of the east side of 6th Avenue, some hundred meters south of the intersection of 46th Street. He is selling cheap African crafts (brass giraffes, leather bracelets, and wooden combs) arranged on a blanket. His lookout,

A WEST AFRICAN TRADER SELLS T-SHIRTS IN MIDTOWN, SUMMER 1997. (PHOTO BY JASMIN TAHMASEB MCCONATHA)

who stands at the east corner of 6th Avenue and 46th Street, keeps a protective eye on him. A tourist arrives and purchases a bracelet. Shortly thereafter, another man, presumably a compatriot, crosses the street and approaches the vendor. This "banker" takes the cash from the sale and returns to midblock on the west side of 6th Avenue, where he safeguards the money.[3] In this way, as we have seen, the Senegalese successfully colonized the sidewalks of Midtown.

As more and more Senegalese arrived in New York City, the vending territory expanded north to 86th Street on the East Side and south to 14th Street in Greenwich Village and Canal Street in lower Manhattan. In some areas, the Senegalese replaced vending tables with attaché cases filled with "Rolex" and other "high-end" watches. Sales of these counterfeit items by unlicensed and therefore non-tax-paying vendors constituted violations of trademark statutes as well as city ordinances. Like their fellow vendors, the attaché men developed strategies to protect themselves from the long arm of legal regulation and punishment. A well-dressed attaché man would stand on a corner with his attaché case open for inspection. In Midtown, a man dressed in a business suit with an attaché case—even an open one—is unremarkable. Like his fellow traders who sell from tables or blankets, he has his lookouts across the street and his money holder at midblock—an arrangement that makes vendors more mobile and less visible. The arrangement also demonstrates how these informal entrepreneurs from West Africa have confounded mainstream assumptions—to their own economic advantage.[4]

When the first two Senegalese traders came to New York City in 1982, they had every intention of participating in the formal, regulated economy of New York City. They sought and received permits to sell wares on New York City's streets. They paid their taxes and an excessive amount of fines. Eventually finding city regulations to be bad for their street business, they decided to let their licenses lapse and to forgo paying taxes to the state. In other words, they had entered the unregulated world of the informal economic sector.

In chapter 2 we touched on how the forces of global restructuring have not only compelled widescale migrations from the third to the first world, but also the exponential growth of informal economies. The term "global capital restructuring" encompasses a multiplex of phenomena: the appearance of a global economy, the implosion of space and time, the shift of manufacturing to diverse sites in the world, the emergence and growth of export processing zones in nations in debt to and facing pressure from the World Bank and International Monetary Fund, the expansion of international finance markets, the feminization of the manufacturing workforce—especially in export processing zones—the emergence of transnational migration patterns, the proliferation and growth of informal economies, and the solidification of economic polarization.[5] The worldwide technological grid that links the diverse elements of the global economy is not, in fact, global. Rather, "it connects selected parts of the globe while it simply spans others. In addition to increasing economic polarization within societies and regions, the so-called global economy has marginalized millions. According to World Bank projections, the number of the world's poor in Asia and Latin America will steadily drop, whereas in sub-Saharan Africa, 'the number of poor will rise by 85 million to 265 million in the year 2000. . . . Sub-Saharan Africa's percentage of the world's poor will double from 16 to 32%.' "[6] These conditions of poverty have compelled West Africans like Issifi Mayaki and Boubé Mounkaila to leave home and family and travel to New York City to set up informal enterprises.

The new migration is but one local consequence of global capital restructuring; it has also prompted widescale social upheavals, especially in "global cities," the contemporary hubs of global economic activities. Global cities, briefly alluded to in chapter 2, are centers in which centralized networks of information, technology, capital, and highly trained professionals are concentrated. As the dispersion of manufacturing from first world urban centers has precipitated a marked decline in manufacturing output in cities like New York, it has simultaneously reinforced the need for technologically concentrated sites—global cities—from which the dispersed grid of manufacturing sites can be managed.[7]

In New York, the global restructuring of capital has increased the polarization of income, unleashed a flood of immigration, and propelled the growth of the informal economy. This social and economic upheaval, which, of course, affects the economic practices of West African street traders, began when service industries formed to manage the global disbursement of manufacturing. These industries recruited highly trained people who had the technological capacities to monitor and control global production: specialists in advertising, investment bankers, accountants, lawyers, real estate brokers. This elite required a large pool of support staff, mostly female, many of whom were hired on a temporary basis. These workers shared low salaries, few health benefits, and little job security. In the shadow of New York City's glitz and wealth, there came into existence a "disenfranchised" working class. "Among them can be counted an army of female clerical workers, other workers who toil in 'downgraded manufacturing' sectors, low-skill workers who provide increasingly specialized consumer services that urban elites demand, and, finally, a growing number of people, like street vendors and gypsy cab drivers, who work outside the formal labor force in the informal economy."[8]

Perhaps the most widely recognized activities in the informal sector are those that involve criminal activities. The importation, distribution, and sale of narcotics, of course, is probably the most notorious. The illicit trade in marijuana, heroin, cocaine, crack, uppers, and downers supports directly and indirectly a broad swath of the recently disenfranchised working class. Phillippe Bourgois's magnificent book *In Search of Respect* demonstrates how the illicit trade in drugs powerfully reinforces informal economic activity and radically affects social relations among these disenfranchised people. It is a mistake, however, to link informal economies exclusively to criminal enterprises, for what makes an economic activity informal is that "it is unregulated by the institutions of society in a legal and social environment in which similar services are regulated."[9] Although informal economic activity certainly encompasses illicit trade in narcotics, it also includes paying a babysitter or dishwasher in cash off the books, failing to fill out Social Security forms for nannies, employing contractors to make home improvements without building permits, manufacturing clothing in residential zones, or selling wares—real or counterfeit—on the street without a vendor's license.

Take the recent case of Vincent Cummins, a native of Barbados, who in 1997 drove an "outlaw" van that competed with New York City's Metropolitan Transit Authority (MTA) buses. MTA buses charge $1.50, pick up passengers at bus stops, and don't guarantee a seat. Cummins charged $1.00, guaranteed his passengers a seat, and on the homeward leg of a trip, dropped passengers off at their doorsteps. Unlike the MTA, van drivers like Cummins made change and traveled their routes frequently. Cummins, however, had no license to operate his van and was therefore in violation of the law. He was careful to avoid the marked and unmarked police cars that had been on the lookout for outlaw vans.

> Cummins would prefer not to be an outlaw. . . . He has been driving his van full time ever since an injury forced him to give up his job as a machinist. "I could be collecting disability," he says, "but it's better to work." He met Federal requirements to run an interstate van service, then spent years trying to get approval to operate in the city. His application, which included more than 900 supporting statements from riders, business groups, and church leaders, was approved by the City Taxi and Limousine Commission as well as by the Department of Transportation. Mayor Giuliani supported him. But . . . the City Council rejected his application for a license, as it has rejected most

applications over the past four years, which is why thousands of illegal drivers in Brooklyn and Queens are dodging the police.[10]

The vast majority of West African immigrants to New York City have worked in the informal sector. Unable to obtain a general vending license, they have worked as unlicensed street vendors. Many of them have sold pirated, counterfeit, or gray market merchandise.[11] This economic activity, it should be noted, constitutes a violation of copyright and trademark legislation or licensing agreements. West Africans who are not merchants may drive unlicensed gypsy cabs. Others may work in an unlicensed import-export enterprise; some of them are employed as unregulated wage laborers. "All are forms of illegality produced by global regimes of power and knowledge, regulatory activity and bureaucratic inaction."[12]

We have already met Boubé Mounkaila, "specialist of leather," who has lived in New York City since September of 1990. From the beginning, he has sold African leather goods and wristwatches on the city's streets. Between 1990 and 1992, he sometimes sold his wares on 34th and Broadway, but he gave up that turf because he lacked a vendor's license. In and around Times Square, his violation of New York City ordinances frequently attracted the attention of the police. Reflecting back on his experiences around Times Square, he said: "I'd go down there with my African bags and sell very well. But I'd have to always watch out for the police. Several times the police came and took my bags and fined me. I told them that I'm a hardworking African trying to make a living. They said that they understood, but that I had to follow the law. They said that I couldn't sell without a permit. They said that if I paid my fine, I could get my bags back. So I paid my fine, got my bags back, and went back to 34th and Broadway. I made much money, but after having my goods taken for the seventh time, I decided to remain in Harlem. There the police leave you alone. The police in Harlem like Africans and don't care if you have a permit or not."

"Do you miss selling in Midtown?" I asked him.

"I miss the money that I could earn in Midtown, but I don't miss the police pressure. When I was there, I also missed the camaraderie of brother Africans." Boubé paused a moment. "And there's no good food around Times Square. In Harlem, you can get good African food."[13]

Until October 1994, Boubé, still unlicensed, continued to sell African leather goods and wristwatches. Between November 1994 and March 1995, after the dispersal of the 125th Street market (see chap. 7), he and his colleague Sala Fari rented store space on Broadway near Canal Street. There they sold African leather goods, wristwatches, baseball caps, gloves, and scarves. Given the excessive rent ($2500 per month), the lack of heat, and the subway construction outside the front door, they spent a mere three months at that lower Manhattan site. Sala, who had an employment authorization permit, eventually went to work as a security guard on Lexington Avenue in Midtown. For his part, Boubé elected to rent space at the Malcolm Shabazz Harlem Market on 116th Street and Lenox Avenue. When city hall and the Masjid came to an agreement about the new market, they decided to split the vendor rent revenue thirty-seventy. City hall also elected to recognize the "legality" of the vendors. After a payment of a hundred dollar registration fee, the Masjid issued each vendor an identification card.

Having paid his registration fee, produced his rent money, and obtained his vendor's card, Boubé secured a stall at the Malcolm Shabazz Harlem Market. He chose a space near the Lenox Avenue/117th Street corner of the market space, a location that attracted a lot of foot traffic. He set up his stall, arranging his Nigerien leather goods on tables but also hanging the large bags from rafters that he had constructed. Knowing the hunger that his clients had for possessing trademarked products, but also conscious of their limited budgets, Boubé purchased from his Asian suppliers an array of "trademarked" wristwatches and baseball caps. Some of the sports caps he sold had labels that explained the product's authenticity.

"I never try to tell my clients that my knockoff caps are originals or even seconds. They know by my word and price that I sell copies."

"Is that important?" I ask him.

"Yes. I want my clients to trust me. I want them to know that I am honest and that I give them a good price for the Nigerien bag they buy. That is the way we have done business."

"How do you determine the price of your copies?"

"We sell them for eight dollars."

As we learned in chapter 4, some of Boubé's best customers are Japanese tourists who routinely visit the Malcolm Shabazz Harlem Market. "My friend the tour operator brings them to my stall."

"The copies," I say, looking at a New York Yankees baseball cap, "look just like the originals."

Boubé smiles. "The Koreans are strong, very strong."

"Do people complain about buying copies?"

"People here expect to buy copies. But they sometimes complain that the hats fall apart easily or that the African bag is torn. They also say that I charge too much," Boubé says. "If the hat unravels after a week or the stitching on an African bag comes undone, I say, fine. If I sell you a hat or an African bag and it is no good after even one month, then bring it back and exchange it for another. That is our way." [14]

In *Simulations*, Jean Baudrillard described how the technological evolution from mechanical to electronic reproduction of images had transformed the world from one that valued the original over the copy to one in which copies—and simulations—had eclipsed the value and importance of originals and "real" life. Reality, in other words, had become hyperreality. [15]

In retrospect, Baudrillard's analysis was brilliantly prescient, but he did not focus concretely on the economic ramifications of simulation. Goods that are copies have flooded the marketplace, especially the ever-expanding informal sector: counterfeit clothing, wristwatches, baseball caps, and handbags, to name only a few product categories. Indeed, counterfeit products generate billions of dollars in annual sales in the United States. We have seen how West Africans, exploiting the economic potentials of Afrocentricity, have marketed clothing and hats that bear the unlicensed inscription of Malcolm's "X." In 1992 the sale of licensed "X" products reached an estimated $100 million. That same year, sales of counterfeit "X," which West Africans, among many others, bought from Asian producers in the Gift District and sold to African Americans in Harlem, were estimated at $20 million—still only a small fraction of the counterfeit product market. [16]

Baudrillard's analysis also points to a displacement of value. In the past, value, as the Dooney and Bourke Company would like its consumers to believe, derived from both the quality of materials used to fashion the good as well as the quality of product workmanship. This rule still applies to many products, but in the mass consumer market, difference in quality between the original and the copy is sometimes negligible. Real and fake Polo trousers, T-shirts, or jackets, for example, are "assembled" by similar people with similar materials. As the proliferation of signs becomes more and more powerful, the issue of quality, in fact, diminishes. The goods sold by many of the West African traders at the Malcolm Shabazz Harlem Market are "largely manufactured in Asia and are all marked with famous names: Ralph Lauren, Polo, Hugo Boss, Guess, Fila and dozens of sports team logos. The goods themselves are almost indistinguishable. They include baseball caps and knit caps, sweatshirts and other cheaply manufactured goods whose only allure is the fame of their trademark." [17]

In an age of simulated reality, what, then, determines the value of the good? The product's value, as Rosemary Coombe and others have shown, is generated more from its trademark than from the actual quality of material or precision of work. This fact explains why corporations that hold trademarks or licenses spend millions of dollars to prevent, investigate, and litigate trademark and copyright violations, which, in the course of one year, may generate millions of dollars in losses.[18] This fact also explains why manufacturers of both originals and copies pay close attention to the reproduction of labels, which, in the end, display a product's real or copied trademark and attest to the good's real or simulated value.

Consider what you get when you purchase an original Major League Baseball cap. First, you see the trademarked image of a player in a batting stance looking at a baseball coming his way. This image is inscribed, "Major League Baseball." Second, you receive an attached card, shaped like a baseball diamond (home plate and three bases), on which is written in all-American red, white, and blue:

Genuine Merchandise

Congratulations on your selection of this genuine article—a product officially licensed by Major League Baseball. It takes hard work and commitment to make the Major Leagues. Every Major League Baseball product is designed and crafted to meet the highest standards of quality and performance. This product represents America's long baseball heritage. With the purchase of this article, you bring home a part of Baseball you can call your own. The Major League Baseball Genuine Merchandise Logo is your assurance of authenticity. Accept no substitute.[19]

Like most holders of trademarks, Major League Baseball licensees want to establish the superiority of their product. In the case of Major League Baseball, the trademark holders also appeal to patriotic sentiments associated with "the National Pastime." Most important, the unknown authors of this card issue a request to the consumer: "Accept no substitute."

It is easy to manufacture a baseball cap that looks just like the real thing. Fake baseball caps, in fact, also have trademarked labels and cards that authenticate the product as "real." In fact, scanning technologies make it easy for manufacturers to reproduce exact replicas of trademarked labels. This process has been called cyberfaking, which is a principal process in what has been called brandnapping. According to *Fortune* magazine, in 1994 product forgery precipitated an estimated $200 million in losses for U.S. companies. Counterfeits are mostly produced in South Korea, Taiwan, and China and find their way to New York City streets by way of Los Angeles. Truckloads of merchandise are then shipped across the United States and unloaded in Korean-owned distribution centers near Canal Street in lower Manhattan as well as in the Gift District on Broadway between 20th and 30th Streets.

The merchandise is then wholesaled to, among other entrepreneurs, West African street vendors.[20]

From the vantage of the street, the key issue, of course, is not whether a product is real or fake; it is rather the difference in price generated by the presence of a trademark. In 1994, genuine Major League Baseball caps cost fifteen dollars at the 125th Street market in Harlem; a copy was only eight dollars. For consumers at informal markets or on midtown Manhattan streets, price is more often than not the determining factor in the purchase of two otherwise virtually indistinguishable products.

Between 1990 and 1994, Garba Hima, a forty-year-old man from the western region of Niger and a regular at the 125th Street market, sold sunglasses in the spring and summer and pirated videos throughout the year. In the spring and summer, Garba arranged his wares on two tables. One table, near the north curb of 125th Street, contained hundreds of sunglasses: cheap ones arranged by like color and design and counterfeit ones, mostly "Ray Bans," which had been packaged in either a faked case or box. He sold the cheap sunglasses for as little as five dollars. For the "Ray Bans" he asked fifteen.

The second table, which he displayed year-round, was situated at the other edge of the sidewalk against the brick wall of a parking garage. On this table, Garba displayed pirated videos in their faked boxes—a combination of newly released films and Kung Fu movies. He positioned the boxes neatly around a television monitor and VCR, which were hooked up to a car battery underneath the table. In this way, clients could verify the quality of the merchandise they sought to purchase.

In the summer of 1994, Garba discussed the ebbs and flows of pirated videos. "When I sold the sex tapes," he stated in Songhay, his first language, "business was very, very good. I always had a group of teenage boys and other men around looking at my samples. I sold a lot of sex tapes. But then the Church Ladies came around and complained about the sex tapes." In fact, these middle-aged and elderly African American women, who were, according to Garba, the local standard bearers of religious morality, threatened to file a complaint with the police if Garba refused to remove the X-rated videos from his tables. He did so in 1993, and his video sales declined. "I don't attract the same crowds as before, but I still sell a lot of Kung Fu videos and new releases. They come here and look at them and buy. Business is not too bad here. Sunglasses in the summer. Videos in the winter."

"Where do you get the videos?"

Garba scratched his chin. "I'm searching for the word," he said. "My English is getting better and better, but still . . ." He looked skyward and smiled and switched into English. "I get them from how you call . . . Mafia. Yes, Mafia."[21]

Piracy today has less to do with outlaw sailors who roam the open seas to steal precious cargo than with the unlicensed reproduction of copyrighted or trademarked goods. It is an open question whether contemporary pirates are controlled by the Mafia, but it is clear that they—whatever their connection to organized crime—are key players in the informal economy. Pirates supply street vendors like Garba and Boubé with bootleg baseball caps, counterfeit jeans and T-shirts, and pirated cassettes, compact disks, and videocassettes. Much to the chagrin of corporate giants like Microsoft, cyberpirates have begun to flood the market with counterfeit software.

Business may be "not too bad" for someone like Garba who sells pirated audiocassettes, compact disks, or videocassettes on New York City streets, but it is booming for the people who manufacture these products. It is estimated that organized groups of pirates extract as much as $250 million a year from Hollywood studios. "Increasingly, they control vertically integrated enterprises engaged in everything from manufacturing blank tapes to distributing millions of finished counterfeits."[22] That figure, of course, does not include illegal sales of pirated audiocassettes and compact disks.

Movie studios are outraged, as are officials charged with enforcing copyright, trademark, and antipiracy statutes. Accordingly, law enforcement agencies in New York City have stepped up their efforts to shut down pirate video operations and seize unlicensed videos. In the summer of 1994, for example, Westchester County officials broke a video ring that operated in Yonkers. Although the packaging was slick, the quality of the videos, according to officials, was poor. "The operation . . . was capable of producing 2,200 counterfeit videocassettes a day, which would be sold for $10 a piece, making it a major supplier of the illegal videos that are sold openly on the streets of New York City and through local video stores throughout the region."[23]

Like most video pirates, these operators took portable camcorders to film openings and taped the films from the audience. They then returned to their video factories. Using hundreds of videocassette recorders, they produced thousands of unlicensed copies of a newly released film. In Yonkers, police found "4,600 video-cassettes, 200 VCR's, scores of televisions, computers, video casings, a laser printer and a plastic shrink-wrap packaging machine . . . along with $104,000 in cash and three vans." This operation alone, according to Douglas Corrigan, who in 1994 worked for the Motion

Picture Association of America (MPAA), would cost Hollywood $4 million a year.[24]

The MPAA has established a force to battle video pirates in this profitable but illegal business. Despite the fact that the MPAA pays $2,500 to anyone who shuts down an unlicensed video lab, the business of video piracy boomed during the 1990s. In June of 1996, for example, law enforcement officials in New York City raided a huge piracy operation run by two Israeli families. They seized "hundreds of VCR's and 100,000 illegally duplicated copies of the very latest Hollywood hits, from 'The Nutty Professor' to 'The Rock' to 'Twister.'"[25] This operation, far more significant than the one in Yonkers, made an estimated $500,000 a week. Although street vendors like Garba Hima say that the Mafia supplies them, it appears that many video pirates have little or no connection to organized crime. In the New York City area, video pirates are usually Dominicans, Arabs, or Israelis.[26] Following the bust of the Yonkers video ring, Garba Hima's supply of pirated videocassettes seemed unaffected. Asked if the periodic police actions against video pirates affected his supply, he laughed. "There is always a way to get videos. No problem."[27]

Moustapha Diop, a Senegalese trader at the Malcolm Shabazz Harlem Market, has sold pirated videocassettes at New York street markets since 1994. Although the New York Penal Code was amended in 1995 to include the distribution and sale of pirated and bootleg products in addition the manufacture of unlicensed products, Moustapha's stall at the Malcolm Shabazz Harlem Market had never been raided. Indeed, between 1994 and 1998, no one questioned the legitimacy of his operation—even though the 116th Street market operates under the supervision of the Masjid Malcolm Shabazz and the City of New York. Although seizures of bootleg CDs, also sold at the market in Harlem, soared by 1,300 percent in 1996, distributors and vendors of bootleg products at the market seemed to operate with impunity.

Between 1994 and January 1998, Moustapha worked as middleman in the distribution and sale of pirated videocassettes. Each week, he received shipments from Arab and Dominican suppliers, who would bring to his stall several large cardboard cartons filled with the latest videos of films that had perhaps premiered earlier that week. He'd arrange these and other longstanding favorites on his table. Like Garba, his stall featured a television and VCR for sampling the products, though his equipment could be plugged into an electric socket courtesy of the Masjid Malcolm Shabazz. Unlike Garba, who sold directly to the public on 125th Street, Moustapha sold his videos to small distributors, mostly African Americans, who, upon stocking their bags and backpacks, wandered through Harlem's streets hawking videocassettes. Moustapha would buy his product at five dollars per cassette and sell it to African Americans distributors for seven dollars. They, in turn, took to streets and sold their videos for ten.

This system worked quite well. African American distributors sold videos to people in their neighborhoods with little if any chance of being apprehended under the revised bootleg law. Their product was concealed in backpacks or bags, and they sold their wares on residential side streets away from the various regulatory restraints of commercial strips and markets. Moustapha's restricted contact with the buying public limited the hassle that sometimes erupts over the sale of pirated videos. "How can you charge so much?" "This product is defective. How can you sell it to us?" And yet the system was not without its glitches. One afternoon, Moustapha got into a heated argument with one of his African American clients who wanted to return a cassette he had purchased.

Moustapha refused to take back the product. "It doesn't have my mark," he insisted, meaning that Moustapha would be paying the client for something that the client hadn't purchased from him.

Moustapha's refusal infuriated the man, who claimed that Moustapha didn't trust him and that Africans didn't trust or have respect for African Americans. The man used foul language and accused Moustapha of being a thief.

"It doesn't have my mark," Moustapha insisted, looking carefully at the cassette in question.

The man eventually stalked off. "I'll never do business with you again. We can't get any respect from these Africans."[28]

Despite these problems, the sale and distribution of pirated audiocassettes, CDs, and videocassettes seemed to be a cornerstone of the Malcolm Shabazz Harlem Market. According to Issifi Mayaki and Boubé Mounkaila, the sale of CDs and especially videocassettes, most of them counterfeits, attracted crowds to the 116th Street market.

In March of 1998, I visited the Malcolm Shabazz Harlem Market. It seemed unusually slow even for a Thursday. Many stalls were empty. Few people strolled through the market aisles. I asked Boubé Mounkaila about the state of the market. He said that in January 1998 the Masjid Malcolm Shabazz forbade the sale of all CDs, audio-, and videocassettes. I asked Boubé why they had taken this action.

"The city," he responded, "put pressure on them to do so."

"But why?" I asked. "They didn't seem to care about the sale of cassettes before?"

"I think Blockbuster Video put pressure on the city. They put pressure on the Masjid. And the Masjid finally told people like Moustapha that he couldn't sell cassettes."

"Not good for the market?"

"Most of the people who come here, want to buy a CD or a video," Boubé Mounkaila said. "When they come, they see our merchandise and they might buy jewelry, a watch, or a bag. Now that they know that there are no videos here, they don't come. Many of the brothers now travel to festivals to make money."

"And Moustapha?"

"He sells somewhere else. Maybe in several months, he'll be back with his videos and the market will be good again," Boubé added with his typical pragmatism.[29]

One way the state regulates personal, professional, and commercial activity is through the construction and reconstruction of law—civil and penal codes. These codes are designed to structure what is deemed—by the powers that be—to be appropriate behavior. Despite the prodigious indirect influence of these codes, they directly affect only a small percentage of a population. The state's ability to issue licenses, permits, and identification cards, however, is much more invasive. It is not an exaggeration to say that in every North American municipality the life of every resident is affected by the need to obtain various permits, licenses, and identification cards. These documents enable one to authenticate one's identity; they also stamp the state's approval—its authority—on one's right to perform a particular activity or to live and work in a given locality. Because individuals must supply the state with personal information when they apply for permits, licenses, or identification cards, the regulatory power of the state also enables it to gather and store information on the residence, age, marital status, approximate salary, occupation, and other personal and legal details about its inhabitants.

State regulation of "official" identity creates everyday circumstances that sometimes rival the surreality of Kafka's fiction. Consider this commonplace example: To apply for a residential parking permit in any given city, one must present to the municipality evidence of one's residence. Usually a driver's license will do. However, people these days move quite often, and the address indicated on one's license may be inaccurate or from out of state. These dated documents do not prove one's current municipal residence and are therefore unacceptable. In the absence of authenticating documents, the municipality may demand a current electric, gas, or telephone bill. If one lacks a proper driver's license and hasn't yet received a bill for electricity, water, or telephone at one's new domicile, no residential parking permit can be issued. The clerk who administers the permits may suggest that the improperly certified driver apply for a new permit. To apply for a new driver's license, one must leave the municipal offices and travel to the offices of the Department of Motor Vehicles—a state office—which may be quite far from the municipal castle. Upon finding the Department of Motor Vehicles, which also regulates vehicular titles, license plates, and registration, one fills out the form, pays the fee, turns in one's old license, has an eye check, takes an exam, and if all goes well, receives a new driver's license. If one has moved to the municipality from out of state, one will have to register one's vehicle, which means applying for a new title (certificate of ownership, sanctioned by state governments in the United States) and passing a car inspection for which one will need to present a certificate of car insurance. If one's "insured" car passes inspection—never, as they say, a done deal—one then pays a title transfer fee and a car registration fee, receives license plates, registration card (mailed to the new domicile afterward), and a sticker for the license plate, indicating when the registration expires. After all these transactions, one may at last be able to return to the municipal offices to apply for and receive a residential parking permit, usually a sticker affixed to the rear bumper of the vehicle.

The potential complexity of registering one's vehicle, obtaining a driver's license or a residential parking permit, of course, is but one strand in the regulatory tangle of everyday life in North America. If individuals do not possess a driver's license, for whatever reason, they will have trouble cashing checks or paying for merchandise with checks. Payment by check necessitates a checking account at a bank, and to open a checking account one needs some form of official identification, perhaps a driver's license, some employment identification, a state identification card, or perhaps a Social Security card, the number of which is used by many regulatory bodies, be they governmental or corporate, to keep track of people. Is it any wonder that so many people in the informal economy bypass regulation by using cash or money orders to pay for unlicensed goods and services from unlicensed vendors?

Cash is not the only answer to the regulatory hassles of contemporary North American social life. There are ingenious ways around regulatory blockage. In New York City, street vendors who do have permits will often rent them to other vendors for a monthly fee. In December of 1994, after the demise of the 125th Street African market (see chap. 7), an African American handbag designer gave Sala Fari the phone number of a friend who wanted to rent his vendor permit. "Call him," the man said. "He'll rent his permit to you and won't rip you off. You can sell anywhere in the city and make some money."[30]

More often than not, however, people sell stolen or counterfeit licenses, permits, and identification cards. Indeed, the same kind of computer scanning technology that is used to reproduce trademarked labels can be used to reproduce official permits and licenses—for a fee. In midtown Manhattan, Senegalese street vendors around Rockefeller Center sometimes wear counterfeit vending permits around their necks.[31] Throughout the Bronx, Brooklyn, and Queens, unlicensed taxi and van operators "authenticate" their operations with "appropriate" permits. In 1993 and 1994, vendors on 125th Street hawked stolen credit, gasoline, and phone cards. Informal entrepreneurs selling counterfeit Social Security cards seemed more discrete. In 1994, they casually strolled among undocumented West African immigrants on 125th Street to see if street vendors needed Social Security cards. If they found interested clients, they wrote down their names and informed them of their fee—five hundred dollars upon delivery. During one of my visits to New York City in 1997, a woman circulated among the West African vendors at the Malcolm Shabazz Harlem Market with a large stack of counterfeit Social Security cards. "Anybody need a Social Security card?" she asked.[32]

For West African street vendors, however, the greatest regulatory struggle stems from their immigration status. As noted in chapter 2, West African traders fit into two immigration categories: documented and undocumented. There are two kinds of documented immigrants among West Africans in New York City. A small number of West African traders are permanent residents—holders of the "green card." As permanent residents, they are free to travel and work as they please. They pay federal, state, and local income taxes as well as Social Security taxes and, as of this writing, qualify to receive most federal, state, and local government services and benefits. In time they will be able, if they so choose, to apply to become naturalized U.S. citizens. An increasingly larger group of West African traders possess employment authorization permits. The Immigration and Naturalization Service (INS) issues these cards to people who have married American citizens and are seeking to reside in the United States or who have been granted political asylum. As mentioned previously, West Africans who hold employment authorization permits must renew them once a year. They, too, pay a variety of taxes and can sometimes qualify to receive certain government benefits and services. They can also work in the formal sector, if they so choose, and travel freely in the United States. If they want leave the United States for any reason, they must receive authorization from the INS. If they do not receive such a travel authorization, their return to the United States may be blocked for a period ranging from three to ten years. In some cases, they may not be allowed to return at all.

During the course of this research (1992–98), the majority of West African street traders in New York City have been undocumented immigrants. These were mostly men—although there were a few women—who obtained three-month tourist or six-month business visas for the United States. They traveled here and remained after the expiration of their visas.

FEDERAL PLAZA (AND INS OFFICES) IN LOWER MANHATTAN, SUMMER 1997. (PHOTO BY AUTHOR)

Lack of documentation compelled these men and women to live beyond the pale of state regulation. Although it was unlikely that the state would deport them, some of them feared the long arm of the INS. They all took precautions. They would pay for food and housing in cash or by money order. They would often avoid going to physicians. They would buy their medications, if they needed them, informally—on the street or from a pharmacist who had both formal and informal dealings. Some of them were afraid to "sign up" for night school English classes for fear of being tracked down (see chap. 8 for a fuller description of these patterns). Many of them spent inordinate amounts of money trying to obtain what they call "papers," the aforementioned employment authorization permit. Given the complexity— not to forget the severity—of recent changes in the immigration law, many West African traders decided that it was better to remain undocumented. Indeed, lack of documentation presented myriad problems for those whose lives were regulated by the state. If traders, however, accepted a life in the informal sector, their lack of documentation could hide them from the state and protect them to some extent from its regulation.

No matter what their immigration status might be, the social lives of West African traders in New York City have been affected by the ebb and flow of immigration debate, policy, and enforcement strategies, all of which have long and convoluted histories. As we have seen, there have been two major waves of immigration to the United States. The first great wave began in the 1890s and lasted until the passage of the Immigration Act of 1924, which not only limited the number of immigration visas, but also based their issuance on national origin. This system favored granting visas to immigrants from northern Europe at the expense of people from Asia and eastern and southern Europe. In 1965, Congress amended the Immigration Act, abolishing immigration quotas based on national origin. The INS made family reunification its priority in acting on immigration applications and appeals. This development led to increased immigration from Latin America, the Caribbean, and Asia and set the stage, in part, for the second great wave of immigration to the United States. Indeed, preliminary data from Census 2000 indicate that 10 percent of the U.S. population is foreign born, suggesting that during the 1990s more new immigrants came to the United States than in any decade in its history.[33]

The abolition of national immigration quotas, of course, did not in itself trigger an explosion of immigration to the United States. Many immigrants sought residence in the United States to escape gruesome wars, especially in Central America. Fundamental economic change, however, seems to be the detonator in the immigration explosion. By the early 1980s, national economies had become globally integrated. This global integration of information, finance, and economic power, in turn, resulted in the development of global cities like New York, London, and Tokyo. Globalization also resulted in spatial dislocations. Manufacturing declined in cities like New York and expanded in sectors—Mexico, the Philippines, and Costa Rica—where cheap labor and tax incentives abounded. These economic dislocations sparked an unprecedented worldwide movement of people, migrating in search of economic opportunity. Many of these immigrants came to the United States, some with legal documentation, some without.[34]

Prior to 1986, economic incentives attracted millions of undocumented immigrants to seek employment and residence in the United States. Given the vastness of space and the depth of population in this country, many undocumented immigrants believed it would be easy to avoid getting caught and deported. They also knew, moreover, that many employers would happily hire them. The new immigrants did not require competitive salaries, and given their precarious legal status, employers could avoid paying for such benefits as retirement and health insurance, let alone making a contribution to Social Security. These perceived economic conditions prompted Congress to pass the Immigration Reform and Control Act (IRCA) in 1986. Provisions of the IRCA fine employers who hire immigrants without documentation. The act also authorized legalization of aliens who could prove that they had lived continuously in the United States since January 1, 1983. The IRCA ignited a spirited debate. Advocates of immigrant rights, on the one hand, claimed that the IRCA discriminated against undocumented workers. Nativist groups opposed to immigration suggested that IRCA employer sanctions would be hard to enforce. They also complained that recently arrived undocumented immigrants could easily produce papers, however bogus, of their continuous residence in the States and thus make their case for amnesty.[35]

Although the reasons for the influx of immigration—legal and illegal—to the United States are complex, it is clear that the flow of immigrants increased exponentially in the 1990s. In the early 1990s, the United States admitted more than 800,000 legal immigrants a year. In 1995, the U.S. authorized the entry of 716,000 legal immigrants. In 1996, the figure jumped almost 30 percent to 911,000 legal immigrants. A Census Bureau survey found that in 1996 eleven of every twenty residents of New York City were either immigrants or the offspring of immigrants. In 1997, according to a Taub Urban Research Center study, immigrants constituted 34 percent of the city's population. The study's projections for the year 2000 increased the number to 38 percent.[36]

Just as legal immigration jumped in the 1990s, so did illegal immigration. In 1996, the estimated number of people living illegally in the United States rose from 1.1 million to a an estimated 5 million. To be counted among the estimated population of illegal immigrants, moreover, one would have to have resided illegally for one year. But there are thousands of illegal visitors who come to work or to see relatives and return home before the twelve-month cutoff. In 1996, New York City had an estimated 540,000 illegal immigrants living within its borders.[37]

The exponential increase in recent immigration to the United States has led to increased efforts to reduce immigration flow and to punish illegal immigrants. Numerous writers and politicians have claimed that increased immigration has had a negative impact on the U.S. economy because the education and skill level of recent immigrants—both legal and illegal—has declined substantially, which means that they will earn less than native-born Americans in their working lives. The presence, in turn, of such a large low-skill and low-wage labor pool has, so the argument goes, negative ramifications for low-skill native-born Americans, leading to their wage declines. The low levels of education and skill, moreover, mean that recent immigrants place a burden on existing social welfare programs. One study suggested that in 1994 the social welfare cost of immigration—both legal and illegal—had bypassed $51 billion. These claims, however, are hotly contested, at least according to a study by the Urban Institute, immigrants have paid out billions of dollars more in taxes than they have received in services.[38]

Citing the negative economic consequences of illegal immigration, there have been a number of policy initiatives to reduce, eliminate, and punish illegal immigration to the United States. In 1994, a federal panel proposed a national computerized register of all people authorized to work in the United States. In this way the government would provide an easy way for employers to check the immigration status of potential employees.[39] In 1995, Congress explored how to fight illegal immigration. One proposal required public hospitals to report any illegal immigrant who had sought medical treatment. The same proposal asked public schools to refuse instruction to the children of illegal aliens. In New York City, this proposal would have affected between forty and sixty thousand children, some of whom were the sons and daughters of West African traders in Harlem.

Rudolph Giuliani criticized these congressional proposals, saying that they did not consider the positive impact of immigration and that they would increase crime and despair in New York City. "It's based on an irrational fear of something different, something strange, that somehow they're going to take something away from us. . . . A lot of it is just undifferentiated fear of foreigners, of people who appear to have different values and different ways of doing things."[40] Despite the protests of Giuliani and other supporters of immigration, other public officials were less sanguine about immigration's social benefits. In August 1996, in response to the perceived cost of illegal immigration to state social welfare programs, California governor Pete Wilson signed an executive order to cut off illegal immigrant access to such state programs as prenatal care, public housing, and child abuse prevention.[41] In 1996, Congress enacted the Illegal Immigration Reform and Immigrant Responsibility Act (IIRIRA), which in effect legalized many of the practices that Giuliani and other supporters of immigrants rights have fought against.

Both the increase in the number of illegal immigrants and the national debates on immigration policy and enforcement have directly affected the lives of West African street vendors. Consider the case of Boubé Mounkaila. As previously mentioned, Boubé came to the United States in September of 1990 on a three-month visa. When his visa expired, he became one of several million undocumented immigrants living in the United States. As his African leather goods business on 125th Street became more and more successful, he decided to apply for an employment authorization permit. Boubé believed that he'd be able to increase his revenues substantially if he had "papers." He also thought that if he had papers, he'd be able to go home to visit his family without being barred from returning to the United States. He had two options: he could marry a U.S. citizen or he could apply for political asylum. Wanting no part of a problem-laden immigration marriage, which would mean his paying an American woman to marry him, Boubé elected to apply for political asylum. In 1993, several of his compatriots had received asylum, after which the INS had sent them employment authorization permits.[42]

In the summer of 1993, Boubé submitted his application for employment authorization to the INS. To meet INS requirements, he had to submit the following completed forms: a fingerprint card (FD-258), a biographic information form (G-325A), an application for employment authorization (I-765), and a request for asylum in the United States (I-589). He had to submit the latter form in triplicate and attach to it two ADIT photographs taken within thirty days of the date of application. The ever-insistent INS required that this photo show a three-quarters frontal view showing the right side of the face and the right ear. He also submitted processing fees for his employment authorization application ($70) and for his request for asylum application ($70). He mailed the whole package to the regional INS processing center in Saint Albans, Vermont, and received some ten days later an INS letter acknowledging receipt of his material. The letter also stated that the INS would reach a decision on his application within ninety days.

Boubé received the first of many INS rejections on November 19, 1993. The INS said that Boubé had neglected to include in his petition a completed fingerprint card. More seriously, they claimed that his request for asylum was "frivolous."

> On November 18, 1993, you filed an I-765 Application for Employment Authorization pursuant to Section 274a.12(a) (8), Title 8, Code of Federal Regulations. This application for employment authorizations is based on your pending Form I-589, Request for Asylum in the United States. CFR 274a.12(c) (8) provides that any alien who has filed a non-frivolous application for asylum pursuant to Section 208 of the Immigration and Nationality Act may be granted employment authorization.
>
> Title 8, Code of Federal Regulation, Section 208.7(a) defines "frivolous" as manifestly unfounded or abusive.
>
> Following a review of your asylum application and any attachments, it has been determined that your Request for Asylum in the United States is frivolous.
>
> You state that you are seeking asylum in the United States because you need to be a legal alien who can work and stay in the United States. You did not answer the majority of the questions on the asylum application. You have not indicated what would happen to you if you returned to your home country. You have not indicated if you or any member of your family have ever belonged to or been associated with any organizations or groups in your home country. You have not indicated if you or any member of your family have ever been mistreated/threatened by the authorities of your home country or by a group(s) controlled by government or by a group(s) which the government of your home country is unable or unwilling to control. You also have not indicated if you or any member of your family have ever been arrested, detained, interrogated, convicted and sentenced, or imprisoned in your home country. These questions were all left blank on your asylum application. You have not made a claim for asylum based on one of the five grounds of persecution on which a claim for asylum may be made.
>
> Form I-589, Request for Asylum in the United States, must be based on your fear of persecution on account of race, religion, nationality, membership in a particular social group, or political opinion. You have failed to show a relationship between your request for asylum and one of the five grounds of persecution on which a claim for asylum may be based.

For that reason, your application for employment authorization, Form I-765, is denied. There is no appeal to this decision. This decision is without prejudice to consideration of subsequent applications for employment authorization filed with the Immigration and Naturalization Service.[43]

In 1993, Boubé's English proficiency enabled him to run his leather goods business successfully, but it had not reached a level where he could completely understand the bureaucratese of an INS rejection notice. The rejection frustrated him a great deal, but as man of great determination, he decided to resubmit his application in January 1994. He made sure that his fingerprint card had been completed correctly and sent it and all other relevant materials to the INS, thinking that this time, he'd receive his papers.

Boubé received his second INS rejection in March of 1994. Like his previous rejection, the notice stipulated that he had not supplied sufficient information about whether he or members of his family might have been persecuted in Niger. Boubé explained that he had heard on the street that Africans like him had received "economic asylum," and that providing information on his economic persecution would have been enough to receive asylum and employment authorization. He had neglected to provide information about his political difficulties in Niger.[44] This time, however, the INS suggested that if he had questions about his application, he could go to the INS office at the Veterans Administration Building in Newark, and find out what he might do to achieve more positive results.

Boubé asked me to accompany him to Newark as a potential interpreter. We took the subway to Penn Station, transferred to a New Jersey Transit train, and traveled to the AMTRAK station in Newark. We then took a taxi to the Veterans Administration Building at 20 Washington Square, and after having signed in with a rather rude guard who complained about "all the immigrants who come here and can't even read or speak English," we took the elevator to the sixth floor. We arrived at the INS office at 11:45 A.M. Three officials were working at what, at least to my eyes, seemed a rather leisurely pace. Boubé filled out a slip and an INS official gave him a number—461.

"Go sit in the waiting room," she told him, "until your number is called." Four people sat in the waiting room. One man had been waiting since the previous day for his appointment. He lived in Virginia, near Washington, D.C., and didn't understand why he had been summoned to Newark. "Why couldn't they interview me down there," he complained. "Here, they can't find my file, and I've been waiting here since yesterday at noon."

Boubé did not suffer these particular indignities. The same woman who gave him his number called it in about thirty minutes. The woman told him, rather sternly, that the INS had again found his application for asylum frivolous. "We found no political grounds for granting you asylum," she informed him. "But you can always reapply."

"But I don't understand," Boubé protested. "I completed everything."

"Your application is frivolous. There is no appeal."

Boubé had expected this hearing to be the last hurdle to clear before being granted asylum and employment authorization. He began to ask the woman another question, but the woman, who was on the other side of a glass partition, walked away. "I will reapply," he said to me as we left the building. "I will get employment authorization, but I do not appreciate these people. They have no respect. Why did they tell me to go to Newark? This whole thing hurts me. It makes me suffer."

On the train back to New York City, Boubé lamented his lack of papers. "If only I had papers," he said. "I could be very successful at business. I understand business in America. I just need papers. I have friends who have just received papers. They say it is a good time to get papers. They are no different than me. Why have they gotten papers and I haven't?"

"Did they fill out the forms themselves, too?"

"Some of them did; others hired a man, a Malian, who knows how to fill out the forms. That's what Moussa Niori did, and he got his employment authorization card in two months. Maybe I'll talk to the Malian and see if he can help me."[45]

Boubé sought the advice of the Malian immigration broker, who urged him to let some time pass before he reapplied to the INS. In the fall of 1994, Boubé hired the Malian broker to fill out his asylum and employment authorization application. In August of 1995, however, his case had still not been resolved. "Last year" he said, "my case would have been resolved. Other people received work authorizations without problems last year. But now it is more difficult with the INS. Now they interview you to make sure you have political problems. I may go to a hearing in October."[46]

In the fall of 1995, the INS informed Boubé that he had been scheduled for an asylum hearing on February 22, 1996, in Lindenhurst, N.J. But he had serious misgivings about hiring an attorney and going all the way to Lindenhurst for this hearing. In early February of 1996, Boubé again asked me to accompany him to the New York City offices of the INS, located in the Federal Plaza in lower Manhattan. He wanted to inform the INS of his new address.

Scores of West Africans, many of them doubtless undocumented aliens, sold a variety of counterfeit goods in the shadow of New York City's INS offices. We entered the ground floor and waited in the INS lines with other

Africans, West Indians, South and East Asians, Latinos, and many Poles. Boubé's number finally came up, and he approached a middle-aged woman who gave him an official Department of Justice change-of-address form, which asked the following questions: name, date of birth, place of birth, place of entry, port of entry, visa status, date of return, and employment history. Boubé asked me to fill it out for him. He claimed to be a visitor, but his date of entry was September 5, 1990. He had been a visitor for more than five years. He also asked me to indicate that he was seeking political asylum in lieu of a departure date. I filled out the form and indicated Boubé's new address. Even though we were in the INS offices, they insisted that the form be mailed to them.[47]

Boubé's hopes were eventually realized. Several months later, the INS informed Boubé that he was to report to their office in Queens for an asylum hearing in May 1996. I offered to attend the hearing as a translator, but by this time Boubé felt comfortable enough in English to represent himself. He also didn't feel the need to hire legal representation. Boubé reported that the interview went well. He said that the INS officers had requested updated photographs and a new fingerprint card. He sent these in and expected to receive a positive judgment sometime that fall. Finally in October 1996, the INS granted him political asylum and issued him an employment authorization permit. Permit in hand, he felt free to travel and also made plans to apply for permanent resident status (a green card).

I asked him if he'd travel to Niger. It had been six years since he'd seen his wife and family.

"Before," he said, "many people with [employment] papers went home. But now, the government doesn't like immigrants so much. The INS must give permission for you to travel home, and it is difficult to get it. If you get it, it's only forty-five days. I want to get the 'big one' [the green card], but that's very hard to get. I will try. If I get that one, I'll have time enough to see my family in Niger."[48]

Boubé's case gives us a glimpse into how the INS regulates the lives of immigrants, especially those who lack documents. Thinking that his employment authorization permit would enable him to travel freely between Niger and the United States, Boubé spent three years and thousands of dollars in his quest for papers. When the INS finally granted him political asylum in October 1996, the question of immigration had become a hot topic of political debate. By then the Illegal Immigration Reform and Immigrant Responsibility Act had been signed into law by President Clinton, an action that made the immigration climate much more severe. Boubé's legal status, however tenuous, made him proud. He realized, however, that the new immigration climate meant that he now needed the "big one," in order to travel freely between Niger and New York City. He also recognized that the effort and expense of getting employment authorization paled in comparison to that of getting the green card.

INS officials have long realized how many undocumented immigrants from underrepresented countries covet the green card. As a result of the Immigration Act of 1990, the INS holds an annual immigrant visa lottery. Although the lottery gives tens of thousands of immigrants a chance to win a green card, it also creates opportunities for unscrupulous operators— lawyers, bondsmen, and other immigration consultants—to "help" their clients submit entries. They sometimes make outrageous claims, guaranteeing that their clients have the best chance of winning. These consultants may charge unsuspecting immigrants anything from ten to eight hundred dollars to fill in the applicant's name, birth date, and place of birth on a piece of paper and place it in an envelope. "You have boiler room operations and phone banks and lawyers," said Alfred E. Cerullo III, the consumer affairs commissioner of New York in 1994, "that are preying on people's vulnerability and anxiety and trust at a time when their lives are at issue."[49] In 1994, the INS received three million entries for the visa lottery. That year, they selected fifty-five thousand winners.

The high demand for INS documentation, of course, triggers a great deal of fraud. It is difficult, though not impossible, to produce counterfeit immigration certificates and cards. It has been relatively easy, however, to find INS officials and clerks willing to accept payoffs from brokers in exchange for their help in procuring documents. In 1994, the street price was $5,000 to $6,000 for a green card, $500 for an employment authorization permit, and $350 for a border crossing card. Between 1992 and 1994, word spread on the street that for the right price, green cards and employment authorization permits could be obtained easily at the Northern Virginia Offices of the INS. "Smooth-talking middlemen took care of the details, bribing immigration service employees with gold jewelry, free vacations, and cash-filled envelopes passed hand to hand in the aisles of a nearby department store. Ghanaians, Lebanese and Salvadorans, among others, flocked to what quickly became a multicultural bazaar. Most came from the Washington area, but others drove hundreds of miles and scribbled phony addresses."[50]

When the Justice Department broke open the case, they discovered that during a two-year period the Arlington office had illegally given four thousand people the right to work and had fraudulently granted legal residency to another thousand. Brokers typically charge immigrants $500 to $700 for work leading to the issuance of an employment authorization permit. From that pool of money, they may give an immigration clerk $100 to $200. In some cases, it might take only several hours for them to obtain work cards for their clients, though the typical wait is two months.[51]

The temptation to accept bribes in exchange for documents is evenly spread through the ranks of INS civil servants. In July 1996, John F. Lonergan, supervisor of two hundred INS inspection and examination employees at Newark International Airport, was charged with falsifying documents that enabled immigrants to enter and reside illegally in the United States. "An indictment handed up by a federal grand jury in Newark accuses Lonergan . . . of conspiring with a document broker . . . to make false statements on forms for allowing aliens living in the United States to re-enter the United States after traveling abroad."[52]

In short, immigration brokers know where to go to get what they want and can advise their clients accordingly. To enhance their business, they spread word on the street of immigration opportunities and encourage people to use their services. Satisfied customers recommend the brokers to other immigrants who are seeking work permits, legal residency, or authorization to travel to their home countries. The majority of immigration lawyers and brokers, of course, do not engage in fraud and bribery. By the same token, the temptation and opportunities for graft are great: high demand for documents and low pay for the clerks who process them. Like the majority of the West African street vendors in New York City, Boubé Mounkaila hired an immigration broker, took the man's advice, and six months later legitimately received his employment authorization permit. Like other immigrants in other circumstances, several of Boubé's acquaintances paid brokers and received their documents through fraudulent means.

The exponential increase in immigration to the United States—legal and illegal—during the 1990s sparked much political debate. Supporters of immigration, as stated above, believe that it contributes to the nation's economic and social strength. Opponents of immigration believe that recent immigration—meaning third world immigration—has hurt the U.S. economy by lowering wages and taking jobs away from lower-income American citizens. By the mid-1990s, the debate had shifted to illegal immigration. By 1996, it should be reiterated, approximately five million people resided illegally in the United States. The Republican-controlled Congress sought, among other things, to curb illegal immigration by enacting tough legislation that would increase border patrol enforcement, increase the number of annual deportations, and make the removal process more expeditious by eliminating judicial reviews of deportation cases. Legislators designed some of the new immigration provisions to punish illegal immigrants. They proposed to eliminate food stamps and reduce access to welfare for legal and, by extension, illegal immigrants. They also threatened, as we have seen, to enact a provision to bar the children of illegal aliens from public schools.

As we have also seen, bolstered by a growing anti-immigrant sentiment in the United States, Congress passed and President Clinton signed the IIRIRA in 1996. The attempt to bar illegal immigrant children from public schools, however, met with stiff resistance. Lawmakers nevertheless adopted many of the other controversial measures, including the elimination of food stamps and reduction of other public assistance to legal immigrants, as well as abolition of judicial review in deportation cases.

One of the toughest new measures in the 1996 legislation repealed provision 245(i) of the Immigration and Nationality Act, a provision that has a direct impact on many West African street traders in Harlem. Enacted in 1994, the provision had allowed by November 1997 an estimated six hundred thousand undocumented immigrants to pay a thousand-dollar fine in an effort to become legal while remaining in the United States. In the absence of this provision, undocumented aliens like Issifi Mayaki or traders with employment permits like Boubé Mounkaila would have to return home to apply for legal status. By leaving the States to do so, they might be barred from returning for three to ten years.[53]

Most of the IIRIRA provisions went into effect on April 1, 1997. Any undocumented immigrant who left the United States before September 30, 1997, and desired to obtain a visa to return would be prohibited from reentering the country for three years. Undocumented immigrants who left the United States a full year after the April 1 initiation date would be barred from returning for ten years.[54]

The approach of April 1 prompted thousands of undocumented immigrants to marry U.S. citizens. Although marriage to a citizen does not guarantee permanent residency or citizenship, it significantly enhances a person's immigration status. In January 1997, for example, the number of marriage licenses issued in New York City jumped 47 percent from the total recorded in January 1996.[55] Two weeks before IIRIRA took effect, Mayor Giuliani, an ardent supporter of immigrant rights, declared that a person's immigration status would not be an obstacle to obtaining a marriage license in New York. This statement meant, in effect, that an illegal immigrant who used a foreign passport with an expired visa as identification would not be denied a marriage license in New York City.[56]

Public sentiment against immigration began to decline after the IIRIRA legislation went into effect. The repeal of provision 254(i) sparked much of the opposition to IIRIRA. Critics stressed how the elimination of the provision would arbitrarily break up families. Facing the September 30, 1997, deadline "at least a quarter of a million illegal immigrants, many of whom have been in United State for years and have jobs and families, are faced with a wrenching choice. They are trying to decide whether to return to their homelands until they can get alien registration cards, known as green cards, making them legal residents, or remain and face the risk that they will never become legal."[57]

A flood of lobbyists, including immigration lawyers, religious groups, businesses, and ethnic associations, flowed into the halls of Congress. Advocates argued that provision 245(i) kept families together and was vital in enabling U.S. businesses to retain skilled workers who came to the country legally, but whose status became illegal because of technicalities or ignorance of American immigration law. Supporters of the provision also argued that the fine paid by immigrants who wanted to remain in the country as they sought legal status produced $200 million in annual revenue. This money, in fact, had become a major funding source for the INS.[58]

Faced with this barrage and the fear that an increasingly diverse voting public would see the Republican Party as "anti-immigrant," the Republican-controlled Congress voted a temporary extension of provision 245(i) to November 7, 1997. In November, Congress passed yet another extension of 245(i). This second extension would remain in effect until January 14 and applied only to "illegal immigrants for whom family members or employers [had] filed visa petitions or labor certifications." The "grandfather clause" permitted at least a million more illegal immigrants to apply for a green card.[59] However, if they missed the January 14 deadline, illegal immigrants would be fully subject to the provisions of IIRIRA. That is, they'd have to return home to apply and wait for their green cards. And if they had resided illegally in the United States for more than six months they'd be barred from returning for three to ten years, depending on the length of their illegal residence.

From the fall of 1997 to the spring of 1998, advocates of immigrant rights intensified their efforts to amend the tough immigration laws of 1996. They sought to amend provisions for the quick removal of aliens who are caught entering the country with fraudulent documents as well as for the compulsory imprisonment and deportation of immigrants convicted of serious felonies. Advocacy groups have also called for the reinstatement of food stamps to legal immigrants. According to Frank Sharry, director of the

National Immigration Forum, this intensification represented a significant shift in public attitudes about immigration. The results of a 1993 poll had indicated that 65 percent of the American population thought that the rate of immigration should be not only controlled but also decreased. In August 1997, a similar poll showed that only 36 percent of the population thought immigration should be decreased from current levels.[60]

By January 1998, the INS reported, an estimated 1.2 million legal and illegal immigrants were settling annually in the United States. In 1998, the Immigration Forum said that "Americans these days are feeling 'less threatened' by immigration and are 'more comfortable with the diversity it brings' than they were a few years ago. . . . The change coincides with recent improvements in the economy compared with the early 1990s and a greater availability of jobs."[61]

It is anyone's guess how public opinion on immigration will change in the coming years. Will Congress soften the tough provisions of the IIRIRA? How will political considerations affect how the INS interprets the regulatory language of the law? Will Congress pass new immigration legislation in the near future? Will states enact new punitive immigration measures or repeal or amend existing ones? The world of politics and state regulation is filled with uncertainties—uncertainties that dramatically affect the lives of people like Issifi Mayaki and Boubé Mounkaila.

The IIRIRA of 1996 compelled Boubé Mounkaila to seek legal residence in the United States. He had spent much time and money between 1993 and 1996 to obtain political asylum and employment authorization. When he began his quest, many holders of employment authorization permits successfully petitioned the INS to return to their homelands to attend funerals or visit ailing relatives. The INS limited these authorized visits to forty-five days. As public opinion toward immigration turned negative in 1994, it became increasingly difficult to receive these authorizations. By the time Boubé received his employment authorization permit in October 1996, he realized that he'd have to become a permanent resident if he wanted to visit his family in Niger and continue to work in the United States. Having followed the twists and turns of the debate on IIRIRA and the repeal of provision 245(i), Boubé decided to apply for permanent residency. Accordingly, he paid the INS a thousand dollars and filed his petition for a visa before the January 14, 1998, deadline. This action has enabled him to await his green card— the "big one," as he calls it—in New York, which means he has been able to protect his considerable inventory and profit from his African leather goods business at the Malcolm Shabazz Harlem Market. Even though it is likely that Boubé will eventually be granted legal residency, he doesn't know when he'll be able to return home.

In 1997, Issifi Mayaki's immigration prospects appeared to be more limited. Unlike Boubé, Issifi never petitioned the INS for a work permit. Because he had no desire to work for wages in the formal sector, he saw no reason to obtain an employment authorization permit. For him, trading is a way of life. "Trading is in my blood. I will never work in a factory or in a store."[62] When the IIRIRA went into effect on April 1, 1997, Issifi wondered about his options. How might he, too, be granted legal status so that he could visit his father in Côte d'Ivoire and his mother in Niger?

In the spring and summer of 1997, Issifi discussed his options with his colleagues. There was no reason to apply for asylum, as he didn't need or desire a work permit. Might his chances for legal residency improve if he married a U.S. citizen? Like Boubé, Issifi had invested considerable sums of money in inventory and his business generated healthy profits. By the same token, he missed his family and very much wanted to return to see them. What to do? Being undocumented, Issifi thought that given the approaching deadlines for filing petitions for visas, he might marry an American citizen. By October 1997, Issifi had not yet decided his course of action.

"Can you find out about if such a marriage is good for me?" he asked me on one of my visits.

"I'll do some research for you," I said. "But I'm not an immigration lawyer. You should consult a lawyer."

"I don't trust lawyers. They charge too much money and give bad advice. See what you can find out and phone me. Call my beeper and no matter where I am. I can call you back."[63]

I consulted a number of sources and discovered that a person who enters the States without documentation and then marries a U.S. citizen can apply for permanent residence. Once the INS has interviewed the couple, and if the marriage is considered legitimate, the immigrant is granted provisional legal status. After that, the immigrant can formally apply for legal status.

In November 1997, I saw Issifi at the Malcolm Shabazz Harlem Market and discussed his situation. I told him what I had discovered.

"If you get married to a U.S. citizen, you need to apply for legal status. That means you need to pay the INS a thousand-dollar fine and file a visa petition before January 14 of next year. If the deadlines passes," I said, "you'll need to return to Côte d'Ivoire or Niger to apply for legal status.

"It's very complicated."

"Because you're undocumented," I said, "you may have to leave to apply for legal status and not be able to return for ten years."

Issifi laughed. "There is no time for all of this. What's the point? Why bother to marry a woman who wants money and nothing more. And even that is not enough to get papers."

"What will you do, otherwise?" I asked.

"I don't know. I miss Africa. Maybe it's time for me to return."[64]

The January 14 deadline passed, and Issifi had neither married nor filed an application for permanent residence. Meanwhile, his younger brother had arrived from Niger by way of Côte d'Ivoire and was now living with him in Harlem. Issifi said that when his little brother had learned enough English and understood the ins and outs of his cloth business, he might return to Abidjan and start a new business. In this way, the business he had developed in New York City would continue to generate revenue for his family.[65] For an undocumented transnational trader like Issifi, the immigration law— tough or not—was beside the point, for his intent was to exploit an economic environment, find a kinsperson to occupy his node on the transnational circuit, and triumphantly return home.

It is clear that state regulation affects the everyday lives of almost everyone in the United States. Most of us possess various forms of identification and certification—driver's licenses, identification cards, titles and deeds to property, validation and parking stickers—that are issued by federal, state, and local governments. In the United States, one usually needs one form of identification, a material statement of one's regulated status, in order to obtain other forms of identification. It is usually a painful process—to put the matter diplomatically—to apply for state or private certifications—so much so that we often protect ourselves from bureaucratic insanities by muddling through them in semiconscious states. Imagine, then, the difficulties of finding one's way through the bureaucratic mazes of American regulation without a shared cultural foundation, without first-language competence in English, and without documentation.

From the vantage of recently arrived West African traders, the regulatory obstacles may seem insurmountable, but despite cultural, linguistic, and legal disadvantages, many of them have brilliantly made their way through a thoroughly regulated America. Like the rest of us, West African traders in New York City may possess a driver's or a hacker's license as well as an array of credit, bank, phone, and identification cards. Some of them have business tax identification numbers. Others carry INS employment authorization permits or perhaps a permanent resident card. In short, they have found ways around the federal, state, and local regulatory impediments that confront them.

Besides being astute observers of American cultural life, economic trends, and regulatory change, West African traders have become keen observers of national, state, and local politics. In chapter 7, we will consider how the politics and the battle over space in New York City have affected West African street trading.

7 | The Spatial Politics of African Trading in Harlem

In mid-October 1994, the 125th Street Vendors Association, a loosely organized "union" of African American vendors and West African traders from Senegal, Mali, Niger, and the Gambia, threatened to shut down 125th Street if Mayor Rudolph Giuliani made good on his campaign promise to disperse the African market from Harlem's main thoroughfare. Although the Nation of Islam, whose ministers preach versions of Islamic purity and African American self-sufficiency, supported the vendors, some members of the union disliked and distrusted Louis Farrakhan. Many of the West African traders wondered how such a man could call himself a Muslim.

Reverend Al Sharpton, who has used his particular orientation to Christianity to articulate his solidarity with hardworking African and African American people, also supported the vendors. Then there were supportive Asian and African American shop owners on 125th Street who thought that the crowds brought in by the African market were good for business. There were, of course, just as many Asian and African American shop owners who thought that the presence of street vendors was bad for business. They said that the vendors engaged in unfair business practices. They complained that vendors cluttered 125th Street with garbage.

Like the Nation of Islam, the Masjid Malcolm Shabazz has promoted Islamic austerity and African American self-sufficiency. Confronting the political showdown between Mayor Giuliani and the 125th Street Vendors Association, the Masjid proposed to regulate the vendors. They suggested that the unregulated 125th Street market be moved nine blocks south of the shopping district to their regulated and city-sanctioned site at 116th Street and

Lenox Avenue, a commercially depressed space. They asked the vendors to pay them a hundred-dollar vending registration fee, which would make them "legal," as well as rents of seven dollars per day. In exchange, they would monitor the new market's security and make sure it conformed to the city sanitation regulations.

The Harlem Business Alliance and the Harlem Urban Development Corporation both endorsed the Masjid's plan. Both organizations had promoted economic ties to West Africa, but neither liked the cluttered, unregulated presence of an open-air African market on Harlem's major business boulevard. Harlem's elected officials, who had vested interests in the neighborhood's economic development, also supported the mayoral crackdown and the Masjid's "generous offer." The Giuliani administration warmly embraced the Masjid's plan. And why not? From its perspective, the plan co-opted a generally revered African American religious institution and provided a peaceful alternative to a potentially violent racial confrontation that no mayor would want. At the same time, city hall would receive 30 percent of the revenues collected by the Masjid, meaning that it would collect taxes from previously unlicensed and untaxed vendors. In exchange, city hall would police the market and clean the streets regularly. The plan also supplied important political payoffs to the Giuliani administration. Giuliani could boast of keeping his political promises. Police Commissioner William Bratton could say that he was following through on his promise to enforce even the most minor city regulations, which, as we saw in chapter 6, are at odds with the practices of the informal economy.

In October 1994, most of the West African traders, many of whom said that their presence invigorated the economy of 125th Street, seemed like powerless pawns in the chess game of New York City's cultural politics. And yet they, like the exceedingly diverse African American community in Harlem, had constructed complex political and cultural discourses of their own. The Senegalese, whom, as we have seen, have been in New York City since 1982, were well represented among the West African traders on 125th Street. Some Senegalese, most notably those well established in various businesses, supported the move of the market to 116th Street. Many Senegalese street traders, however, opposed the mayor's crackdown. Ethnic and regional conflicts, historically deep, exacerbated these political differences among the Senegalese. It is less likely for Senegalese from the Casamance, the south, to be tied into the northern economic and religious networks controlled by the Wolof and Serere, who are majority peoples. By 1994, moreover, many Senegalese in New York City claimed to be devotees of the Mourid Sufi order, which, according to street vendors from Mali and Niger, had invested

THE "POLITICAL" VIEW FROM BOUBÉ MOUNKAILA'S VENDING TABLE, SUMMER 1994. (PHOTO BY AUTHOR)

capital in the Masjid Malcolm Shabazz, giving the Masjid's market plan a putative behind-the-scenes Senegalese connection. Vendors from Mali reacted to the imminent dispersal of the 125th Street market with pragmatic resignation. Although they all wanted to remain, they refused to march with the 125th Street Vendors Association on October 17, 1994, the day that city hall disbanded the market along Harlem's commercial thoroughfare. Some of them decided that they would pay the hundred dollars it took to register at the Masjid's 116th Street market; others, who blamed the market's demise on the Senegalese, refused to pay money to people who wanted to ruin their trading businesses. Most of the established traders from Niger, like those from Mali, elected not to march with the 125th Street Vendors Association. Thinking that the cost of trading on Canal Street—as much as twenty-five hundred dollars a month in 1994—would be too expensive, some of them agreed to move their operations to 116th Street; others refused to do so. Many Nigeriens blamed the market's demise on the greed of the African American community, for which they had little respect and much distrust.[1]

Unlike most of their compatriots from Niger, Moussa Boureima and Idrissa Dan Inna decided to march with the 125th Street Vendors Association on October 17. Neither man had been in the United States for more than a year. Moussa had left Abidjan, where he sold watches and clothing in the

THE "POLITICAL" VIEW FROM BOUBÉ MOUNKAILA'S VENDING TABLE, SUMMER 1994. (PHOTO BY AUTHOR)

capital in the Masjid Malcolm Shabazz, giving the Masjid's market plan a putative behind-the-scenes Senegalese connection. Vendors from Mali reacted to the imminent dispersal of the 125th Street market with pragmatic resignation. Although they all wanted to remain, they refused to march with the 125th Street Vendors Association on October 17, 1994, the day that city hall disbanded the market along Harlem's commercial thoroughfare. Some of them decided that they would pay the hundred dollars it took to register at the Masjid's 116th Street market; others, who blamed the market's demise on the Senegalese, refused to pay money to people who wanted to ruin their trading businesses. Most of the established traders from Niger, like those from Mali, elected not to march with the 125th Street Vendors Association. Thinking that the cost of trading on Canal Street—as much as twenty-five hundred dollars a month in 1994—would be too expensive, some of them agreed to move their operations to 116th Street; others refused to do so. Many Nigeriens blamed the market's demise on the greed of the African American community, for which they had little respect and much distrust.[1]

Unlike most of their compatriots from Niger, Moussa Boureima and Idrissa Dan Inna decided to march with the 125th Street Vendors Association on October 17. Neither man had been in the United States for more than a year. Moussa had left Abidjan, where he sold watches and clothing in the

Treichville market. Moussa hailed from Tessoua, Niger, an enclave of Hausa, and like his father before him, he had been a long-distance trader. Like Issifi Mayaki, Moussa's family remained in Niger. He had one wife and eight children, two of whom were adults. Unlike Issifi, Moussa spoke only rudimentary French, and aside from a few market phrases, no English. Despite these drawbacks, his street business had flourished on 125th Street, and the prospect of losing it to some incomprehensible political dispute angered him. Speaking of the upcoming October demonstration, Moussa said: "The market is only a little good. We are weak. We will come here tomorrow at 9:00 A.M. and follow the Americans."[2]

Idrissa Dan Inna easily made the decision to march in the 125th Street Vendors Association demonstration. In Niger, he had been active in trade union politics. Indeed, he claimed to be the president of a vendors union in Niamey, the capital of Niger. Throughout his adult life, he had fought to protect the rights of workers in his home country. Like Moussa, he didn't speak much English. Like some of his compatriots in New York City, he spoke French haltingly. He said that he had come to the United States to trade. "I made much money in Niger, but there is no money left there," he told me. He arrived in New York City on February 28, 1994, one month after the World Bank had devalued the CFA franc by 50 percent. "The lowering of the CFA wiped me out, so I came to New York."[3] Idrissa's main problem had been insufficient English. He estimated that his lack of linguistic skill had reduced his intake by 50 percent. By October 1994, Idrissa's calculation had become a scholastic exercise, for Mayor Giuliani had declared the African market illegal.

Idrissa saw the order to disperse the 125th Street market in strictly political terms. For him, the crackdown resulted from an alliance between city hall, the Senegalese, and the Masjid Malcolm Shabazz—an alliance that would increase revenues to its partners at the expense of the street vendors. As a matter of principle, he refused to move his business to 116th Street. Why pay money, he said, to people who are trying to ruin his business. In defiance of the mayoral order, he stated that he'd set up a table—without inventory—on 125th Street on October 17.[4]

The evening of October 16, Idrissa and Moussa attended a vigil sponsored by the 125th Street Vendors Association. Because they couldn't understand what the speakers said, they asked several of their compatriots to translate for them. Each speaker stressed the injustice of the mayoral order, which they cast in the clear-cut terms of racial politics. Hard-working black folks, they said, had a right to work on the streets of their communities. The order to disperse street vendors, they said, resulted from a plot on the part of whites and Asians to take control of Harlem. The speakers also stressed that the march should be peaceful and orderly.

Based on their impressions of the speeches, Moussa and Idrissa went ahead with their plans to march. On the morning of October 17, they dressed in military fatigues and army boots. At 9:00 A.M. they assembled behind a black, green, and red Garveyite banner held by two African American street vendors. When Morris Powell, the leader of the 125th Street Vendors Association, gave the signal, Moussa and Idrissa began to march with the others. As they slowly walked down 125th Street, they, like the other demonstrators, chanted, "No food, no peace. No food, no peace."

As they walked, they saw a group of their compatriots standing among the spectators along the sidewalk. They waved for them to join the group. "Come and join us," they both said in Hausa and Songhay. "Come join us and march."

None of the Nigerien spectators accepted their invitation.

The cultural and political study of spaces like Harlem's 125th Street has a long history in anthropology. Until recently, most anthropologists followed the Aristotelian dictum that space is a static "given" that mirrors the social and cosmological order. Claude Lévi-Strauss suggested that the spatial patterns found in Bororo villages reflect the dual organization of the sociosymbolic order of that Amazonian society. Similar assumptions are found in Marcel Griaule and Germaine Dieterlen's article on Dogon space, in which the patterns of fields and compounds are said to reify themes of Dogon cosmology. In writing of African towns, David Hull suggests that "community layouts mirrored the laws of nature and the forces of philosophic thought. So humane were African towns and cities that they were regarded by their inhabitants as the concrete expression of their inner thoughts about man, nature and the cosmos."[5]

For their part, geographers have often taken a much more dynamic approach to the analysis of space. Many of them have followed Maurice Merleau-Ponty's phenomenological orientation, in which space is a universal force used by the constituting mind; it is not "given," but constituted:

> Space is not the setting (real or logical) in which things are arranged, but the means whereby the positing of things becomes possible. This means that instead of imagining it as a sort of ether in which all things float, or conceiving it abstractly as a characteristic they have in common, we must think of it as the universal power enabling them to be connected. . . . Is it not true that we are faced with the alternative of either perceiving things in space, or conceiving

space as the indivisible system governing acts of unification performed by the constituting mind.[6]

Thus space is continuously negotiated and renegotiated; it becomes an arena of confrontation.

In the early 1990s, many anthropologists began to adjust their spatial gaze to a more geographical focus. Grappling with the increasing spatial, political, and conceptual complexities of globalization, many scholars critiqued the assumed isomorphism of space, place, and culture arranged "logically" on a field of social relations. For authors such as Akhil Gupta and James Ferguson, "the fiction of cultures as discrete, object-like phenomena occupying discrete spaces becomes implausible"—especially for men like Issifi Mayaki and Boubé Mounkaila who live along increasingly permeable borders of transnational space. Such a transnational space has "rendered any strictly bounded sense of community or locality obsolete. At the same time it has enabled the creation of forms of solidarity and identity that do not rest on the appropriation of space where contiguity and face-to-face contact are paramount."[7]

The static notion of space has been rendered superfluous by what David Harvey has called the "condition of postmodernity," which has given rise to the implosion of space and time, the explosion of mass migration, and the erosion of national boundaries.[8] Thus, by 1997, it was no longer unusual to see men from rural West African villages hawking T-shirts emblazoned with Malcolm's "X." In a few short years these traders had completely transformed the 125th Street corridor into an African market. "The ability of people to confound the established spatial orders, either through physical movement or through their own conceptual and political acts of reimagination, means that space and place can never be given."[9] It also means that the constitution of space—in our case the spatial constitution of the 125th Street African market—carries with it serious political ramifications.

Like most of his compatriots from Niger, Boubé Mounkaila decided not to participate in the 125th Street Vendors Association demonstration on October 17, 1994. Boubé, in fact, thought it prudent to remain at home—at that time a tenement on 126th Street near Lenox. As the demonstration began, he sat on the stoop and surveyed the scene in front of his house. Several men clustered on the southeast corner of 126th and Lenox. A contingent of six Nation of Islam followers, dressed in dark suits, white shirts, and bow ties, marched down Lenox Avenue. A mounted policeman trotted by on his steed.

Dressed in light blue jackets, police responsible for "community relations" talked to a group of Harlemites across the street from Boubé's building.

Boubé had already been down to the proposed 116th Street market. "Not one vendor has gone there to set up," he said. "Not one. No one will go there. You'll see."

Boubé was eager to learn more about the demonstration. What would people say? Would anyone get hurt? Would the police arrest anyone? "I don't like American politics. I'm a businessman. I work hard. Politics ruins my efforts." He expressed confidence that no matter the political situation in New York City, he'd weather the current storm. "What I really don't like is politics among black people here, like the politics between the Nation of Islam and the Masjid Malcolm Shabazz." He appreciated the Nation of Islam's support of the West African street vendors, but also realized that support had a deep political history. He also thought that the Masjid Malcolm Shabazz and their "Senegalese allies" wanted too much money. "They want us to pay them nine dollars per day and give them a hundred-dollar license fee to get a badge and a stall number. I will not do it. They want to get as much money from us as possible and then get rid of us."[10]

The previous evening, Boubé had asked his compatriots to come to a palaver to discuss their options. At the palaver most of his colleagues had said that they would not demonstrate. Most had also agreed that they wanted little to do with the new market at 116th Street. Garba Hima had announced that he wanted to move to a new city. Some of the others had been thinking about moving their businesses to White Plains Mall or Penn Station. Others were contemplating a move to lower Manhattan—Canal Street, West Broadway, or Chambers Street. They all declared Monday, October 17, to be a holiday— no work.

From the stoop, Boubé greeted several compatriots and then suggested a walk down Lenox to the site of the 116th Street market. As we walked, Boubé commented on the neighborhood. "Once you go south of 125th Street, the neighborhood gets bad." He pointed to several burned-out buildings. "These are all for drugs, you know, crack. People will not want to walk nine blocks from 125th to 116th Street. Do you think tourists will come to the new market? . . . Never! They will be scared to take the subway to 116th Street. There are bandits everywhere."

We reached 116th Street and Lenox around 11:00 A.M. The Masjid had freshly blacktopped a large rectangular surface, a perhaps half a city block in area. Bright yellow lines and numbers indicated stall spaces. A ten-foot chain-link fence enclosed the space. Three wide openings provided entrances to the market. We walked into the space and found only one merchant there, a representative from the Masjid Malcolm Shabazz. He sat at a table where he hoped to register traders. So far, no one had registered.

"You see," Boubé said. "No one will come here. I'll take my business somewhere else."

We crossed to the west side of Lenox and started back toward 125th Street, passing smoke shops, carryouts, burned-out tenements, and clusters of men and women loitering on the wide sidewalk. Boubé suggested that these people could well be "bandits," and a good reason for people to avoid the new market. He pointed out a smoke shop on 123rd Street that the police had raided. They had found a cache of arms inside. Several people said hello to Boubé, including a young Hispanic woman.

"She's a crackhead," he observed. "She trades sex for crack."

Closer to 125th Street, the salty smell of half-smoke sausages blended with the aroma of mustard as we walked by yet another carryout. "The place we just passed," Boubé said, "is the most dangerous place in Harlem. There is crack and guns in all of the houses. It's very bad."

It was about noon when we reached 125th Street. Although the demonstrators had long since marched down Harlem's main thoroughfare, the police remained. Mounted officers rode by. Metal crowd control barriers separated street from sidewalk. Police cruisers and paddy wagons lined the street. Dressed in riot gear (helmet, eye shield, body armor, mace, nightstick) dozens of uniformed cops patrolled the streets.

Across the street, Boubé noticed a group of his compatriots sitting on the wall of the flower garden in front of the Adam Clayton Powell State Office Building. A motley assortment of people milled about the plaza there: a contingent of Nation of Islam followers, standing at attention in front of the office entrance; groups of young African American men dressed in fatigues; older African Americans armed with cameras, video and still; print and photojournalists with prominently displayed press badges; a cluster of Japanese tourists, talking animatedly; more street police in riot gear; community outreach officials; and detectives and plain clothes officers.

The Nigeriens seemed angry and frustrated.

"Why is it that personal interest destroys the good of everyone," one man from Niger observes. "They say that four hundred vendors have signed up. That's a lie. No one who sells on 125th Street has signed up. If they have signed up people, they're probably from the Bronx or Brooklyn—not Harlem. Lies, my brothers. Lies." The man went on to say that the police sweep would be just the beginning of a protracted struggle between African street vendors, African American and Asian business owners, elected officials, the Senegalese, the Nation of Islam, and the Masjid Malcolm Shabazz.

"All of this politics," Boubé lamented. "I don't understand it all. Why are people here always at one another's throats. And why do people here want to hurt us Africans? We work hard and we don't hurt anyone. Why do they want to make life so difficult for us?"[11]

The politics of space in New York City has a long and contentious history. For the past century and more, merchants have complained about peddlers, peddlers have complained about merchants, and both merchants and peddlers have complained about the duplicities of elected officials. Moreover, the success of informal markets has usually precipitated political problems in cities like New York.[12] We have already discussed how the presence of Senegalese vendors selling "cashmere" in front of Bergdorf-Goodman on 5th Avenue provoked a strong response from Mayor Ed Koch. In 1985, the police drove them from New York City's most prestigious space.

The growth and success of the informal African market on 125th Street also brought with it a bevy of political problems. Like the Fifth Avenue Merchants Association, the organism that petitioned Mayor Koch to "clean up" 5th Avenue, the Harlem Business Alliance lobbied the Dinkins administration to disperse the "illegal" vendors. With the support of Harlem's elected officials (federal, state, and city), the administration decided, albeit reluctantly, to enforce the city's vending ordinance that forbade unlicensed vendors from selling goods (except for books) on the streets. The enforcement plan proved to be a dismal failure. In protest against Dinkins's decision, the newly formed 125th Street Vendors Association staged a demonstration that shut down 125th Street for one day. Although the police voiced their willingness to disperse the protesters, Dinkins, fearing the violent consequences of a police-vendor confrontation, backed down.

The 125th Street market continued to grow following Dinkins's capitulation. In March 1993, vendors reported hearing rumors about the imminent dispersal of the market. "We hear these things all the time," one merchant said. "But we're not worried. The last time they tried to shut us down, we shut down all of 125th Street."[13] That March, most of the vendors seemed more worried about the effect of cold weather on sales than the impact of city hall's regulations. Rumors nonetheless persisted throughout the spring and into the summer.

On August 19, bureaucrats from the New York City Department of Business Services distributed the following letter to the vendors on 125th Street.

TOURISTS SHOOT THE 125TH STREET MARKET, SUMMER 1994. (PHOTO BY AUTHOR)

DEAR VENDOR:

The New York City Department of Business Services with assistance from the 125th Street Local Development Corporation, the Harlem Business Alliance, Community Board #10, the 125th Street Vendors Association and members of the business and street vendor communities have been working together to improve business conditions on 125th Street.

You should be aware that the law currently prohibits almost every form of street vending that now exists on 125th Street. This is why we are now proposing to establish an open-air market for street vendors on 126th Street between Adam Clayton Powell Blvd. to St. Nicholas Avenue as a way to provide an alternative legal site for vendors. We will also work with vendors currently at Malcolm X Blvd. from 125th to 126th Streets on a plan to legally remain at this site. This solution is being presented to you as a way to provide a legitimate place for you to conduct your business.

In order for you to participate in this program, you should fill out the vendor registration form and mail it to the New York City Department of Business Services, 110 William Street, New York, N.Y. 10038, Attention: Intergovernmental Business Affairs Division. This information will be used for vendor identification cards to determine the exact location of street vendor spaces and other requirements for the street vendor market.

We appreciate your cooperation and assistance to make the 126th Street alternative site a success. Thank you for your time and attention.[14]

The vendor registration form requested the following information: name, address, telephone number, the nature of goods sold, and the number of tables used for vending. Many vendors provided the requested information; some furnished false names, addresses, and phone numbers; others simply refused to comply with the request for information.

In the end, it didn't matter whether the vendors complied with the Department of Business Services request, for city hall solved the problem of unlicensed vending on 125th Street the usual way—by doing nothing substantive. City hall held meetings with the concerned parties: the 125th Street Local Development Corporation, the Harlem Business Alliance, and the 125th Street Vendors Association. People vented their frustrations, and city hall scheduled additional meetings, which led to more vented frustrations, more meetings. Meanwhile, the African market continued to grow. Despite these ongoing negotiations, all parties knew that nothing would be resolved until after the mayoral election in November 1993. "When Dinkins was a teenager," one West African vendor stated, "he peddled on the streets of Harlem. He will not deny us our living."[15]

In November 1993, Mayor Dinkins lost his reelection bid to Rudolph Giuliani, the Reagan-appointed former U.S. district attorney for New York City. One strong reason for Giuliani's victory was his pledge to make New York more "livable," by which he meant crime-free. Considering this seemingly insurmountable pledge, Giuliani's choice of William Bratton as police commissioner became his most important and politically significant appointment. Prior to his tenure in New York City, Bratton had secured his reputation by successfully policing Boston. In concert with Giuliani's views, Bratton believed in consistent and energetic enforcement of city regulations. This belief meant that one polices a city from the bottom up—through the enforcement of minor regulatory infractions that sometimes cause minor headaches for citizens. Such enforcement, according to Bratton's theory, compels people to believe that there is some semblance of law and order on the streets. In this way one begins to bring order to the chaos of urban society and, as a consequence, makes a city more livable.[16]

Soon after his appointment, Bratton held a press conference and presented a detailed outline of his pragmatic philosophy of law enforcement. He spoke about the presence of "squeegee men" in Manhattan. These men, mostly unemployed African Americans unlicensed by city hall, approached motorists stuck in Manhattan traffic and proposed to wash their windshields for a modest fee. In some instances, they washed windshields without the consent of motorists and aggressively demanded money. Although such unregulated activity hardly constituted a major law enforcement problem, it was a nuisance in Commissioner Bratton's universe. By eradicating the nuisance, following Bratton's logic, one would take a small but significant step toward making New York City a better place to live—at least for those who commuted to Manhattan.[17]

Commissioner Bratton's proclamation can be read as a declaration of war against the informal economy of New York City in which the exchange of goods and services is unregulated by the state.[18] As we have noted already, informal economic activities include most forms of street vending, unlicensed gypsy cab service, as well as all forms of unlicensed building projects—to name only a few.[19] To enforce overlooked city regulations, then, is to crack down on the informal economy.

Early talk from Giuliani and Bratton led to much speculation among West African vendors on 125th Street. Would Giuliani act quickly to close down a market that was in gross violation of New York City ordinances? As it turned out, the beginning of the Giuliani administration did not mean the immediate end of the African market. In fact, the market expanded in February and March of 1994, usually a slow season. Reeling from pervasive political instability as well as economic uncertainty following the World Bank's decision to devalue the West African franc, new waves of West African immigrants had arrived in New York looking for commercial opportunities. They quickly found places for themselves at the African market on 125th Street. According to some Harlemites quoted in the *New York Times,* as many as a thousand vendors might line the sidewalks of 125th Street on some weekends.[20] In the spring and summer of 1994, more rumors swept down 125th Street sidewalks: Commissioner Bratton was organizing an imminent police action; Mayor Giuliani would soon issue an order to relocate the vendors to 126th Street and St. Nicholas Avenue. Some of the West African vendors reacted to these rumors with anger. "I will never move from here. No one will go over there to buy our goods." Boubé Mounkaila reacted with the equanimity of a pragmatic Muslim trader. "We are here to do business. If they decide to move us, we will go. We will be all right wherever they send us. We are here to make money, not to cause trouble."[21]

During the summer of 1994, the Masjid Malcolm Shabazz erected a large sign on an abandoned lot on the northeast corner of 116th Street and Lenox Avenue. It read, "Coming Soon, Masjid Malcolm Shabazz International Plaza." The sign listed the following sponsors: the Masjid Malcolm Shabazz, the Harlem Business Alliance, the 125th Street Local Development Corporation, Community Board Number 10, and the 125th Street Vendors Association.

Soon after the appearance of the 116th Street sign, members of the 125th

Street Vendors Association circulated a flyer that denied their sponsorship of the International Plaza. The flyer stated that one of the former officers of the 125th Street Vendors Association was guilty of misrepresentation. When asked about this political bickering, vendors from Niger said that it was not uncommon for African Americans to play politics.[22]

As business leaders and elected officials of Harlem lobbied the mayor to remove the street vendors from 125th Street, rumors of an imminent police action circulated through the market. Most West African vendors believed that the city would eventually evict them, but not until after the summer.[23] Meanwhile the battle lines had been drawn. Federal, state, and Harlem officials joined forces with the Masjid Malcolm Shabazz, the Harlem business community, and the Giuliani administration—political groups with very different agendas. They suggested moving the vendors to the proposed site of the Masjid Malcolm Shabazz International Plaza on 116th Street and Lenox Avenue. Led by Morris Powell and backed by Louis Farrakhan's Nation of Islam and the Reverend Al Sharpton, the 125th Street Vendors Association vehemently opposed this plan.[24]

Tensions were understandably high by the time Mayor Giuliani had set October 17 as the date for moving the African market. Several days before the imposed deadline, the Department of Business Services circulated the following notice, written in English, Spanish, and French, to the shoppers on 125th Street.

TO ALL SHOPPERS ON 125TH STREET:

If you patronize the street vendors who sell on 125th Street and its immediate vicinity, then this notice is for you. Beginning Monday, October 17, 1994, street vending will no longer be allowed on 125th Street and its immediate vicinity.

That's why we want you to know that as of that date (October 17, 1994) all of the street vendors carrying your favorite goods will be operating from two new markets on the corners of 116th Street and Lenox and 117th Street and Lenox. The new markets are only a few blocks away and they offer many conveniences and advantages over 125th Street.

For instance:
- the markets will be cleaner
- the vendors will be more organized
- because of the markets, there will be less over-crowded sidewalks on 125th Street
- less over-crowded sidewalks should reduce the opportunity for crime and dangers posed to your safety

• you can shop in an environment of relative comfort. You can buy
your usual product from the same vendors at no more than the usual
prices.

So please, beginning October 17, 1994, bear in mind that your vendors
whom you've always patronized will be at new markets on 116th and 117th
Streets and Lenox Avenue, sponsored by the Malcolm Shabazz Masjid. Your
vendors in their new location need you more than ever! Help make them a
success.[25]

I took a copy of this notice and showed it to several West African vendors.
They scoffed at city hall's plan. A Malian vendor said that the move to 116th
Street was nothing more than a plot to profit the Masjid Malcolm Shabazz
and its putative Senegalese cohorts. "The Senegalese," he said, "see this
move as a way to crush other West African competition and make much
money for themselves."[26] On 125th Street, vendors did not pay for their
spaces, which meant that the City of New York did not receive tax revenues
from them—the very definition of informal economic enterprise. As we
have seen, under the plan sponsored by the Giuliani administration and the
Masjid Malcolm Shabazz, the vendors would pay a flat fee of seven dollars
per day for their spaces, each of which would be marked by painted lines and
numbers. City hall agreed to take only 30 percent of these revenues, leaving
70 percent to the Masjid Malcolm Shabazz.[27]

Two days before Mayor Giuliani's police action, West African vendors
speculated about the plans that the Masjid Malcolm Shabazz had for them.
All the vendors I talked to suggested that the 116th Street site would be
temporary. "We'll be there for only one year," one vendor predicted. "By that
time, the Masjid will have gotten enough money to build a new mosque on
the site. What will happen to us then?"[28] This view was confirmed by Lance
Shabazz, who on October 17 told Jonathan Hicks of the *New York Times* that
the Masjid would build a mosque at the 116th Street site. "So this [open-air
market at 116th Street] is just a temporary arrangement. . . . When the new
mosque is built, what's going to happen to the vendors then? I don't think
the city has considered any of this."[29]

On the eve of Mayor Giuliani's police action, Morris Powell, head of
the 125th Street Vendors Association, was defiant, saying that his members
planned to stay put "even if they bring in the National Guard. We're not going anywhere." For their part, the New York City Police Department seemed
determined to control the public order by maintaining a high profile. "We're
going to have a sufficient contingent to make sure that public safety is maintained," Assistant Chief of Police Wilbur Chapman told the *New York Post*.[30]

Police also mentioned that vendors who defied the mayor's order to leave 125th Street might face arrest and fines as high as one thousand dollars.

Meanwhile an ad hoc group known as the Concerned People for the Development of Harlem, which did not specify its membership, underscored the issue of race in the politics of the African market. They circulated a flyer that put Asian and white store owners on notice: "If we are not allowed to do business among our own people . . . then we're not going to allow any other non-black entity to continue to exploit our consumer market. If our children don't eat we will make damn sure your children don't eat off our people's spending power."[31] The imminence of police action, as already mentioned, prompted West African vendors to hold palavers where they seriously discussed their economic and social futures. Many of the vendors expressed a kind of critical resignation, which reflected their ambivalence toward the cultural politics of New York City. "We have no power here. What is our choice? We do not want trouble. We will make the best of a bad situation."[32]

Issifi Mayaki couldn't fully understand why Mayor Giuliani wanted to disperse the African market. "The market is good. There are many people. We all seem to get along. There is a great deal of business transaction. Our presence is even good for the shopkeepers. Our presence and our goods are so fine that they bring busloads of tourists who come to see the African market."

"Maybe people here don't like the presence of an African market in America," I suggested.

"Yeah," Issifi said. "They just don't like Africans. That's all. They want us to go back home."[33]

We have already seen how space was negotiated at the African market on 125th Street. In many respects the market reproduced markets in West Africa. There were no formally assigned market stalls and no one paid a fee for a market space. One's space was usually occupied early in the morning and kept until sunset. Vendors rarely contested this informal rule. Over time, Africans from specific countries (Niger, Mali, the Gambia, and Senegal) had appropriated specific areas of the sidewalk on 125th Street and on Lenox. In this way, one could find Nigeriens or Malians in certain areas, though this casual rule was not exclusive. As in West African markets, certain groups sold specific items. In New York City, Malians sold cloth; Gambians traded beads and African crafts; Nigeriens offered T-shirts, sweats, and hats; Senegalese sold African dolls and sunglasses; and Jamaicans provided African art. When new vendors came to the market, their compatriots would "make space" for them—all informally.[34]

What was it about these spatial processes—and about space in general—that sparked such controversy? It is clear that the symbolism of spatial relations can be a powerful political tool—a continuous reminder of one's power or of one's powerlessness, of one's hopes and desires and of one's despair and anger. From the West African perspective, it was business as usual to have a thousand street vendors squeezed into informally allotted spaces along 125th Street, where they'd sell goods as they bantered with local residents and tourists. Their forebears had conducted business in West Africa in a similar manner; it is an open, flexible, and profitable way to engage in commerce. From the perspective of the Harlem business and political establishment, the presence of a thousand unregulated street vendors on 125th Street represented a throwback to the past rather than an opportunity for the future economic development of Harlem. Such development, they reasoned, would provide much needed employment to Harlem's residents. They saw the informal market as an impediment to economic and social progress; it was a symbolic thorn in their sides that had to be removed and destroyed. Some of the shop owners liked the crowds that the informal market attracted; some of the shop owners thought the market crowds hurt their businesses. Some of the shoppers liked the informal, festive air of the African market, but did not like the garbage and trash left in its wake.

As is often the case in local politics, the political and business establishment, knowing how to exercise its power, convinced Mayor Giuliani to disperse the market. The vendors, for their part, did not leave quietly.

October 17, 1994. There were no vendors on the street. They had been replaced by fleets of blue paddy wagons and police vans. Men dressed in suits walked along the sidewalks, talking into their walkie-talkies. The clatter of hoofs announced the arrival of a contingent of mounted police. Young men and women with press cards walked stiffly up and down the street, taking photos and writing notes. Older Harlemites strolled by the scene carrying their own video cameras and notebooks.

At 10:00 A.M. the police blocked off 125th Street and Lenox Avenue. Shortly thereafter a group of demonstrators, mostly African Americans, began their march down 125th Street. Considering the throngs of street vendors on 125th Street, the number of demonstrators seemed slim—perhaps no more than 150 marchers. They were literally surrounded by police—in vans, in paddy wagons, on foot, on horseback. The demonstrators formed a core, which the police sealed off. Encircled by the police, the demonstrators moved slowly down 125th Street. "No food, no peace," they chanted. A few West African street vendors joined the march.

The demonstrators gathered on the plaza of the Adam Clayton Powell Building. Morris Powell, short, gray, and formless in his military fatigues, stood on a platform to speak. He wore a kente cloth hat and beads. A motley group gathered around him: vendors, a few Japanese tourists, a smattering of white civil servants, and people from the neighborhood, many of them older African Americans.

Mr. Powell began to speak and immediately injected the issue of race into his discourse. "We will not move," he said. "We have a right to be here. We must stop the move of whites to take over 125th Street." Another speaker talked of police racism and brutality. He said there was a conspiracy to rob African Americans of their own self-determination. He also said that the cops were nothing less than the Gestapo and that Mayor Giuliani was a disgrace. A woman stood up to speak. She, too, described the realities of racism in America, saying that African Americans needed to feed their own children before letting others feed their children with the dollars of African Americans.

Someone gave Mr. Powell a bullhorn. He asked the demonstrators to begin marching in an orderly fashion. Soon thereafter, the police arrested Mr. Powell for the unauthorized use of a bullhorn. Police arrested twenty-one other demonstrators, some of whom had knocked down barriers and confronted store owners. After the rally and arrests, the crowd dispersed, but the police remained in force to patrol the sidewalks. Except for fast food restaurants, all the businesses along 125th Street were shuttered. After his arrest, Mr. Powell vowed to continue to boycott "non–black owned stores." On the other side, Chief of Patrol Louis Anemone said: "We'll be here forever, if necessary." [35]

As promised, the 125th Street Vendors Association attempted to boycott businesses on 125th Street owned and run by nonblacks. Supported by the Nation of Islam, the Reverend Al Sharpton, and Khallid Muhammad, the vendors set up picket lines in front of these businesses. On October 18, the police arrested Sharpton for "illegally" selling Bibles on 125th Street. On subsequent days, picketers lambasted African American shoppers for frequenting white and Asian-owned stores. Perhaps many of the shoppers grasped the irony that at least some of the picketers missed: the forces behind the crackdown had less to do with racial politics than with economic incentive. Consider the commentary of E. R. Shipp in the *New York Daily News*:

This week picketers, egged on by the likes of Khalid Muhammed—are spending their days outside stores they say are owned by whites and Koreans, shouting slogans like "Close 'em down" and berating anyone who insists on shopping rather than acceding to their boycott.

They miss the point: It's not just white and Koreans who want to bring some semblance of order to the chaos on 125th St., Harlem's main commercial strip. Indeed, it's downright insulting when Powell and his ilk ignore the fact that black business, civic and political leaders have been after the mayor—from Koch to Dinkins to Giuliani—to do something about the situation. Giuliani took his sweet time, but he's finally listening to responsible Harlemites.[36]

Writing in the *New York Amsterdam News,* Abiola Sinclair took a position more moderate than either Morris Powell or E. R. Shipp. Sinclair had bought from both black and Asian store owners as well as street vendors. She supported the right of the vendors to be on 125th Street, but believed they should be regulated: "My position is they should be regulated. Not in front of bus stops, hydrants, etc. Not blocking the sidewalk to the extent that people can't pass by. They should also be ticketed for keeping a dirty space. I've seen Africans and African Americans set up in the morning, leave the spot dirty, and they pay it no attention. They leave it that way or worse. Those large concrete tubs were meant for flowers not trash."[37] An editorial in the *New York Post* likened the 125th Street market to a "veritable Third World bazaar."[38]

Such official talk about order as opposed to chaos, cleanliness as opposed to clutter, and regulation as opposed to informality echoes the arguments of the Fifth Avenue Merchants Association in its partially successful attempt to clear midtown Manhattan of Senegalese "clutter" in 1985. Such discourse seeks to replace third world chaos, filth, and informality with first world order, cleanliness, and regulation.

Given the diversity of political opinion, racial ideology, and spatial preferences about the dispersal of the 125th Street African market, it was hardly surprising that the boycott had mixed results. Four days after the police action, Commissioner Bratton visited 125th Street and said that he was pleased that the picketing vendors had not denied shoppers access to stores. He vowed to maintain a considerable police presence as long as necessary and said—to counter charges of police racism—that similar vending regulations would be enforced in other parts of the city. "It's getting cold," he said. "I believe nature will end up controlling the situation."[39]

By the fourth day of the 125th Street boycott, the number of picketers had dwindled, the vendors had gone, and the crowds had left. Even though the police profile was still high, their behavior remained low-key. The 125th Street Vendors Association boycott of non–black owned businesses, in fact, petered out in less than one week. Many forces worked against its success.

First, although many residents of Harlem thought that the informal market had disrupted commerce on 125th Street and that the street vendors should be dispersed or, at the least, regulated, many disagreed with the logic that connected the mayoral crackdown to the boycott. Second, vendors, like anyone in New York City, needed income. Some of them, including many West Africans, relocated their unlicensed operations to other parts of the city: Canal Street, Chambers Street, 14th Street between 6th and 5th Avenues. The great majority of the West African vendors reluctantly relocated to the Masjid Malcolm Shabazz's new market at 116th Street and Lenox Avenue.

Four days after the removal of "illegal" vendors from 125th Street, the *New York Times* published an editorial that supported Mayor Giuliani's action, but also urged city hall to grant some assistance to the displaced street vendors.

> Before this week, the business strip on Harlem's 125th Street was annoyingly— and dangerously—overcrowded. As many as 1000 illegal vendors of all kinds operated an outlaw market that left sidewalks impassable. Parents had to push children's strollers in the streets.
>
> Legitimate businesses faced obstructed doorways, summonses for dirty sidewalks and unfair competition from vendors who paid neither rent nor taxes. As the congestion escalated, fistfights broke out among the vendors over contested spaces.
>
> The Giuliani administration has now solved the problem by relocating the vendors to vacant lots on 116th Street and by creating special licenses for them, allowing more than 400 to become legitimate, taxpaying entrepreneurs. Those who continue to operate outside the lots will be prosecuted. . . .
>
> However, with the congestion problem solved, the city and the local business association need to consider whether 125th Street has been swept *too* clean of street life. On a recent sunny afternoon, strollers and shoppers were sparse. If thin foot traffic becomes persistent, shop owners could find themselves scrambling to bring back the crowds. . . . Too little foot traffic is just as damaging as too much.[40]

The *Times* observations have turned out to be prophetic. Since October 1994, independent store owners on 125th Street have seen foot traffic dwindle, revenues shrink, and rents expand. The inclusion of Harlem in a Federal Empowerment Zone, the agenda of the Harlem business and political establishment, brought in $300 million in federal, state, and city funds earmarked for the economic expansion. The availability of these considerable funds helped to trigger the corporatization of 125th Street—both the Body

Shop and Haagen-Daaz, for example, have opened stores on the "One Twenty Five." As a consequence, "rents have soared, and some of the small businesses that struggled through the lean years have been squeezed. Others are unsure if the influx of money will benefit or harm them." [41]

"The shop owners," Issifi Mayaki said some two months after the demise of the African market, "were greedy. They didn't want to share 125th Street with us. Now they are sorry. I've been to several community meetings. The merchants of 125th Street say that business is down, way down, since we left. Some of them want us to come back."

"Do you think that will happen?" I ask.

"No, not really. There's too much politics involved." [42]

The same *New York Times* editorial that warned of the economic perils of too little foot traffic on 125th Street also urged city hall to help reestablish the displaced vendors by advertising their new locale on 116th Street. In December 1994, there was little evidence of any city effort on the vendors' behalf. At the peak of the 1994 Christmas season, vendors outnumbered shoppers at the Malcolm Shabazz Harlem Market.

Despite these foreboding economic signs, Issifi Mayaki, like most of the displaced West African vendors, immediately signed on at the Malcolm Shabazz Harlem Market. He had no grudge against the Masjid Malcolm Shabazz and felt that the Masjid's registration and rental fees were fair. Several Nigeriens, all Hausa, moved to the new market. One sold counterfeit watches; two others sold leather hats, novelty baseball caps, gloves, and scarves. West Africans from Senegal and Guinea, as we have seen, established video enterprises. They sold pirated cassettes wholesale to African Americans who would take them into Harlem to sell them corner to corner, door to door. Despite this dynamic activity, the market seemed quite dead, even on a weekend two weeks before Christmas in 1994. Issifi said that people did not yet know about the market. Worse yet, he suggested that the space, with its ten-foot chain-link fences and visible police patrols, seemed too much like a prison, an image that kept many prospective buyers away. [43]

Many of the West African vendors, however, moved their operations away from Harlem. In November 1994, as already mentioned, Boubé Mounkaila and his partner, Sala Fari, took their business to Canal Street in lower Manhattan. For twenty-five hundred dollars a month, they rented a storefront just up the corner from Broadway and Canal Street. They shared this unheated space, which had been a gift shop, with two Octavian Indians, Luis and Maria, from Ecuador, who displayed handwoven wool sweaters. Since Boubé and Sala paid more than Luis and Maria, they reserved the right to display their wares—a few African textiles and several kilim bags imported from Turkey—in the window. They also hung African leather bags, baseball caps, and ski hats from pegboards on the walls and installed a mirror adjacent to the entrance to the store.

Several factors conspired to bring on the failure of Boubé and Sala's enterprise. Because of their high month-to-month rental fees, they needed a high sales volume to make profits. Although they made sales every day, especially during the lunch hour, they did not sell enough to offset operating costs. The fact that the store was cold, poorly lit, and some distance away from the always-crowded Canal Street also reduced their sales. To make matters even worse, the city began a subway construction project just in front of the store soon after they moved in. The obstructed sidewalk kept customers from wandering in, and the constant noise of the jackhammer did not encourage those few who did venture in to linger. Sala complained about the high costs and lack of income. Although Boubé could pay his rent and food costs and could also invest in new inventory, he gave up his phone and stopped sending money to his family in Niger.

Some of their compatriots who had rented storefront shelves on Canal Street fared somewhat better, despite rents of three thousand dollars a month. Both El Hadj Harouna Souley and Mounkaila Bari, two Songhay men, had been on Canal Street since 1992. They sold hats, scarves, and gloves and made enough money not only to meet their professional and personal expenses, but also to send funds to their families in Niger. El Hadj Harouna and Mounkaila were both in their forties, and it was hard to stand outside in the cold weather twelve hours a day, seven days a week. They persevered, however, for as El Hadj Harouna put it, they had "a responsibility to [their] families."[44]

Boubé Mounkaila and Sala Fari remained in their Broadway shop for four months. In March 1995, Boubé brought his business back to Harlem and sold Nigerien leather goods from a stall at the Malcolm Shabazz Harlem Market. His fortunes ameliorated almost immediately. In short order, he paid off his phone bill, reinvested in new inventory, and sent small of amounts of money to his family in Niger.

Since Sala possessed an INS employment authorization permit, he chose to work as a security guard at a leather goods shop on Lexington Avenue in Midtown. To maintain his identity as a trader, he rented a stall at the Malcolm Shabazz Harlem Market and sold baseball caps on the weekends. Because his stall was at the back of the market, his weekend business never prospered. In September 1996, Sala left New York City for Greensboro, North Carolina, which had a rapidly growing West African community and where he continued to combine trade with work in the formal sector.

Nigeriens began to move to Greensboro just after the demise of the 125th Street market. As Garba Hima, who had procured a work permit in October 1994, explained: "I heard that there was work for Africans in Greensboro, North Carolina. I flew there, found a job, found an apartment, flew back to New York City, packed my belongings and took a bus there." At first Garba held two jobs—at a raincoat factory and at a McDonald's. Once he established himself, he moved into a more spacious apartment. From the outset, he urged his compatriots to come to Greensboro. "The weather is warm here. There are many Africans working in factories. We have a nice mosque. Apartments and food are cheap. No crime. And people are friendly. They treat you with respect."[45] Like Sala Fari, Garba Hima also continued to trade informally.

Greensboro continued to attract Nigerien merchants. At the time of the Giuliani police action, Idrissa Dan Inna, former trade unionist in Niger and a member of the 125th Street Vendors Association, vowed never to sell goods at 116th Street's Malcolm Shabazz International Plaza. He maintained his vow. Like several of the West African vendors in Harlem, he had procured an employment authorization permit, and following the demise of the 125th Street market, he found work in a Brooklyn tool and die factory. He often worked long night shifts, and eventually his health suffered. In October 1995, he left New York for Greensboro, where Garba helped him to find jobs at a McDonald's franchise and the raincoat factory. Like Garba Hima, he urged his New York compatriots to come south for decent jobs, warm weather, safe streets, and inexpensive apartments. In March 1996, El Hadj Harouna Souley and Mounkaila Bari gave up their stalls in lower Manhattan for factory jobs and informal trading in North Carolina. In June 1996, Mounkaila Bari welcomed his Nigerien wife to North Carolina. In the summer of 1997, she gave birth to a baby girl.

The West African merchants who remained at the Malcolm Shabazz Harlem Market adjusted to the economic realities of the 116th Street space. Several men with employment authorization permits left the trading life to become factory workers, security guards, or drugstore clerks. Traders like Boubé Mounkaila diversified their product lines. Engaging in a trading strategy employed by their forebears, Hausa merchants like Moussa Boureima and Issifi Mayaki became mobile merchants. During the many lulls at the Malcolm Shabazz Harlem Market, they followed a circuit of African American cultural festivals and made money by marketing Afrocentricity.

The trade at the Malcolm Shabazz Harlem Market took a serious downturn in January 1998. Between 1994 and 1998 traders sold pirated videos, CDs, and cassettes with impunity. This trade, according to Issifi Mayaki and

Boubé Mounkaila, had become the key to success at 116th Street. Videos, CDs, and audiocassettes, they said, attracted many clients to the market who would then stay to browse and buy a handbag, a watch, or a baseball cap.[46] Reacting to political pressure brought to bear by Blockbuster Video and the film and recording industry, city hall suggested to the Masjid Malcolm Shabazz that the illegal sale of videos, CDs, and audiocassettes would have to stop. In January 1998, the Masjid told its vendors who sold these items that they could no longer do so. The dispersal of the pirated video and audio trade severely limited the foot traffic at the 116th Street market. Boubé Mounkaila stated that the trade in pirated videos and CDs would eventually return. His business was secure enough to weather this economic lull, but his Hausa colleagues, like Issifi Mayaki, now had to spend much more of their time on the road. In March 1998, they traveled to Chicago and Detroit. In April 1998, they went all the way to Houston as well as to Orlando and Atlanta.

"It is very tiring to travel so much," Issifi said in April 1998, calling from his van somewhere in Mississippi, "but we have no choice. We are tired, but we cannot ignore possibilities for business."[47]

There is something heroic about this group of West African traders. Fleeing economic hardship, they arrived in America with little money and less technological expertise. Mastering the language of American capitalism and skillfully recreating their trading networks, they have managed to earn enough money to expand their enterprises as well as to care for their large families in Niger, Mali, Senegal, Guinea, and Burkina Faso. Confronting regulatory obstacles and disruptions to their businesses, they found legal loopholes that allowed them to continue trading. Many of them procured immigration papers that could eventually lead to permanent residency or citizenship. Faced with the ebb and flow of the informal economy, they have reacted with the flexibility of professional traders who know how to weather the hard times and how to profit when times are good.

West African street traders are an impressive lot. They are adaptable, street savvy, and smart. And yet one wonders if they are immune to the considerable stresses of being immigrants. How do these savvy traders feel about their lives in the United States? How have they adapted to being separated from their loved ones for as many as eight years? How have they coped with their alienation, their loneliness, and their sexual isolation? It is to these questions that we turn next.

144   In 1997, Moussa Boureima, who by then had lived and worked on the streets of New York City for more than three years, was suffering more and more from rheumatism. The condition, which made his knees ache, his ankles swell, and his joints stiffen, had been aggravated by the fact that he sold his merchandise outside—in the damp chill of fall and winter as well as in the stifling humidity of summer—at the Malcolm Shabazz Harlem Market. Despite his continuous discomfort, Moussa was hesitant to see a physician.

"I don't speak much English," he said, "not enough to explain what's wrong with me. Last year I found a doctor on 72nd Street. He speaks French. He gave me a shot and my pain went away, but it came back. I don't want to go to a hospital. I have no papers. I don't want any trouble."

We have already touched on many of the difficulties the question of "papers" presents for West African street vendors in New York City. Men without papers usually have no health insurance. They may be unable to obtain a driver's license, though some of the traders have found ways to do so. They may be timid about signing up for night school, though several of the traders have learned English in this manner. They often refuse to report thefts to the police.

Aside from his health, Moussa had a number of other very serious concerns throughout 1997. From the money that he earned from the sale of baseball hats, gloves, and scarves, he had to pay $450 per month to rent an apartment in a substandard building in the Bronx. He also had to pay for his electricity, gas, and telephone. His daily transportation on the subway, food costs, medical expenses, as well as necessary investments in new inventory, quickly sapped his financial resources. After he paid his monthly bills, he sent the remainder of his money to Tessoua, Niger, to support his wife and eight children.[1]

At least half of the West African traders in New York City are part of the estimated five million undocumented immigrants who live in the United States. Many undocumented West Africans avoid hospitals, doctors, and nurses because of their fear of detainment and deportation. Although no West African trader that I've met has been deported, many of them have expressed fears of detainment.

The reasons for these seemingly unfounded fears are clear-cut. No trader wants to be sent home in disgrace, let alone languish in an INS detention center. During many informal conversations between August 1992 and March 1998, West African street vendors asked my opinion on current events. Many of them read the *New York Post*. More of them got their news from television. Some of the traders watched the news in English; others tuned into a French-language station in New York City. During lulls in the market, they invariably discussed new cultural trends gleaned from MTV and periodically debated international, national, and local politics culled from local and cable news programs. These viewing habits made them critically aware of shifting U.S. attitudes toward immigration.

"Why are people so against us?" Issifi Mayaki asked me in August of 1995. "They say that even though we don't pay taxes, we use your services. We don't. All we do is work, work, and work to make money to send to our families. If there is a problem, we rely on one another for money and services. We are not criminals. We don't rob or steal. Why not worry more about drug dealers and petty thieves than about hard-working people like us?"[2]

In the summer of 1995, there was much talk of immigration politics at the Malcolm Shabazz Harlem Market. Traders expressed concern over Congress's proposals that would bar the children of illegal immigrants from public schools and force public hospitals to report undocumented aliens seeking medical treatment. Mayor Giuliani's sharp criticism of these proposals won the praise of West African traders. Giuliani, himself the son of immigrant parents, condemned both ideas. He said that to bar from the public schools some forty to sixty thousand students whose parents were undocumented would create tens of thousands of new street kids, leading to an increase in crime. He also said that it was morally wrong to refuse to treat sick people in public hospitals. "It's just out of a sense of decency," he said. "I can't imagine, even in parts of the country where views are harsher than they might be in New York, that they're basically going to say, let people die."[3] Indeed, in 1985, former New York City mayor Ed Koch signed executive order 124, which prohibited city employees from supplying information to the INS on the unregistered immigrants they served—unless the immigrant had been involved in a crime. The executive order remained in effect until a provision of the 1996 Illegal Immigration Reform and Immigrant Responsibility Act superseded it. Refusing to accept this outcome, Mayor Giuliani sued the federal government in U.S. district court in October 1996. The court found in favor of the federal government. The city appealed the lower court ruling to the U.S. court of appeals, which in May 1999 upheld the federal district court ruling.

This sequence of events has served to reinforce the already entrenched wariness of West African immigrants living in New York City. They have learned to take public assurances, like that of Giuliani's in 1995, with a grain of salt. Their central concern has been, Can people who misunderstand us be trusted? Although several public officials seem to support the rights of immigrants, the West African street vendors I've met are convinced that most Americans view them with disdain and resentment. These negative attitudes, they say, are clearly expressed in the way that the INS treats inmates at its detention centers.

The traders often brought up for discussion the cases of two West African detainees who had received media attention—Fauziya Kasinga of Togo in 1996 and Edwin Bulus of Nigeria in 1997. The INS had subjected these two detainees to horrible treatment. The more notorious case was that of Fauziya Kasinga, a young woman who had fled Togo to avoid a cliterodectomy. Kasinga's family, she reported, insisted that she become the fourth wife of an older man who demanded that her clitoris be removed. Thinking she'd be granted asylum, Kasinga had escaped her family and country and attempted to enter the United States with another woman's passport, bought from a Nigerian man in Düsseldorf, Germany. Rather than hearing her case, the INS had detained Kasinga immediately after her arrival at Newark International Airport on December 17, 1994. She was then sent to the infamous Esmor detention center in Elizabeth, New Jersey.

At Esmor, guards placed her in a windowless cold room and told her to strip off her clothes. Because she was menstruating, she asked to keep on her underwear, but the guard refused. She sat on the room's toilet shivering. At one point she saw a male guard spying on her. Eventually guards gave her a pair of sandals, both for the right foot, and a stained pair of underwear much too large for her. When she used the showers before 6 A.M. to perform ritual ablutions before the early morning Muslim prayer, a rule violation, guards put her in an isolation cell for five days. In June 1995, fights broke out at Esmor in protest of poor jail conditions and extended incarcerations. Guards tear-gassed and beat the detainees during the disturbance. An investigation followed. The INS "issued a report after the melee that documented many of the abuses Ms. Kasinga said she had endured. The agency concluded that the poorly paid guards had treated the inmates with capricious cruelty."[4]

Following the Esmor incident, the INS moved Kasinga to the York County prison, then to the Lehigh County prison, both in Pennsylvania. In January 1996, the INS moved her from Lehigh back to York, where, owing to a lack of space, Kasinga was put in maximum security, along with Americans convicted of drug dealing, robbery, and murder. At York, guards routinely strip-searched Kasinga. After almost two years of legal wrangling—and, perhaps as a result of public sympathy for her case—the INS released Kasinga in late April 1996.

The more recent case of Edwin Bulus also caught the attention of West African traders at the Malcolm Shabazz Harlem Market. The INS had detained the twenty-eight-year-old Bulus upon his arrival at John F. Kennedy Airport in May 1995. Bulus claimed that he had fled Nigeria to save his life. In February 1995, the Nigerian government had arrested his brother, a military officer, who had been accused of plotting to overthrow the regime of General Sani Abacha. Fearing the worst, Bulus, who was a pro-democracy advocate in Nigeria, had gone into hiding. In March 1995, failing to apprehend Bulus, the military had arrested his parents, both of whom would die in prison. The Nigerian government eventually commuted his brother's death sentence to twenty-five years.

Bulus entered the United States on a resident alien card that did not belong to him. INS officers detained him at the airport and sent him to the Esmor detention center, where during the disturbance of June 1995, officials, according to Bulus's claims, threw away his birth certificate and transferred him to Union County jail in New Jersey: "In the county jail, Bulus said, guards stomped on him, forced him to kneel naked for hours, pushed his head in a toilet, left him to sleep naked on a bare mattress and subjected him to racist invective. Twelve guards were subsequently indicted for beating and degrading 25 Esmor detainees, including Bulus."[5]

During two years of INS detention, Bulus, who suffers from clinical depression, was repeatedly transferred among various county jails in New Jersey and Pennsylvania. He was sent twice to the INS detention center in Miami. His previous requests for political asylum were denied because he was unable to produce identity papers. His several appeals for parole, pending a new ruling on his political asylum, have been turned down. His attorney has asserted that guards have repeatedly beaten him. As of late 1999, he was still in detention.

From the perspective of West African traders, especially if they are undocumented, the importance of these and other horror stories about INS detention lies less in the specific details of the cases than in the graphic descriptions of the brutal conditions of INS detention centers like Esmor. Although it is unlikely that undocumented traders already in residence would be treated as harshly as people detained for illegal entry into the United States, the horror stories about INS detention make those traders extremely prudent in their dealings with outsiders.[6]

Fear of INS detention and deportation compels many traders like Moussa Boureima to avoid any municipal service, like public hospitals, in which they must provide some form of identification. Traders often, however, find other ways to seek medical treatment. Through his network, Moussa Boureima found a French-speaking physician who agreed to receive payment in installments. Other traders, most of whom have no health insurance, use private or neighborhood walk-in clinics. In the case of emergencies, they try go to the emergency room of a private hospital. When thugs severely beat one of the older Nigerien traders in 1993, he received extensive, life-saving treatment at an expensive private hospital. Because the cost of the treatment was far beyond the man's capacity to pay, Nigerien traders in Harlem collected money among themselves to help their compatriot settle his hospital bill and to pay for his airfare back to Niger, where he recuperated in his family compound.

If traders are suffering from an earache or a systemic infection, some of them will purchase antibiotics without prescriptions in a particular pharmacy or from pill pushers on the street. One trader who in 1994 complained to me of skin eruptions and joint aches purchased "antibiotics" from a man he described as a Nigerian pharmacist who worked at a Harlem pharmacy. He said that the pharmacist had been a physician in Nigeria and was studying for his American medical license. The man had asked the trader about his symptoms and then sold him pills. He showed me the pills that had been put in an unlabeled container. I wondered if the lack of a label troubled him. He responded by taking a pill from the container, putting it in his mouth and swallowing it.

"The doctor is an African brother," he said. "He's an African just like me and I trust him. He gave me a good price, too."[7] The trader suffered no adverse reaction to the course of mystery medicine. The next time I saw him, one month later, his condition had cleared up and he felt strong again.

There are West African street traders, however, who place little or no faith in modern Western medicine. In New York City, these men rely on traditional West African healers. Some of these healers are Muslim clerics, or marabouts, who specialize in healing. They treat people in one of several fashions. If the cause of a physical ailment is determined to be spiritual, the marabout may write a sequence of numbers on a piece of paper, recite a corresponding passage from the Qur'an, spit on the paper, fold it into a tight bundle, and instruct his client to encase the paper in a leather pouch and wear it on a string around neck or waist. In Francophone West Africa, these pouches are called *gris-gris*. For spiritual illnesses that have somatic manifestations, the marabout may use black ink to write a powerful Qur'anic verse on a tablet. He then washes the passage from the tablet with water, making sure to collect the inky fluid in a glass. The patient is then asked to drink the contents of the glass.

Illnesses generated by physiological rather than spiritual causes are treated with herbal medicines—the dried stems, leaves, and roots of medicinal plants shipped to New York City from West Africa. The plants arrive in New York City in one of two ways. There are traders, like El Hadj Tondi, who, when coming to New York City every six weeks or so, bring along several sacks filled with dried medicinal plants. Between 1990 and 1994, El Hadj Tondi sold these plants at the 125th Street market. After the demise of that market, he moved this side operation—he principally imports West African cloth—to the Malcolm Shabazz Harlem Market at 116th Street. In August 1994, El Hadj Tondi showed me a bag of medicinal herbs he had brought to the 125th Street market. The burlap sacks contained, he said, two kinds of powdered tree bark, which when mixed with milk, coffee, or water, is ingested to combat *weyna*. In Songhay *weyna* refers to "hot" illnesses. He recommended *changari turi* for mild cases of *weyna* (bloated stomach, weakness in the limbs and body aches) and offered *zam turi* for more serious cases of *weyna* (diarrhea, blood in the stool combined with lower back pain and weakness in the limbs, especially just above the knees). "You either put water in a teaspoon and fill it with powder or put three pinches of powder into a cup of coffee or a glass of milk. I give my countrymen the medicine they want. If it works for them, they will pay me. If it doesn't work, they don't pay me."[8]

El Hadj Tondi, however, is a businessman, not a healer. Itinerant healers like Alpha Turi, a sixty-year-old man from Niger, routinely treat West African patients in New York City. Between early 1992 and October 1995, Alpha Turi said that he had traveled ten times between Niger and New York City. In 1994, when I first met him, he identified himself as a traveling cleric who led his countrymen in prayer and resolved disputes. He also sold cloth at the 125th Street market. In October 1995, he said that he had brought with him a large assortment of medicinal herbs, as well as plants used in Songhay magic. Indeed, he had brought such rare plants as *nine baso* and *kobe*, which are used by Songhay sorcerers (*sohanci*). In addition, he had a supply of *godji deli*, which, when burned, works as a powerful sedative. He even possessed *yulumendi*, a powerful love potion much coveted both in Niger and in New York City.[9] As it turned out, this mild-mannered man with a smooth angelic face framed by a neatly trimmed white beard, had become an important figure in the community of West African traders in New York City. His presence, however intermittent, gave West African traders a wide choice of remedies for the social and spiritual vicissitudes of city life.

Since coming to New York City in September 1990, Boubé Mounkaila, whose robust health obviates the need for modern or traditional medical treatment, has lived in three apartments. For six weeks he lived in an SRO (single room occupancy) hotel in Chelsea, which he disliked. "Too many roaches and bandits," he said, "and the place smelled bad, too."[10] Since then, he has lived in Harlem, first in a building on 126th Street and then in an apartment on Lenox between 126th and 127th Streets. He lived alone in the first apartment building, the hallways of which stank of stale onions and cabbage. His neighbors included two other Nigerien immigrants, who lived on his floor; a Senegalese immigrant married to a Puerto Rican woman who was a U.S. citizen; two Senegalese merchants; and a large Puerto Rican family. He lived in a one-room second-story walk-up, with a toilet and bathing facility at the end of each floor's dark hallway.

Illuminated by a single fixtureless light bulb, Boubé's room was a stark rectangle, perhaps twenty feet by ten. Two lumpy cots had been pushed against opposite walls near the apartment's one window, which looked out over an alley strewn with broken glass, the rusting carcasses of stripped cars, and garbage. White paint cracked with age covered a radiator just under the windowsill. Two plastic deck chairs awaited their charges at the head of each cot. A small television rested on a low table next to one of the deck chairs. On the far side of the room, a battered chest of drawers stood next to the door. Boubé had put his radio/tape/CD player on top of the chest and had arranged in neat piles his collection of CDs and cassettes—mostly rap (Public Enemy was his favorite rap group), African pop, and rhythm and blues. Toward the front of the apartment, Boubé's refrigerator hummed. Washed dishes had been stacked in a drainer to the right of the sink. A hot plate had been placed on a kitchen counter to the left of the sink. Boubé had just enough room to lean his mountain bike, a prize possession for an enthusiastic cyclist, against the wall near the apartment door. The room had no closets. As was the custom in mud-brick houses in rural Niger, Boubé hung his clothes from nails strategically hammered into the walls. He had two suits for, as he put it, "formal invitations" at the Nigerien United Nations mission and elsewhere, many dress shirts, and dozens of T-shirts with African American themes. A large calendar with an image of the Kaba in Mecca, the holiest place in Islam, hung on the wall near the refrigerator.

When I first visited Boubé in his apartment in April 1994, he told me that he paid his landlord four hundred dollars a month for his room, a sum that did not include utilities. At that time he was supporting not only his wife and daughter, but also his mother, his father having died some years earlier. He also regularly sent money to his two sisters and their families.

These expenses created a financial strain. Boubé's worries about money, like those of most peddlers, were seasonal. At the 125th Street market, he might take in seven to eight hundred dollars on the weekends in the spring, summer, and fall. During the week, however, he might gross two hundred dollars on a good day. In the winter, these sums declined precipitously. He also expressed concern over his living conditions.

"They take advantage of us," he said. "Look at this place. A small room without a toilet. And I pay four hundred per month plus utilities. They know that many of us don't have papers, and they expect us to pay in cash and not cause problems. What choice do we have?" Boubé wanted to move to a two- or three-room apartment with a bath and toilet, but his monthly expenses prevented him from doing so. "I want to leave here," he said, "but when I finish paying for food, gas, electricity, telephone, inventory, parking and car insurance, and family expenses, there's not much left."[11]

Nevertheless, in January 1995, Boubé was able to move to a three-room apartment on Lenox Avenue. A local entrepreneur owned the building. When I visited Boubé's new apartment on a rainy afternoon in March 1995, we saw a man getting into his Jaguar. He was dressed in a black leather jacket and wore a Stetson. "That's my landlord," Boubé said. "He likes Africans." Boubé explained that when he had moved in two months earlier, he had some cash flow problems. His phone service had been terminated. The new landlord, however, charged him just four hundred dollars a month for a space considerably larger than his previous apartment and allowed him to stay rent-free for the first month. Sometimes he let Boubé use his phone. "And he is always respectful," Boubé stated emphatically. "He's a fine man."[12]

Boubé's apartment was on the third floor and looked out on Lenox Avenue. The stairwell was dark and creaky and smelled fetid even in winter. Mailboxes were located on the first floor, but because mail was so frequently stolen, Boubé had a box at the local post office. Above the mailboxes was a

sign: "Anyone caught throwing garbage out the window will be punished."
In March 1995, Boubé's neighbors included his compatriots Sala Fari and
Issifi Mayaki, who shared an apartment, several African American men, and
a young white man who studied at Columbia University. The new apartment
consisted of two rooms, perhaps seven foot by twenty. One room remained
empty. Boubé planned to make this space his salon, although he didn't yet
have furniture for it. In the other room, Boubé installed a curtain as a divider.
He positioned a new double bed and a chest of drawers near the window. He
adorned the bedroom walls with prints of African American women. His
temporary sitting room consisted of plastic deck chairs and several low coffee tables. A cheap cotton carpet with "oriental" designs stretched between
the chairs and tables. On one table he had put a large boom box. The second
table supported a television and VCR. Boubé explained that he had bought a
multisystem television so he could play PAL as well as VHS videocassettes.
Many of the French and African videocassettes, he said, could be viewed only
on the PAL system. "I used to have a much larger TV," he mentioned, "but
I sent it to my older brother in Abidjan. He asked for it and I had to send it
to him. It cost fourteen hundred dollars."[13] In the small foyer that separated
the two front rooms from the kitchen and bathroom, Boubé had hung three
images on the wall: a poster of the Dome of the Rock in Jerusalem, a print
of a beautiful African American woman, and a picture of Jesus.

"Why the picture of Jesus?" I asked, during a visit in 1995.

"A woman from Canada gave it to me. We spent almost one whole day
talking at the market and she gave me the photo. She thought that because
I am Muslim I'd refuse to take the picture. But I like all religions."

Boubé's mountain bike was curiously absent.

"I gave it to an African American child who said he needed it to get to
school." Boubé said that he missed riding his bike and that it had been expensive, but offered no further explanations for this generous act. Changing
the subject, Boubé asked if I wanted to watch some television.

Looking at his watch, he channel surfed until he came upon *Top Cops*,
one of his favorite shows. In *Top Cops*, policemen recreate the stories of
their most notable arrests. He also tuned in to Broderick Crawford's *Highway Patrol* every week and found shows featuring Oprah, Jerry Springer,
Jenny Jones, and Richard Bey irresistible. At the conclusion of *Top Cops*, he
switched to *The Richard Bey Show*, which happened to focus on men who had
abandoned their pregnant girlfriends and refused to take any interest in their
future children. First the women complained about the deficiencies of their
men to an enthusiastic live audience. Up to this point the guilty boyfriends
had been waiting in a soundproof booth; they were now led, blindfolded, onto

the stage. Once his guests' blindfolds had been removed, Richard Bey introduced himself; explained the stage, the bright lights, and the hoots, whistles, and catcalls; and asked the men to tell their sides of the story. As for most people who watch this kind of television spectacle, the public airing of intimate details both repelled and attracted Boubé. Invariably, he believed that the men had wronged the women. "Men should take responsibility for their women," he said. "It is the Muslim way."[14]

Housing is a central problem for West African immigrants in New York City. Although conditions in SROs are often deplorable, many West Africans continue to live in this kind of housing. Perhaps the best-known African "village" in New York City is the Park View Hotel at 55 West 110th Street. Francophone West Africans who live there call it "Le Cent Dix." The building is in a state of advanced disrepair. In 1994, city hall cited it for a variety of code violations that included the presence of leaks, urine, feces, roaches, trash, and garbage in public access. Cracked and peeling plaster walls that line the dark hallways have attracted drug dealers and other hustlers. "Still, along with a few other Manhattan single-room occupancy hotels, this rundown, two-hundred-room warren of dark hallways and gloomy corridors has provided the first and enduring taste of America for hundreds of peddlers, taxi drivers, students and others from the nations of West Africa, fresh off jets from Dakar or Abidjan."[15]

In 1992, the owner of the building, Joe Cooper, said that perhaps three-quarters of the residents were West Africans. In 1995, fewer than half the occupants were from West Africa. Cooper said that deteriorating conditions compelled West Africans who had the funds to seek other lodging or to return to West Africa. The owner complained that the more recent occupants in the hotel were destructive. As soon as he fixed something, he asserted, someone destroyed the repairs or created new problems. The local police, however, say that crime is not widespread at the Park View.[16]

In the mid-1990s, the juxtaposition of Africans and African Americans led to some social tension. "Several Africans said they had been disappointed to encounter hostility from blacks in the neighborhood, reporting with bitterness that they were sometimes accused of selling the black Americans' ancestors into slavery."[17] The Africans also lashed out at what they said was an unwillingness of African Americans to work. In contrast, many African Americans at the Park View praised their African neighbors, saying that they were friendly, respectful, and hard working.

If the West African residents at "Le Cent Dix" hate the building in which they live, why have so many remained there? "They stay, in part, because they do not know where else to go, and because, despite everything the 'cent dix' offers something very essential: fellowship. Charles Kone, from the Ivory Coast, summed up this painful mix: 'It's misery. . . . There's no security, no maintenance.' But he added: 'I knew when I got to the airport, there was a place I could go. It's like a corner of Africa.' "[18] Indeed, at the Park View Hotel, West Africans have set up convenience stores and established communal kitchens. From the vantage of many West African residents, it has become a "vertical village."

These "vertical villages" in New York City are well known in far away West Africa. Experienced West African businessmen, like El Hadj Tondi, routinely instruct first-time travelers to look for African taxi drivers upon their arrival at John F. Kennedy Airport. These drivers, so it is said, know to take the new arrivals to one of several SRO hotels in Manhattan. When Boubé Mounkaila came to New York City in September 1990, he found a West African taxi driver, a Malian, who took him to a SRO hotel in Chelsea.

The principle of social cooperation among these immigrant traders, apparent even in New York's rundown SRO hotels, is deeply embedded in the cultures of most West African societies. We have seen how the practice of Islam is centered on cooperative economics and the establishment and reinforcement of fellowship in a community of believers.[19] We have also examined how personal and professional networks create a sense of fellowship. Many West African traders at the Malcolm Shabazz Harlem Market share professional information, exchange goods, and encourage business for each other.

When Issifi Mayaki first came to New York City, bringing inventory to expand his trade, he didn't expect to remain for more than six months, the length of his visa. Itinerant West African art and textile dealers in New York City usually stay in one of several SRO hotels in Manhattan. Thus, Issifi's first "home" in America was a single room that he shared with other Nigerien art dealers at the Hotel Belleclaire.

The Hotel Belleclaire, a rundown SRO, is located at 77th and Broadway, a rather posh neighborhood on the Upper West Side, just ten blocks north of Lincoln Center and close to such gourmet shops as Zabars and Citronella. It has ten floors of gloomy hallways, all of which smell of mildew and stale sweat. Issifi lived on the seventh floor at the south end of the hotel. His room, which he usually shared with three other Hausa, was a twenty-by-twenty-foot cubicle with only one window, which looked out at another building. A shower and toilet awaited them a few paces down a dark and dank hallway.

In 1997, the same room, which had been continuously occupied by Hausa from Niger, Ghana, and Côte d'Ivoire, was furnished with two sin-

THE HOTEL BELLECLAIRE, UPPER WEST SIDE, SUMMER 1996. (PHOTO BY AUTHOR)

gle beds, one by the window, the other placed by the east wall. There was also one small chest of drawers and a small sink and countertop, on which rested a hot plate with two burners. A skillet and a saucepan dulled by years of cursory cleaning sat unused on the burners. The once white wall directly behind the hot plate looked as if someone had smeared it with seedy turmeric paste. Those stains gave way to grime that patterned the rest of a wall dulled by age, dust, and inattention. Cobwebs hung like canopies from the ceiling corners. On the east wall, someone had hung a calendar featuring the image of the Kaba. Two clocks framed the calendar. One clock indicted time in New York City, the other in Abidjan—six hours earlier. Knowledge of time differences, the traders said, facilitates intercontinental business transactions, not to forget contact between families separated temporally, spatially, and perhaps existentially.

Suitcases lay open under the beds. Several other suitcases had been stacked in the room's one closet. Cloth folded into bales had been piled up against the walls like so many sacks of grain. Wooden statuettes lay like dead bodies on a frayed carpet that covered the creaky wooden floor. Other statuettes had been laid to rest under the beds. Masks had been squeezed between suitcases, stuffed into the closet, and shimmied between the thin lumpy bed mattresses and the walls. Plastic patio chairs filled in the spaces between the beds. A telephone fax machine awaited its next message on a low table between two of the patio chairs. A recently bought cell phone remained packed and unused in its box—perhaps an imminent export to West Africa.

In 1993, Issifi shared this room with three or four traders. If four men stayed in the room, they slept two to a bed. When on some occasions the room filled with five or even six men, the younger men took turns sleeping on the floor. They often shared breakfast—coffee, tea, and perhaps some bread slathered with margarine. On colder days, one man might prepare hot porridge. They usually lunched at the Warehouse in Chelsea, where they received and stored their inventory. Two women had established an African restaurant at the Warehouse, and many of the men, who spent long hours there, took advantage of their reasonable prices for food that reminded them of home: rice, meat, and gumbo sauce; *igname* smothered in a zesty tomato sauce; bitter-leaf sauce with beef; chicken in peanut sauce. Some evenings they might eat at La Caridad on the corner of Broadway and 78th Street. La Caridad is a Caribbean (Creole)-Chinese restaurant whose spicy and cheap dishes resembled the food of West Africa.

Issifi didn't expect to live long in these conditions, certainly no more than half a year. Every several weeks, one of the room's occupants would leave, and another Hausa would arrive from Africa. If an itinerant trader quickly depleted his inventory in profitable sales, he would have the luxury of returning to Abidjan well before his six-month visa had expired. But when Issifi lost his textile inventory, he also lost his return home and found himself trapped in New York City. He had to make new arrangements, relying on compatriots also trading in Harlem to obtain credit to start a new enterprise. Word of his difficulties spread through this informal network, and in short order, he moved in with fellow Hausa Sala Fari, who lived on 126th Street in Harlem—on the same floor as Boubé Mounkaila. Sala lived in a small apartment divided into three small rooms: two bedrooms in which large king-sized beds took up much of the space, and a salon/kitchen containing five rickety wooden chairs and a very 1950s aluminum card table with a red Formica top. A twenty-four-inch television, which, according to Sala, was usually on and tuned to MTV, even if no one was watching, occupied one of the salon's corners. In the opposite corner stood a low table supporting a telephone/fax and an answering machine. Here, at least, Issifi had his own bed in his own cramped room. He still had to share the bath and toilet with the other occupants of the second floor.

In January 1995, Boubé Mounkaila introduced Sala and Issifi to his landlord, who suggested that they might like to rent a recently vacated three-room apartment in his building. They looked at the space and liked it. To their surprise, the landlord quoted a monthly rent that was fifty dollars less than they had been paying. In February 1995, Sala and Issifi signed a lease for the three-room apartment on Lenox Avenue and moved in one floor below Boubé Mounkaila.

Following the demise of the 125th Street market in October 1994, Sala Fari and Boubé Mounkaila gradually drifted apart as trading partners. After his abortive attempt to establish a business near Canal Street in lower Manhattan, Boubé moved his African leather business to the Malcolm Shabazz Harlem Market. Sala, however, refused to work at the 116th Street market. He blamed the Masjid Malcolm Shabazz for ruining the lucrative 125th Street market. In principle, he could not bring himself to pay them rent. Instead, he found work as security guard in the formal sector. Even so, he did not want to give up the trading life. On some weekends he traveled to African American cultural festivals, where he sold baseball caps and T-shirts. In August 1995, thieves in Washington, D.C., stole his entire inventory. Destitute and discouraged, he received informal credit through his personal network to buy new inventory and start over. He petitioned the Masjid Malcolm Shabazz for space. They assigned him a stall at the rear of the market where his hats, gloves, and scarves didn't attract much buyer attention.

Frustrated, Sala moved to Greensboro, North Carolina, in January 1997 to join a small, but vibrant West African community there. At first he moved in with Garba Hima, the first Nigerien to colonize Greensboro. In time he made enough money to afford his own apartment. His departure left Issifi alone in the three-room flat, but not for long. In March 1997, he flew his youngest brother to New York City.

Issifi now shared space with his blood kin. This fact made him quite happy, for one can, he said, trust one's kin. "He will have to learn English, and then I will train him, and teach him the business." Issifi said that his brother has been distributing flyers for a car stereo shop on Canal Street. His brother's English was improving. "In time he will learn the business. Then I can travel and not lose opportunity here in New York. In time, I will return to Abidjan and leave him to tend the business. He will then do as I do now—help support his family from America."[20]

Between early 1996 and the summer of 1998, Issifi spent an increasing percentage of his time on the road, following the circuit of African American and third world cultural festivals. There were two reasons for this change. First, African American and third world cultural festivals had become quite popular; they often drew large crowds of people who wanted to spend money in the name of ethnic identity. Men like Issifi, as we have seen, have been quick to recognize the economic potential of this socioeconomic trend. Second, the Malcolm Shabazz Harlem Market had not fulfilled the hopes of its sponsors. According to many West African traders, the market had been declining since early 1997.

Responding to this turn of events, Issifi took to the road. In the fall, spring, and especially the summer, the peak season for cultural festivals, he was often away weeks at a time, returning to New York City periodically to replenish inventory. Although he had a telephone in his New York City apartment, he invested in a beeper, so he could be paged, and a cell phone so he could speak to friends, associates, and family from the van that transported him and his cargo from city to city, festival to festival. In January 1998, he commissioned a new sign that in his absence hung in his stall at the Malcolm Shabazz Harlem Market; it read: "Gone to Festival/Will Return Soon. Please call 1-888-555-1234."

Such travel meant that more often than not Issifi and his companions slept in cheap motels, sometimes four to a room, two to a bed. Issifi had come a long way since he first set foot in New York City. But although he had weathered a crippling setback and was once again making enough to help support his family in Niger and Abidjan, the quality of his life seemed not to have changed all that much. He began at the Hotel Belleclaire, sharing a cramped space with four or five of his compatriots. When he was an itinerant textile merchant, at least, he didn't have to spend so many hours in old, poorly ventilated Econoline vans, crisscrossing interstate highways in search of fleeting profits. On the road, he fought fatigue and frustration. Some trips were worth the physical and financial effort; some were not. But as Issifi is fond of saying: "We are here. We must work. We have no choice."[21]

Although the vast majority of West African street vendors I've talked to in New York City express profound appreciation for the economic opportunities they enjoy and exploit in the United States, they have invariably complained of loneliness, cultural isolation, and alienation from mainstream American social customs. These conditions, moreover, seem to have an impact on the subjective well-being of men like Moussa Boureima, Boubé Mounkaila, and Issifi Mayaki.

Social psychologists have isolated a number of interconnected factors that appear to influence a person's subjective well-being. These include perceptions of control, feelings of competence, subjective health, and availability of and satisfaction with social support.[22] A sense of control over one's life is perhaps the key factor that affects the well-being of men like Moussa Boureima and Issifi Mayaki. If one feels "out of control," one is more likely to be socially isolated.[23] Social psychological research suggests, moreover, that social isolation can subsequently increase the risk of physical deterioration, mental illness, and even premature death.[24]

Immigration, of course, usually reinforces social isolation. Intensified by cultural difference, feelings of isolation from the larger social environment can have a significant impact on physical and psychological well-being. Isolation limits the range of activities and interactions in which people can participate; it also reduces feelings of control and competence. Cultural alienation—living in a social environment where one cannot control, affect, or shape one's surroundings—can lead to feelings of powerlessness and helplessness.[25] This perceived "lack of control" once compelled Moussa Boureima, who was sick, to avoid hospitals; it once convinced Issifi Mayaki that he could do little to resolve his regulatory dilemmas with the INS.

One of the greatest detriments to feelings of well-being, according to many of the West African street traders I've talked to, is the absence of family. Their families, usually constructed as lineages, are primary sources of emotional and social support. Caught in regulatory limbo, Issifi Mayaki has been unable to return to West Africa to see his family, whom he misses. This situation has frustrated him and has sometimes made him mean-spirited. For most of the West Africans living in New York, it goes without saying that family is paramount. Even though many of them feel isolated and lonely in New York City, they have come to America, they say, to support their families back home.

> For the African psyche, the collective or the group is the ideal. For the African, the clan, the ethnic group is the base for unity and survival. The unit of identity among Africans is "we" and not "I." According to an Ashante Ghana proverb, "I am because we are; without we I am not and since we are, therefore I am." Therefore all shame, guilt, pain, joys and sorrows of any particular individual are partaken by the group. The major source of identity is, therefore, for the African the group, beginning with the smallest unit: the family.[26]

Although this statement essentializes Africa and Africans and misses the fascinating tensions that collectivism triggers in individuals routinely subjected to group pressures and responsibilities, it nonetheless captures a fundamental cultural difference between West Africans and most Americans. For most West Africans the ideal, if not the reality, of a cohesive family that lives and works together is paramount. This ideal, however remote, has survived regional, national, and international family dispersion. It drives men like Moussa Boureima, Issifi Mayaki, and Boubé Mounkaila to phone their kin in West Africa regularly; it compels them to send as much money as possible to help support their wives, their children, and their aging mothers, fathers, aunts, uncles, and cousins.

The absence of family has several psychological ramifications for West African traders in New York. Besides support, families provide a sense of trust and feelings of competence. As Issifi Mayaki has said, one can usually trust one's kin. The closer the blood ties, the greater the degree of trust. Absence of family therefore creates an absence of trust, which is, for anyone, a stressful situation. For young men, the absence of wives means that they are also in a kind of sexual and social limbo. They share profound cultural and social mores with their wives, in whom they place great trust. In Niger, for example, marriage binds families in webs of mutual rights and obligations. Men expect their wives, even during their long absences, to remain faithful to them. To avoid opportunities for infidelity, long-distance traders often insist that their wives live in the family compound, surrounded by observant relatives who not only enforce codes of sexual fidelity, but also help to raise the family's children. Many of the men, especially if they are traveling, believe it is their inalienable right to have sexual relationships with other women. As Muslims, moreover, they have the right, if they so chose and are financially able, to marry as many as four women. These are some of the cultural assumptions that many lonely and isolated West African traders bring to social relationships with the women they encounter in New York City. To say the least, these assumptions clash violently with contemporary social sensibilities in America.

El Hadj Moru Sifi, like many Nigeriens in New York City, felt the pain of sociocultural isolation during his time in America. A rotund man well into his fifties who hailed from Dosso in western Niger, El Hadj didn't like the food, detested what he considered American duplicity, and distrusted non-Africans. Between 1992 and 1994, he sold sunglasses on 125th Street. Work and sleep constituted much of his life. El Hadj supported two devoted wives in Niger. "Our women," he told me in August 1994, just prior to his departure, "know respect for their men. They also know how to cook real food. None of these Burger King and Big Macs. Rice, gumbo sauce with hot pepper, and fresh and clean meat. That is what I miss. I want to sit outside with my friends and kin and eat from a common bowl. Then I want to talk and talk into the night. I want to be in a place that has real Muslim fellowship."

During his two years in New York City, El Hadj said that he had remained celibate—by choice. He didn't trust the women he met. The women, he said, took drugs, slept with men, and sometimes gave birth to drug-addicted babies. "Many of these women have AIDS. I've had nothing to do with them. Soon, I will be in Niger in my own house surrounded by my wives and children. I will eat and talk well again."[27] Many West African traders in New York City share El Hadj Moru's attitudes. Like him, they have remained celibate.

Much younger than El Hadj Moru Sifi, Boubé Mounkaila has not been celibate during his time in New York City. Like his brother traders, he misses his family, including a wife whom he has not seen in many years and a daughter born several months after his departure for America. Sometimes, when he thinks of his family, said Boubé in 1995, "my heart is spoiled. That's when I listen to *kountigi* music."[28]

From the time he arrived in New York City more than a decade ago as a twenty-eight-year-old undocumented immigrant, Boubé has had an active social life. He is a tall, good-looking man who can be charming. He also has become fluent in what he calls "street English." Because he sells African leather goods, including many small bags, most of his clients are women. On any given day, a woman, sometimes younger, sometimes older, might be sitting in front of Boubé's stall waiting patiently for him to close up shop. In speaking of Boubé, some of his compatriots shake their heads and say: "Ah Boubé, he likes the women too much. He must be careful." Boubé has also befriended several tourists. Several female tourists who have visited the Malcolm Shabazz Harlem Market have been much taken by him. In particular, two European women, both in their mid-twenties, have visited repeatedly over the years.

Boubé's domestic circumstances are exceptional among West African traders in New York City. For most of the traders, life is not at all dramatic; it follows the course of a man like El Hadj Moru—one works, eats, and sleeps, with occasional interludes or with a long-standing relationship with one woman. Issifi Mayaki's situation has been more typical. A handsome and well-dressed man who speaks good English, Issifi celebrated his fortieth birthday in the year 2000.

As we've seen, he went out for a few years with an African American woman, Monique, who in 1996 was employed as a social worker. Issifi met Monique when he sold cassettes and CDs on 125th Street in 1994. She expressed interest in Issifi, who told her that he had a wife and children in Africa. Monique said that that was okay and that she appreciated Issifi's forthrightness. They began to see one another, but maintained separate residences.

When Issifi began to travel to festivals far from New York City, his relationship with Monique began to unravel. She didn't like him traveling to festivals. This displeasure led her to object to his frequent phone calls to his wife in Niger. When he told her about plans to travel home to see his family, she didn't want him to go. She didn't want to share him with anyone, which is why Issifi says that American women consume their men. That, he says, is not the African way. This cultural clash became the source of unending contention and eventually Issifi and Monique drifted apart.[29]

Other traders have other domestic arrangements. Abdou Harouna, who like El Hadj Moru comes from Dosso in the Republic of Niger, is not a trader, but a gypsy cab driver. Abdou, who sometimes calls himself "Al," came to New York City in 1992. In March 1993, traders on 125th Street introduced me to him. He had doubled-parked what he called his *voiture de service,* a large Pontiac Bonneville of a certain age, near Boubé Mounkaila's display tables.

He commented favorably on my command of Songhay. "How long are you staying in New York?" he asked. "If you have time, come riding with me." In Niger, it is customary for taxi drivers to ask their friends to ride shotgun with them.

I told him that I probably didn't have enough time to ride with him. "I'm leaving New York in two days, on Sunday."

He handed me his card. "Call me. I'll give you a ride to the airport."

"Did you drive in Niger?"

"No, no," he said smiling. "I'm learning here in New York. Call me. I'll take you to the airport."

In 1994, Al married an African American woman, not because he wanted a way to obtain immigration papers, but because he wanted to spend his life with Alice, who is a primary school teacher. Al and Alice have a young daughter and live in Harlem. "Alice," Al said, "has a pure heart. She is a good person, and I'm a lucky man."[30]

One of the Nigerien traders, Sidi Sansanne, has two families: one in the South Bronx and another in Niamey, Niger. At the young age of forty, Sidi has become a prosperous merchant. He runs a profitable import-export business, which requires him to travel between Niamey and New York City seven to ten times a year. Sidi is perhaps the ideal of West African trading success. He came to the United States in 1989 and sold goods on the streets of midtown Manhattan. He invested wisely and realized that the American market for Africana was immense. He saved his money and went to Niger to forge commercial ties with artisans. Having established his multinational network, he began to import to the United States homespun West African cloth, traditional wool blankets, leather sacks, bags, and attaché cases, as well as silver jewelry, mostly the attractive Agadez cross forged by Tuareg smiths from northern Niger.

In time, he established a family in New York City, obtained his employment authorization permit, and in 1994 became a permanent resident—a green card holder. As a permanent resident, Sidi is able to travel between the United States and West Africa without restriction. Because he travels to and from Africa so frequently, he has become a private courier. For a small fee, he takes to Africa important letters or money earmarked for the families of various traders. From Africa he carries letters and small gifts to his compatriots in New York City. The freedom to travel also enables Sidi to find new ateliers in Niger. During his six-week sojourns in Niger, he of course tends to his other family.

This pattern is a transnational version of West African polygynous marriage practices. In Western Niger, for example, prosperous itinerant traders establish residences in the major market towns of their trading circuit. In this way, they pay equal attention to their wives and children and avoid the inevitable disputes that are triggered when co-wives live in one compound.

Sidi is particularly proud of his youngest son in New York City. The boy attends public school in the South Bronx and has been put in a program for gifted students. In the summer of 1995, Sidi boasted of his son's performance. "He is so smart. He's very good in math, and never forgets anything. He was the top student in his class. The school gave him certificate."

"Has he been to Niger, yet?" I asked.

"No, not yet. I speak to him in Songhay, but he doesn't yet know his country. But I will send him to Niger when he old enough for middle school. I don't want him to go to middle school in New York. The schools are not good, and he'd be exposed to bad people. I'll send him to Niger so that he will learn discipline from his relatives."

"Would he go to public school in Niamey?"

"No. I've got the green card, so I hope to send him to the American School in Niamey. That way, he'll know French as well as English and he'll be able to choose a university in Africa, France, or the United States. He'll be a real citizen of the world."

"But Sidi," I interjected, "you're already a true citizen of the world."[31]

As can be seen, there are West African traders in New York who have adapted well to city life. And yet, no matter what their public or private situation in New York might be, they invariably complain about the loss of African fellowship in America. This sense of loss takes on many dimensions. Traders often have complained, for example, of the formality of American social interchange. In March 1998, a Malian art trader said to me that America was like a prison.

"There are so many rules here," he said. "Your time is scheduled. You can't just drop by and see someone; you have to make an appointment. People are in too much of a hurry. They take no time to talk to one another. Everything is so tight. In Africa we are freer. Even if you're a stranger, people will invite you into their house and talk to you. Here, that never happens. America is a prison. In Africa, there is more fellowship."[32] This perception is part of what compels some West Africans in New York City to endure deteriorating conditions in vertical villages like that of the Park View Hotel, "Le Cent Dix," at 110th and Lenox in Harlem.

The West African desire for fellowship in a foreign land entails the construction of communities, a set of associations that offers them a sense of belonging and a buffer against the stresses of cultural alienation.[33] The notion of community, of course, has been central to the ethnographic enterprise. Community studies have been important in the history of both sociology and anthropology. In sociology, the landmark study was Robert and Helen Lynd's *Middletown*. In their highly descriptive book, however, the Lynds did not attempt to construct a theory of community. Robert Redfield took up that task in the 1940s in *The Folk Culture of Yucatan* (1941) and later in *The Little Community* (1955), in which he depicted the community of Teplotzlan as bounded, harmonious, and homogenous. Redfield's work inspired the criticism of Oscar Lewis, who had studied the same community but found a very different kind of society. Where Redfield uncovered harmony, homogeneity, and social adjustment, Lewis found violence, sociopolitical schisms, and social maladjustment.[34] As Sherry Ortner has recently pointed out, Lewis's criticism still rings true to contemporary anthropologists, who have for the past fifteen years underscored the fragmentation and hybridity of sociocultural processes and organizations. Although the concept of community has been plagued with epistemological and conceptual problems, Ortner thinks it is a notion well worth preserving. For her, "the importance of community studies . . . is this: such studies have the virtue of treating people as contexualized social beings. They portray the thickness of people's lives, the fact that people live in a world of relationships as well as a world of abstract forces and disembodied images."[35]

In her study of the Weequahic High School class of 1958, for example, Ortner develops the notion of the postcommunity—a community constructed in an era when people rarely spend their entire lives living in one neighborhood.[36] More specifically, Ortner isolates four types of postcommunities: the neocommunity, the invented community, the translocal community, and the community of the mind. The *neocommunity* is a community that has expanded slightly beyond the space that originally bonded members, but in which there is still a density of social relationships. The *invented community* is a community constructed far from the original bonding space. In it members create a new community of highly clustered social contracts based on common experience—having attended the same high school, for example. The *translocal community* is a community in which demographic or economic forces have broken up the original group. Ties are maintained through an affiliation with a certain religion, social club, or ethnic group. This kind of community is characterized by the periodic ebb and flow of social contacts and social networks. The *community of the mind* is reinforced through what Paul Connerton has called commemorative ritual in which the values and themes of the original community are relived or remembered.[37]

Several of the postcommunity types that Ortner outlines can be extended to the social worlds of West African traders in New York City. Congregating at the African market on 125th Street or more recently at the Malcolm Shabazz Harlem Market on 116th Street, they've constructed an invented community of "African brothers," linked by shared economic pursuits and Africanness. The traders also participate in translocal communities, following the circuit of African American and third world cultural festivals and forming periodic links with fellow Africans as they travel across the United States. Finally, they are linked to their families and economic networks in West Africa in a community of mind—of memory—primarily through Islam. No matter where they are, Muslim West African traders try to pray five times a day and obey the various dietary and behavioral dictates of Islam. One of the central themes of Islam, in fact, speaks to a community of the faithful, the Ummah.[38] The themes of this community of mind are reinforced through daily prayer, daily behavior toward others, and by Jummah services. During Jummah, localized groups of believers are asked to assemble at the Friday mosque, the site of Muslim prayers on the Sabbath. During these services, the imam delivers readings from the Qur'an and sometimes speaks to the faithful about the values of their religion.

Islam unquestionably structures the everyday lives of West African traders at the Malcolm Shabazz Harlem Market and elsewhere in New York City and keeps alive their sense of identity in what, for most of them, remains an alien and strange place. In conversations with my trading friends, the subject of Islam invariably comes up, especially when we touch on the quality of life in the United States. They say that in the face of social deterioration in New York City, Islam makes them strong; its discipline and values, they say, empower them to cope with social isolation in America. It enables them to resist the divisive forces they see ruining American families. But the greatest buffer to cultural dislocation is the perception, held by almost all the traders that I've encountered, that Islam makes them emotionally and morally superior to most Americans.

We met El Hadj Harouna Souley at the beginning of this book. This Nigerien trader had made the expensive pilgrimage to Mecca when he was just thirty-four, a feat that defined his financial success in commerce even nine years later in New York. In many ways, El Hadj Harouna embodies his compatriots' sense of Islamic moral superiority. Between 1994 and 1997, he sold T-shirts, baseball caps, and sweatshirts from shelves stuffed between two storefronts on Canal Street in lower Manhattan. Like most West African traders, he is a member of a large family. He has one wife, fourteen children, four brothers, five sisters, nieces and nephews, not to forget his father's and his mother's brothers and sisters and their respective children. His father has been dead for many years; his mother passed away more recently.

On a rainy afternoon in December 1995, we sat under an awning on the steps of Taj Mahal, a radio and electronics store on Canal Street near West Broadway. He pointed out two seemingly down and out street hawkers, both African Americans, employed by the owners of Taj Mahal.

"You see those men there?" El Hadj Harouna said. "They only know their mother. Sometimes they don't even know who their father is. That's the way it often is in America. Families are not unified. Look at him," he said, referring to the older of the two hawkers. "He's from Georgia. His family sends him money every month, and as long as I've known him he hasn't once returned there to visit them. Why don't people here honor their parents? Why don't families stick together—at least in spirit? I want to get back to my family compound where we can all live together," El Hadj Harouna stated emphatically. "Can parents depend on their children to take care of them when they are old? I don't think so. I've seen children who sit at home and eat their parents' money, but they think that they owe their parents no obligation. My children phone me every week and ask me to come home. If I am old and have no money, my children will look after me. I will do no work. I will eat, sleep, and talk with my friends.

"My Muslim discipline gives me great strength to withstand America. I have been to Mecca. I give to the poor. I rise before dawn so that I can pray five times a day, every day. I fast during Ramadan. I avoid pork and alcohol. I honor the memory of my father and mother. I respect my wife. And even if I lose all my money, if I am able, Inshallah, to live with my family, I will be truly blessed."[39]

•••

West African community structures in New York City take on several forms. I have described and analyzed the newly emergent informal communities generated by networks of economic and social support. We have seen how kinship, ethnicity, and nationality affected the density of contact and degree of trust and cooperation. In addition to these personal networks there are translocal communities based on national origin. These are formal associations like L'Association des Nigeriens de New York, L'Association des Maliens aux USA, L'Association des Senegalais aux USA, and the Club des Femmes d'Affaires Africaines de New York (a New York African businesswomen's association). These associations are usually connected, if not organized, to the diplomatic missions of the various Francophone African countries. Meetings at which issues of mutual concern are discussed are held about once a month in the evenings, usually at a particular nation's United Nations mission. The associations hold receptions for major Muslim and national holidays. They collect funds to help defray a compatriot's unexpected medical expenses. In the case of a compatriot's death, they also contribute funds to ship the body back to West Africa for burial. L'Association des Nigeriens has raised money to buy food for hungry people in Niger. There is also, of course, the community of the faithful, which has a continuous, if abstract presence; it gathers once a week, for Jummah services.

It would be easy and perhaps facile to suggest that these West African communities, formal and informal, economic and personal, translocal or imagined, supply community adherents with financial and emotional support. Such support, it could be argued, also provides social harmony and a sense of belonging that protects members from the disintegrative stresses of cultural alienation. On one level this statement is most certainly true. Belonging to the community of the faithful provides a religiously sanctioned set of explanations for the West African's situation in America. Participants in the Association des Nigeriens engage in a mutually reinforcing set of rights and obligations based on mutual citizenship. The organization represents the interests of Nigeriens in New York City. Participation in personal networks yields both economic benefits and, in some cases, the concrete fellowship desired by most West African traders in New York City.

Closer inspection of these community forms, however, reveals a more complex scenario. Although West African traders speak highly of their various "national" associations, their participation in the regular activities of the organizations—the monthly meetings—is infrequent. There are a few traders, of course, who are active members, but the majority of the traders I've known have neither the time nor the inclination to attend association meetings or events. The meetings are held in the evenings at the Nigerien mission on East 44th Street between 1st and 2nd Avenues. Many traders do not want to travel there from Harlem or the South Bronx after a long day at the market.

More important, the presence of the association in New York City brings into relief a primary tension in Nigerien society—that between members of the educated elite and less educated peasants. In western Niger, illiterate peasants sometimes express a distrust of the literate civil servants whom they sometimes refer to as *anasarra*, which can mean, depending on the context, "European," "non-Muslim," or "white man." Less educated Songhay, including village traders, sometimes say that the civil servants who command state power are *anasarra*. Having learned the white man's language and his ways, they have become foreigners in their own country. In Niger, this strong statement may well be a means of articulating class differences. A similar distrust has been expressed in New York City. In February 1994, one weekend trader, a former Nigerien civil servant and no friend of the government of Niger (GON), claimed that the Association des Nigeriens had deceived the merchants. "There is a clear division," he said, "between educated and uneducated Nigeriens in New York City. The association recently collected money from the street merchants and says that the money goes to help people in Niger. In fact," he said, "the money helped to pay the electric bill at the Nigerien mission to the UN and the traders didn't know." Considering that this man had been a member of the educated elite that he had just criticized, I checked out his story, which was corroborated by an "official" Nigerien in New York City. In 1993 and 1994, it was no secret that the GON was so strapped for funds that it had trouble meeting many of its obligations. The Nigerien trader, however, was not sympathetic. He blasted the president of Niger's visit to the UN in the fall of 1993. "The president stayed at the Plaza Hotel with his entire entourage—an enormous expense. They also paid round-trip airfares for three different groups of dignitaries. They are members of the three most significant political parties. They also lodged at the Plaza."[40] This multiparty invitation, he said, tripled the cost of Nigeriens attending the meeting of the UN General Assembly.

Prior to the February 21, 1994, meeting of the Association des Nigeriens aux USA, the officers wanted the merchants to contribute forty to fifty dollars to the association fund. The former civil servant urged his fellow traders to boycott that meeting. He said that only one merchant from 125th Street, the most prosperous man on the sidewalk, went to that meeting. "Is it right that they should exploit these men who work hard for dollars out here in the cold, while they sit comfortably in their offices? I cannot go to this kind of meeting and sit quietly. No!"[41] Although the man's commentary is admittedly a bit extreme, it underscores fundamental differences between educated and uneducated Nigeriens that have been transported from West Africa to New York City.

By the same token, participation in economic networks can produce negative as well as positive results. In Issifi Mayaki's case, his participation in a network of international textile traders, one based on the trust of cooperative economics, led to betrayal and the loss of his inventory. Boubé Mounkaila lost the entire contents of his Econoline van, which had been parked in a secure, fenced-off space in Harlem. The complicity of one of his economic associates enabled thieves to enter the guarded space and steal his goods.

Membership in the community of the faithful creates a spiritual bond among adepts of Islam. Like any religion, their faith provides explanations for the absurdities of life no matter when or where. It supplies a ready set of explanations for the sociocultural problems of Muslims living in societies in which Islam is not a major sociopolitical force. For West African traders in New York City, Islam, as a way of life, is morally superior to other faiths practiced in the United States. And yet being a member of the community of the faithful does not ameliorate one's financial difficulties, nor does it eliminate the fright of illness or existential doubts brought on by cultural alienation.

Seen in this light, community, however defined or typified, produces a framework, both abstract and practical, within which members struggle to make their way. The struggle is easier in known environments, more difficult in alien settings. No matter where these struggles take place, no matter the mix of social, economic, and political resources, some people prove to be more competent than others are. The communities that West Africans have constructed for themselves in New York City, then, provide resources for, but not necessarily solutions to, their individual confrontations with social life in America.

The key, perhaps, to comprehending the variable adaptability of West African traders in New York is to focus on their cultural competence. The notion of competence has a long history in the social sciences. In linguistics, it refers to the capacity of speakers to master the grammatical rules of a language in order to produce comprehensible sentence strings.[42] Obviously, in their effort to understand this capacity, linguists looked at children's acquisition of language, observing in a sort of natural laboratory how very young children master specific linguistic rules to attain complete competence by the age of four.[43] Sociolinguists, however, extended the notion of competence beyond the rarefied arenas of syntactic and semantic analysis to consider the rules speakers need to master in order to interact competently in various social contexts.[44] This work compelled anthropologists interested in socialization to consider how children acquire culture and develop a fully formed cultural competence.[45]

In sociology, scholars combined some of these linguistic and anthropological insights in microanalyses of social interaction. They attempted to isolate the social rules one needs to know in order to interact appropriately in ever-shifting social contexts. The works of the late Erving Goffman constitute a much-cited body of this research. Throughout his work Goffman suggests how learned "rules" shape interactive behavior.[46] And yet at the end of his distinguished career, Goffman exploded the academic myth that logically perfected rules might explain something as complex as interactive competence. In *Forms of Talk,* Goffman's last book, he undermines the putative coherence of "conversational rules," using the example of an interruption:

> An adjacent hearer can elect to let the matter entirely pass, tacitly framing it as though it were the stomach rumblings of another's mind, and continue on undeflected from his task involvements; or, for example, he can hit upon the venting as an occasion to bring the remaining company into a focus of conversational attention for a jibe made at the expense of another person who introduced the initial distraction, which efforts these others may decline to support, and if declining, provide no display of excuse for doing so. In these circumstances the whole framework of conversational constraints— both system and ritual—can become something to honor, to invert, or to disregard, depending as the mood strikes. On these occasions it's not merely that the lid can't be closed; there is no box.[47]

In other words, sociolinguistic competence is so complex, creative, and variable that one is hard pressed to reduce it to sets of explanatory rules.

In psychology, there are differing views of competence. One perspective relates to therapeutic practice. "Cultural competence (along with the broader concept of multiculturalism) is the belief that people should not only appreciate and recognize other cultural groups, but also be able to effectively work them."[48] In this view, competence refers to the therapist's sensitivity to "other" cultural systems. Another view relevant to the case of West African traders in New York City is that competence measures a person's ability to adapt to an environment, which, as it turns out, is an early psychological definition of intelligence.[49] In their early models, psychologists linked adaptability to performance. They argued that the variation in personal performance could be explained by measurable differences in cognitive ability. Put another way, the greater one's intelligence, the greater one's capacity to adapt to shifting situations in changing environments.

More recently, however, psychologists have considered a more dynamic perspective. These scholars believe that differences in competence stem not only from relatively stable cognitive predispositions, but also from environmental differences, contextual variations within similar or different environments, and temporal shifts. "According to these recent contextual perspectives, competence (or incompetence) is produced through transactions of the individual with his or her social, material, historical and psychological contexts."[50]

The linguistic, sociolinguistic, anthropological, and early psychological models of competence tend to be narrowly defined, which limits their usefulness. A contextualized model of cultural competence, however, which emphasizes a person's range of choices, degree of control, and capacity to plan, can be felicitously extended to our consideration of the cultural competencies of West African traders in New York City. In the previous chapters of *Money Has No Smell*, we have considered the social, material, historical, and psychological dimensions of West African traders' experiences in New York City. The traders, as we have seen, have skillfully used their cultural traditions to build personal and economic networks that result in a variety of communities. These communities, in turn, provide them the potential for economic security, social cohesion, and cultural stability in an alien environment.

Despite this rich set of resources, some traders have succeeded better than others have. Why is it that Boubé Mounkaila is a more successful businessman than Moussa Boureima is? Why is it that even when there are economic lulls at the Malcolm Shabazz Harlem Market, Boubé remains in New York City, while his compatriots are compelled to travel far and wide in search of opportunities? Why does Boubé make elaborate plans to improve both his business and personal life, while many of his compatriots complain of hopelessness and powerlessness? There are no simple answers to these questions, but linguistic competence certainly plays a major role in adaptive success.

There is a wide diversity of linguistic competence among the traders. Men like Boubé Mounkaila and Issifi Mayaki speak English well. Boubé Mounkaila's linguistic competence helps to make him socially confident. His facility in English has enabled him to construct transnational exchange networks with Asians, African Americans, and Middle Easterners and hence to expand his operations. Using his skills in English, Boubé arranged to purchase a vehicle, buy automobile insurance, and obtain a driver's license. Boubé also employs his considerable linguistic skills to charm his mostly African American customers. Mastery of English, in short, has increased Boubé's profits and expanded his social horizons considerably. The same can be said for Issifi Mayaki and scores of other West African street vendors.

Lack of competence in English, however, can result in missed opportunities. By 1997, Moussa Boureima and Idrissa Dan Inna had been in New York City for more than three years. Even so, they still spoke very little English. In 1994, they enrolled in a night school course sponsored by a church in Harlem, but they both dropped out after one week. "I don't know," said Idrissa, who sold West African hats and bags on 125th street at the time, "I just can't learn English. I don't have the head for it. I know it hurts my business. I can't really talk to the shoppers about the goods."[51] When confronted with various financial, social, or personal problems, men like Moussa and Idrissa have to rely on more fluent traders, which affects their self-image negatively and makes them even more socially isolated.

Although West African street vendors in New York City display various linguistic abilities, they must all confront the problem of cultural competence. Many of them seem to have mastered the culture of capitalism, but their lack of a more general cultural competence has had serious negative consequences.[52] In this important domain, one of the key issues is that of trust. According to Islamic law, as we have seen, traders are expected to be honest and trustworthy in their dealings with suppliers, exchange partners, and customers.[53] Among West African traders, almost all of whom are Muslims, trust is paramount. Many of the traders come from families and ethnic groups long associated with long-distance trading in West Africa, and that proud family tradition also reinforces Muslim principles in their economic transactions. Not surprisingly, in a new and very different culture, the traders' trust has sometimes been betrayed. Thus, Issifi Mayaki's textile inventory was lost to an exchange partner. Betrayals cost Boubé Mounkaila his inventory. And yet these men had the individual resilience and competence to use community resources to rebound from these defeats and move along their paths in New York City. Other traders who have suffered similar setbacks have drifted into isolation, changed occupations, or returned to West Africa.

In the summer of 1995, as we have seen, Moussa Boureima and Sala Fari spent several weeks traveling throughout the American South and Midwest. Loading and unloading a van owned by yet another Nigerien, Soumana Harouna, they were one of several Nigerien crews that followed the circuit of African American festivals. Although this regimen taxed their physical stamina, it restored their financial health. As a result of strong festival sales, Moussa sent fifteen hundred dollars to his wife and children in Tessuoa, Niger. Sala sent a thousand dollars to his mother and father in Fillingue, Niger. This good fortune came to an abrupt end in Washington, D.C., when thieves broke into their van and stole thousands of dollars of merchandise. They did not report the theft to the police.

"My life is trade," Sala said. "But how can I trade here when thieves destroy my hard work."[54] Before the theft, Sala had carried on as a trader, despite a string of disappointing economic setbacks. After the theft, a demoralized Sala worked as a wage laborer and traded on the weekends. Moussa Boureima, however, not having papers, could not opt to work in the formal sector. He continued on as best he could at the Malcolm Shabazz Harlem Market, complaining in French about the dismal conditions at the market, an alien environment that rendered him powerless, and rheumatism that comes and goes. "We are here," Moussa said each time we had a conversation, "what else can we do?"

West African traders in New York all confront similar social problems. The traders come from cultures that place a premium on collective solidarity rather than individual assertiveness, societies in which family allegiance is usually given priority over personal desire. This means that rather than allowing themselves personal luxuries, the traders feel obliged to send money home to their families, who are supported by dollars earned day in and day out on the streets of New York City. Because they have come to the United States to support their families in West Africa, many traders experience firsthand what it means to be poor in the United States. They usually live in the most crime-infested neighborhoods in New York City—Harlem, the South Bronx, and Brooklyn—where many of them have been robbed, where some of them have been beaten. They often live in small groups of three or four in cramped apartments overrun by roaches and rats. During lulls in the market, lack of funds may force them to give up their telephones, curtail their use of electric power, avoid necessary medication, and ignore physical pain. Their uncertain legal status as immigrants, whether registered or unregistered, compels some of them to avoid city services. Some of them fear the INS, which rarely, if ever, detains or deports "illegal" immigrants already residing in the United States. Because many of the traders are unlicensed street vendors selling goods that violate trademark and copyright statutes, they must be wary of the police, who can fine them and confiscate their goods.

Most West African traders come to New York City as single men, leaving behind their wives, children, parents, and complex extended families. The fact that most of them are able to help support their families in West Africa does not diminish the loneliness they feel for their kin, neighborhoods, and villages—for the connectedness of social life in West Africa. Many men like El Hadj Moru Sifi have been profoundly alienated from social life in America. On the streets of Harlem, they speak regularly to their compatriots and customers. They work, eat, and sleep with only the slightest exposure to American social life. They count their days in America, waiting to have made enough money to return home with honor. Some are so unhappy that they return home without honor.

To confront these seemingly insurmountable problems, West Africans have extended some traditional social and economic practices to New York City. They have constructed a variety of communities that provide them resources with which to combat cultural alienation: legal help to resolve immigration difficulties or trademark or copyright troubles; funds for emergency medical treatment; informal insurance against ever-present theft; celebrations that promote pride in West African culture and honor Islam. These communities have enabled some, but certainly not all, of the traders to successfully adapt to city life in New York.

Some of the people who have written about West African traders in New York City have described them as pioneers, as savvy merchants who revitalize markets and neighborhoods. "In choosing to migrate to the United States," Donna Perry writes, "Wolofs display a kind of savvy that many Americans themselves lack."[55] In this way, they become almost heroic figures, using their economic acumen to exploit niches in informal economies. This skill enables them to support their families in Senegal, Mali, Niger, and the Gambia—nations suffering from a variety of economic dislocations.

It is beyond question that some of the West African traders in New York City conform to this profile. Many are savvy businessmen who have earned substantial profits in the United States. And yet there are other traders who, for one reason or another, are less successful. Many of them have experienced financial worry and emotional distress. The communities that West Africans in New York have constructed do not, then, define their city lives; rather, they provide resources—economic, social, and cultural—that ease the stress of living in an alien environment. More specifically, these communities enable many, but not all, West African traders to enhance their subjective feelings of well-being and control. But the sense and reality of community, as has been suggested, is no panacea for ills associated with state regulation, poverty, and sociocultural alienation. For West African traders, then, the congruence of historical, material, social, and psychological forces molds their city lives. These forces not only define a sense of community, but also shape cultural competencies that affect adjustment to an alien environment.

176

In the actual use of expressions we make detours, we go by side roads. We see the straight highway before us, but of course we cannot use it, because it is permanently closed.   *Wittgenstein,* Philosophical Investigations

Long before Wittgenstein, people in Niger understood that straight highways are permanently closed not only in expressive culture, but also in the way that life proceeds. Among the Songhay peoples of western Niger, for example, life is seen as a series of winding paths, all of which end by branching off in different directions. These ends and beginnings are seen as points of misfortune. Men are said to have thirty points of misfortune, women forty.[1] If one chooses the wrong path and walks off in a dangerous direction, one will invariably suffer the consequences: a poor millet harvest, a streak of commercial losses, a series of thefts, a truck accident resulting in injury, a lingering illness, the premature death of a child, or perhaps, one's own death.

In West Africa, the path is also a metaphor that extends beyond existential practice to more professional pursuits: learning to fish or weave, cook or farm; understanding how to husband livestock or butcher meat; recognizing when and where to buy low and sell high. Indeed, given its significance in the history of Islamic civilization, the way of commerce is a centrally important path in Muslim West African experience. It is a path on which merchants see the straight highway before them, but realize that they will find the greatest profits on the side roads that meander through commercial experience.

• • •

Many years ago, Issifi Mayaki chose to follow the way of commerce, the way of his father and father's father. As a young man, he left his dusty village near Maradi, where his mother still resides, and followed the path to Abidjan. Like thousands of young West African merchants-in-training, he learned about trading by watching his father and his father's associates. He knew from his father's example as a long-distance trader that business has never been localized. He realized that to earn solid and lasting profits in the Abidjan market, the clever merchant had to attract a wide diversity of clients— including, of course, relatively wealthy Europeans. From his early schooling, he learned French and could speak that language fluently. When he began to learn about trading in African textiles, he soon recognized that in order to flourish as a merchant, he would have to learn several new languages: Dyula, the language of West African trade, and English, the language of the most avid buyers of antique textiles. Dyula enabled him to communicate with most of the textile suppliers in Côte d'Ivoire, as well as with other merchants who did not speak Hausa, his maternal language. English brought him friendships with British and American people—traveling entrepreneurs, expatriates, diplomats, and Peace Corps volunteers. These friendships brought him into contact with European culture, the partial knowledge of which helped him to understand his clients' needs, wants, and wishes.

When several of his colleagues began to ship and distribute African art in the United States, Issifi realized that America represented a fertile market for his textile inventory. Through his personal network in Abidjan, he planned a new journey. Upon coming to New York City, he suffered through the horrible loss of his textile inventory, moved from the Upper West Side to Harlem, shifted his business from textiles to cassettes and CDs, and finally came back to selling original and reproduced African textiles. Throughout his remarkable history, Issifi familiarized himself with American popular culture (especially popular trends in urban Africa America) and dealt with state-sponsored statutes that inhibited his commercial enterprise. He also adapted to state regulations that restricted his personal freedoms, for a time involved himself in a relationship with an African American woman, arranged for his younger brother to come and live with him, and shifted his creative energies to an American version of long-distance trading. Issifi has continued to travel along the side roads of America in search of profits at African American and third world cultural festivals.

While he has engaged in what appears to be a monumental series of linguistic, social, cultural, and economic adaptations, Issifi has managed to support his family in West Africa. Every month he sends money to his mother, wife, and children in Niger. When angry mobs in Côte d'Ivoire severely beat his father in 1997, Issifi sent money to pay for an expensive hospital stay and medications.[2] Issifi's family responsibilities have been a continuous strain on his finances, but he cannot shirk them. Despite the inevitable frustrations these responsibilities entail, Issifi bears his burden with quiet grace and dignity. He reads the Qur'an for inspiration. He speaks softly, is always well dressed, and presents himself with the kind of genuine humility that suggests a man comfortable, as the French say, in his skin.

Although he is steadfastly a Nigerien Hausa, Issifi Mayaki, like many other West Africans, has become a citizen of the world—a pragmatic master of transnational side roads. Despite the many roadblocks he has confronted on his path, he usually finds a way around them. So far, his preparation, skill, vigilance, and patience have enabled him to negotiate his points of misfortune successfully. Even though his thoughts and practices remain very much in the shadows of contemporary mainstream American experience, Issifi has become a player in the global economy. Issifi and many of his compatriots are significant participants in the informal economies that have burgeoned during postmodernity. Many of these traders are entrepreneurial innovators.[3] Most of them participate in the construction of dispersed transnational communities that provide their members with the kind of social and economic support that can help to ease the stress of contemporary transnational social life. The most culturally competent of the traders in New York City, people like Issifi Mayaki and Boubé Mounkaila, take full advantage of the resources that the communities of which they are members are able to provide. In this way, their economic flexibility and sociocultural agility is expanded and their profits are increased. Men like Issifi, as we have seen, have much to teach us about how urban social life works in contemporary America.

Men like Issifi also have much to teach contemporary anthropologists. Their example reminds us of the central anthropological significance of understanding the nuances of kinship and social relations. For a person like Issifi Mayaki, nothing is more important than his social relations—the viability of family, the maintenance of mutually nurturing friendships, the endurance of networks based and built on relations of mutual trust. With varying degrees of effectiveness, Issifi and his brother traders have continuously negotiated and renegotiated their social lives. In so doing, they have established new trading partnerships and have dissolved others. They have mastered the culture of capitalism as they have reinforced the traditions of long-distance African trading. They have staked out individual space in a market culture as they have engaged in a cooperative economics dictated by Islam and by long-standing West African commercial practices. They have adapted to the unfamiliar stresses of city life in New York as they have reaffirmed their African identities.

Given the thick texture of Issifi's life in New York City, how should contemporary anthropologists approach the multistranded complexities of the transnational spaces of contemporary urban worlds? My experiences on the streets of New York City suggest that contemporary anthropologists might well embrace a theoretically flexible orientation to contemporary social worlds. In *Money Has No Smell*, I have attempted to demonstrate how history, the culture of capitalism, popular culture, entrepreneurial practice, global economics, social hybridity, state regulation, local and national policies and politics, and community forms have variously affected the city life of West African traders in New York. The breadth of this abstract subject matter, however, should not prevent us from telling the compelling stories of those we attempt to represent. From the beginning of this research, my goal has been to understand how macrosociological forces twist and turn the economic and emotional lives of real people like Issifi Mayaki, Boubé Mounkaila, and Moussa Boureima. Striving to achieve this balance required me to employ a variety of social theories to illuminate the lives of individuals in a little known, but highly dynamic corner of urban America. By linking theory and narrative, I have attempted to add flesh to the bones of rarefied discussions of global forces. The complexity of studying a transnational space, I think, requires this kind of epistemological diversity.

During the past twenty years, much has been written about the "end" of anthropology. Can one "do" ethnography in fragmented postmodern worlds riven by the politics of identity? Cultural critics have said that ethnography is an anachronism and have suggested that anthropology, "a quaint science," will become increasingly irrelevant in the twenty-first century.[4] The results reported in *Money Has No Smell* and other recent works in urban studies suggest—at least to me—a more encouraging scenario. With time, effort, and a degree of methodological innovation, it is more than possible to illuminate a complex social reality through the combination of narrative and theoretical exposition.[5]

Since coming to New York City, the West African traders that we have met in these pages have made fateful decisions that have affected their well-being. Garba Hima learned to speak English quite well during his four years on 125th Street. He sold sunglasses and pirated videos, but did not like city life in New York, which for him was too noisy, too crowded, and too filled with crime and insensitivity. Sensing the end of the 125th Street market, he hired a Malian immigration broker who helped him to obtain an employment authorization permit. Then he began to investigate new cities as potential business sites. He traveled to Philadelphia, Wilmington, Delaware, Baltimore, and Washington, D.C. In January 1995, he flew to Greensboro, North Carolina. In one day, as we have seen, Garba found work at a raincoat factory and a place to live. He then flew back to New York City, packed his bags, and returned to Greensboro. Since going south, he has moved three times and lived alone in an apartment. In the spring of 1998, he returned to Niger, where he speculated in cars. He has been traveling to Germany to buy Mercedes, Audis, or Volkswagens. He then drives them across the Sahara Desert to sell them for considerable profit in Niger and Togo.

Idrissa Dan Inna hasn't yet learned to speak English fluently, which, in 1994, made it difficult to compete for sales on the street. He soon left his linguistic frustrations on the sidewalks of 125th Street. In short order, he hired a Hausa-speaking immigration broker to steer him through the process of obtaining an employment authorization permit. He obtained the permit only three months after filing his papers. Work permit in hand, he soon found a job in a factory in Brooklyn. Low wages, long hours, and the relatively high living costs of New York City compelled him to seek opportunities elsewhere. In time, he moved to Greensboro and found work in a textile factory. Garba Hima housed him until he could make other living arrangements. He eventually bought a car and earned enough money to support his family. His English was still deficient, however, when he returned to Niger in December 1998. Like Garba Hima, Idrissa bought cars in Germany and drove them across the Sahara to sell them in Niger, Benin, and Togo. In 1999, he returned to Greensboro.

El Hadj Harouna Souley spent almost three years selling baseball hats, gloves, scarves, and T-shirts along Canal Street in lower Manhattan. He grew tired of the high rents he had to pay for shelf space in a storefront. He also grew weary of bone-chilling New York winters and stifling Manhattan summers. He had wanted his son, the oldest of eight children, to come to New York and take over his stall, but given his high operating costs, he was unable to send for him. Instead, he too went to Greensboro, where he immediately found factory work and an apartment to live in.

The rotund El Hadj Moru Sifi, as we have learned, did not like city life in New York. He remained in the States long enough to amass a respectable sum of money, which enabled him to return to his family in Niger. Word has it that he has established a business in Niger and that his two wives take turns preparing him sumptuous dishes of rice and millet smothered with zesty sauces. El Hadj Moru does not intend to return to New York.

Soumana Harouna, whose Ford Econoline van carried goods and merchants in search of profits at African American and third world cultural festivals during the summer of 1995, now limits his travels to the streets of New York City, where he continues to drive a Medallion taxi. At the end of the 1995 season, after thousands of miles of travel and several minor accidents, he retired his van. He has not bought another.

The most seasoned travelers among New York's Nigerien traders are unquestionably El Hadj Soumana Tondi and Sidi Sansanne. El Hadj Tondi, the "father" of many Nigerien "children" in New York, once divided his time between Niamey, capital of the Republic of Niger, Abidjan, and New York City. Between 1994 and 1996, he came to New York City every six weeks to deliver shipments of West African cloth, bring mail, and check on his "children." In 1997, he began to spend more time in Niamey, but he continued to come to New York City once every two to three months. Sidi Sansanne still has two residences and two families: one in the South Bronx and one in Niamey. He now imports cloth and leather crafts from Niger and wholesales them to individual traders and to boutiques up and down the East Coast.

Abdou Harouna is still comfortably settled in New York. He lives in central Harlem with his wife and their daughter. After more than eight years as the driver of what he calls *une voiture de service*, his driving has improved remarkably. "I haven't had an accident in several years," he says, "and I don't get lost so much anymore."

Moussa Boureima has remained at the Malcolm Shabazz Harlem Market. In the winter, he sells scarves, hats, and gloves. In the summer, he offers baseball caps. His rheumatism has improved. He no longer sees the French-speaking physician but goes to Bellevue Hospital. "It's expensive," he says, "but they give me shots once a month and I feel better." He lives alone in the South Bronx. His first roommate, Idrissa Dan Inna, moved away in 1995. His other roommate, Amadou Bita, moved to a building closer to the Malcolm Shabazz Harlem Market. Moussa worries a bit less about his health. His English remains rudimentary. He has no papers and hasn't made plans to obtain them. "It's very hard now," he says, "to get papers." In fact, he plans to return to Niger in 2002.

Boubé Mounkaila has expanded his Harlem operation considerably. In April 1998, he rented four stalls at the market, where he continued to sell African leather goods, watches, and baseball caps. In 1997, he wanted to open an African restaurant in the East Village, but was unable to find a suitable space. By 1998 he had taken the necessary steps, moreover, to become a permanent resident. When he receives his green card, he will return to Niger for a long visit.

Issifi Mayaki has become a mobile merchant. Although he travels the side roads of America in a recently purchased van, he is by no means isolated, for his beeper and cell phone enable him to stay connected to business associates, friends, and family in the United States and West Africa. If, by chance, his successful travels in the American bush transport him to the Gap, he might well forgo an invitation to dinner to browse and perhaps buy.

In the summer of 1998, I wandered over to 53rd Street in Manhattan. There was still a sidewalk display of African Art on a midtown Manhattan sidewalk just down the street from MOMA. The Malian man who had been selling statues and masks during the 1995 Christmas season was no longer there. He had been replaced by a younger man and two women, all Malians, who had taken over the space. They sat on three plastic milk crates strategically placed on the sidewalk next to their parked van. As they waited patiently for shoppers to take an interest in their pieces, they bantered in Bamana.

The American art merchant who displayed exotic African objects along with authenticating photographs of himself buying art in Mali had long since departed, leaving nary an echo of his romantic rap about traveling in Africa. In his place, I found an African American dealer who represented Haitian artists and a Japanese woman who sold black and white photographs of New York City architecture. Having wandered the streets of the city for so long, I thought without surprise about the ebb and flow of the transnational street economy on New York sidewalks, as ever present as the tide.

Notes

Prologue

1. See Steiner 1993; Taylor, Barbash, and Steiner 1992.
2. In February 1999, a special patrol of the New York City Police Department (NYPD) shot Amadou Diallo forty-one times. He died where he fell. To make the police killing all the more tragic, Diallo was a pious Muslim of gentle character. His death can be attributed not only to the increasingly lethal hubris of the NYPD, but also to Diallo's limited knowledge of American street culture. His poor command of English was rendered even more halting by a frightful life or death situation.
3. See MacGaffey and Bazenguissa-Ganga 2000, 9. There are similarities between the populations of Central African traders in Paris described in *Congo-Paris* and West African traders in New York City described in *Money Has No Smell*. The migration of African traders to these two cities has resulted from similar global and political forces. Informal traders in Paris and New York have faced many similar social problems resulting from immigration politics and state regulation. There are, however, profound differences in their trading practices. As we shall see, among West African traders, who are Muslims, commerce is an honorable profession. Traders are members of highly structured networks and follow a strict set of commercial procedures that are stipulated in the Qur'an. Violation of these procedures brings disrespect and shame. Among Central Africans, trade is less esteemed and religion has no central role in their individual trading activities (ibid., 14).
4. The most noteworthy examples are Bourgois 1995; Desjarlais 1997; and Duneier 1999.
5. Desjarlais 1997, 40–41. The methods used in this book are somewhat similar to those employed in two noteworthy studies of street life in New York City. In his award-winning book *In Search of Respect* (1995), Philip Bourgois describes the social lives of crack cocaine dealers in East Harlem. He, too, engaged in long-term fieldwork and altered the identities of the people he interviewed. Unlike Desjarlais or myself, he made extensive use of a tape-recorder. The second study, *Sidewalk* (1999), by Mitchell Duneier, is an outstanding account of mostly homeless men and women who sell books on the sidewalks of Greenwich Village. Like Bourgois, Duneier tape-recorded

street conversations. Unlike Desjarlais, Bourgois, or myself, Duneier reveals the identities of his informants. He argues that this kind of revelation increases his accountability. He also suggests that it would be methodologically astute for more social scientists to reveal the names of their respondents—all in the name of accountability. One could claim that Duneier is staking out higher ground. Knowing the names of his informants, anyone could ask them if Duneier's representations are accurate. What works well in Duneier's study, however, may not be appropriate in other research contexts. Among West Africans, for whom privacy is a major issue, using real names would be unethical. Furthermore, it would be especially troublesome to reveal the names of merchants who may be unregistered immigrants who sell counterfeit goods on the street. As is often the case in social science, an ecumenical approach to field methodology is usually the best path to follow.

6. Interview with El Hadj Harouna Souley, December 14, 1994.

Chapter 1

1. Interview with Issifi Mayaki, January 4, 1997.
2. See Foner 1995, 2000; Mahler 1995, 1996.
3. See Appadurai 1990, 1991; Gupta and Ferguson 1992; Bhabha 1994. In a recent essay, Thomas has suggested that the concept of hybridity espoused by the likes of Appadurai is too general. He argues that "some of the enthusiasm around hybridity reproduces cultural hierarchies that anthropologists have disputed in the past and might continue to oppose. In the art world especially, I find that the interest in hybridity enables critics and curators to celebrate their own capacity for acknowledging cultural difference, while refraining from engaging with the stories and works that emerge from ground remote from their own" (1996, 9).
4. Black Expo is a traveling trade show that highlights and promotes African American business enterprises.
5. Nossiter 1995, 23, 25.
6. Sarah Castle, personal communication.
7. JoAnn D'Alisera, personal communication.
8. Foner 1995, vii; preliminary results from Census 2000.
9. See Stoller 1996.

Chapter 2

1. According to the New York City Taxi Commission regulations, Medallion cabs (yellow cabs licensed by city hall) can legally pick up fares. Gypsy cabs are allowed on the street but are considered limos; they cannot pick up fares on the street, but must respond to phoned or radioed requests for service. In Harlem and the Bronx, however, gypsy cabs often pick up passengers in direct violation of a rarely enforced New York City ordinance.
2. Bohannon 1962; Clark 1994, 186–88.
3. Gregoire 1993, 107; Lewis 1980, 15–19; Amin 1971; Gugler and Flanagan 1978; Painter 1988; Rouch 1956; Stoller 1997.
4. See Brenner 1993.
5. See also Ebin 1990 and O'Brien 1971.
6. Gregoire 1993, 113.

7. See Steiner 1993; Taylor, Barbash, and Steiner 1992.

8. See Rouch 1956.

9. Interview with Issifi Mayaki, January 4, 1997.

10. Interview with Issifi Mayaki, November 15, 1996. Gregoire (1992) notes that among traditional and contemporary Hausa merchants in Niger, the availability of credit is the single most important criterion for trading success.

11. Large corporations like General Motors outsource to save money and streamline their workforce. Instead of having GM workers manufacture the parts that go into GM cars, the corporation contracts with small firms to supply the parts. The result is an increase in corporate profits and a reduction of the corporate workforce. GM's policy sparked a strike in 1996.

12. Export processing zones are usually found in third world countries under debt pressure from the International Monetary Fund or the World Bank. In the hope of raising capital, these countries declare special zones where multinational corporations can manufacture goods cheaply and profitably through the sanctioned, beyond-the-local-law exploitation of a mostly feminine workforce. Most of the shirts, pants, and dresses one buys in North American stores are manufactured in export processing zones.

Kantner and Pittinsky (1996) have isolated four socioeconomic processes connected to globalization: mobility, simultaneity, bypass, and pluralism. *Mobility* concerns the increased ease of movement of capital, innovation, information, and labor across national boundaries; it is what Appadurai (1996) refers to as "flows." These flows have accelerated with the advance of technology. *Simultaneity* refers to the fact that similar goods are concurrently available in many different regions. "The time lag between the introduction of a product or service in one country, and the roll-out in other markets is declining precipitously, especially for new technologies" (Kantner and Pittinsky 1996, 3). *Bypass* underscores how innovative entrepreneurs use alternative channels to bring their goods to individual consumers. Using computer technology, scholars can publish their own books or journals, thereby "bypassing" established academic institutions. Sending a package by way of UPS "bypasses" national mail services. *Pluralism*, an economic process, focuses on the decentralization of economic activity from "monopolistic centers" (Kantner 1995).

These four broad processes, according to Kantner and Pittinsky, have changed American economic life in the following ways: the economy has shifted from manufacturing to services; there is much more competition from foreign producers of goods; facilities are increasingly owned (in part) by foreign investors; businesses are leaner and more flexible—the result of downsizing to meet the rapid changes in the global economy.

Globalization, of course, has had profound sociological consequences on the nature of the workplace, labor conditions, employment security, migration. "Globalization—mobility, simultaneity, bypass and pluralism—is characterized by powerful and dramatic social and economic change. Studying globalization's social impacts provides a window through which scientists may glimpse a world of dramatically re-defined economic and social life" (Kantner and Pittinsky 1996, 17). Kantner and Pittinsky's analysis is useful as far as it goes. It does not, however, include the dimension of culture and doesn't consider the social and cultural ramifications of hybridity in the streets—as at the Malcolm Shabazz Harlem Market. One of the purposes of this book—and of ethnography in general—is to provide some flesh to abstract discussions of global processes.

On informal economies, see also Coombe and Stoller 1994, 251; Harvey 1989; Sassen 1991a; Mollenkopf and Castells 1991.

13. Mittleman 1996, 265; see also Sassen 1991b.

14. Callaghy and Ravenhill 1993.

15. One of the Nigerien traders on 125th Street, Idrissa Dan Inna, arrived in February 1994, two weeks after the World Bank orchestrated the devaluation of the West African franc. The devaluation, he said, ruined his business in Niger. With twelve children to feed, he took action by liquidating his inventory in Niger, buying a round-trip ticket between Niamey and New York City and obtaining an American tourist visa. On arrival in New York City, he sold the return portion of his ticket and used the money to buy new inventory. After several days in New York, he was in business on 125th Street.

16. Sassen 1991b, 1994b.

17. Sassen 1991b, Mollenkopf and Castells 1991. In a recent issue of *Urban Affairs*, James W. White (1998) mounts a sustained critique of Sassen's global city model. He claims that Sassen's model suffers from economic reductionism and even ethnocentrism. It is a product, he says, of an almost crude Marxism. He suggests that there is no compelling evidence to argue that in global cities there is increased dualization—a widening gulf between rich and poor living in cities without middle-income residents (who have fled to suburbs). He also suggests that the model is oversimplified and exaggerates the convergence of urban processes, which tends to create urban similarities where differences exist. His most important criticism, though, focuses on the economic determinism of the model. In the model, he writes, the state is outplayed and outclassed by capital, meaning that states have little power to shape the economic destiny of their cities—especially global ones. In the same issue Sassen defends the model, but agrees that the impact of the state in global cities is an issue that merits new research. These arguments, of course, are on the macrosociological level. They expose economic and social processes that have personal consequences for people living in urban areas. There is, however, no cultural aspect to these cogitations. Although they provide a fine socioeconomic context for books like *Money Has No Smell*, they do not concretely describe how globalization affects the lives of people.

18. Coombe and Stoller 1994, 252; see also Portes, Castells, and Benton 1989.

19. Ebin and Lake 1992; Coombe and Stoller 1994; Stoller 1996.

20. Ebin and Lake 1992; Coombe and Stoller 1994; Stoller 1996.

21. Bluestone 1991; McCay 1940; Osofsky 1971; Thomas 1995.

22. See Rouch 1956; Cohen 1969; Brenner 1993; Gregoire 1993.

23. In 1996, a Senegalese trader in lower Manhattan who possesses an employment authorization permit told me of how the INS turned down his request to visit his ailing mother in Senegal. They required official documentation of her illness.

24. See Thomas 1994.

25. See Bourgois 1995.

Chapter 3

1. See Jean Rouch's 1956 article as well as his incomparable film, *Jaguar* (1964). For other studies of the life of Hausa migrants in West African towns, see Cohen 1969 and Schildkrout 1978.

2. Interview with Issifi Mayaki, November 15, 1997. Of the four groups of traders that A. G. Hopkins isolates in his *Economic History of West Africa* (1973), the professional

merchants have the greatest historical importance—and the greatest relevance for understanding contemporary trading practices among West Africans in New York City. Although there are several widespread groups of traders, discussion in this book is limited to Dyula and Hausa merchants. Both groups constructed what Abner Cohen has called trade diasporas, "a nation of socially interdependent, but spatially dispersed communities" (cited in Meillassoux, 1971, 267). In the trade diaspora, ties of kinship, culture, and language facilitate the flow of goods and market information, all of which enhances the profitability of trade. West Africans in New York, it should be noted, have constructed trade diasporas of their own, using many old practices to adapt to the peculiar cultural and economic circumstances of contemporary North America.

3. Cohen 1969, 8–9.
4. Ibid., 9.
5. Ibid., 19.
6. Ibid., 19–22. See also Gregoire 1992 on the importance of credit in Hausa economic networks and Schildkrout 1978 on Hausa communities in Ghana.
7. Cohen 1969, 99.
8. Ibid., 99–100.
9. See Rouch 1956.
10. Braudel 1972, 467; see also Bovill 1995; and Hopkins 1973, 79.
11. Wolf 1982, 37.
12. Hopkins 1973, 58.
13. Ibid., 37.
14. Ibid., 58.
15. Hopkins 1973, 62; see also Sahlins 1972.
16. Interview with Issifi Mayaki, November 15, 1996.
17. Ibrahim 1990, 5.
18. Ibid., 7.
19. Ibid., 75.
20. Mennan 1986, 285, 286.
21. On the sale of grapes, see Ibrahim 1990, 86–87; on the sale of idols and forbidden foods, see Mennan 1986, 287.
22. Ibrahim 1990, 87–88; see also Mennan 1986; Hodgson 1974.
23. Interview with Boubé Mounkaila, August 14, 1996.
24. See Bovill 1995; Hopkins 1973; Wolf 1982. Phillip Curtin (1975) has written about the history of the trade diaspora of the Soninke people, who like the Hausa are predominantly, Muslim. See also Meillassoux 1971, 1991. Even with a modest commercial technology, small-scale traders in West African diasporas "could carry out all necessary commercial functions on their own, independent of specialized facilities for banking, marketing, and the like. Each commercial enclave could then stand alone, without having to depend for essential functions on a multifunctional urban center" (Curtin 1975, 64). In this way, specialized traders extended their diasporas from town to town along trade routes, exercising both their efficiency and independence. "Since the Soninke were the dominant people of the northern savanna between the Niger bend and the Senegal, it was only natural that their diaspora to the south carried the first known long-distance trade into West Africa" (ibid., 62).

Most of the Soninke diaspora consisted of what Curtin calls "clerical-commercial communities." Traders established the earliest of these communities well before 1500. Some of the communities emerged on overland routes to the southern gold mines; others appeared at strategic points along the upper Niger or along routes that branched southward off the Niger toward Asante. In time, the people in these communities adopted one of several Malinke languages. Eventually, many of them referred to themselves as *dyula*, the Malinke word that denotes "merchant."

Not all of the diasporic Soninke settled in Asante, however. Jahaanke cleric-traders, who originated from Jahba on the Niger River, settled on the Bafing River in Senegambia. Like the Dyula of Asante, the Marka, a Soninke population that established itself south of the Niger bend, adopted Malinke ways. Curtin also suggests that the Yarse, traders who today live in Burkina Faso are also Soninke in origin. Other Soninke trekked north to Walata to profit from the salt trade in the desert; still others journeyed south to Kankan in northern Guinea to deal in the north-south kola trade (ibid., 69).

In time, two major Soninke trade diasporas established themselves in the Senegambian bush: a traditional Soninke community in the Gajagga region, which retained Soninke language and culture, and the aforementioned Jahaanke of Jahba on the Bafing River, who adopted Malinke ways. The clerical status of the Gajagga Soninke enclaves, which traced their origin to Wagadu, the seat of the Ghana Empire, provided them protection from marauding armies, ensuring the Soninke clerics a go-between status that enhanced their capacity to broker deals. The cleric-traders of Gajagga valued their autonomy from local political authority. But the enclaves didn't operate in the absence of authority. All of the clerical Soninke enclaves in Senegambia, for example, owed moral alliances to the Draame, the most important clerical lineage among the Soninke groups. The moral leadership of the Draame provided "the mutual solidarity that bound merchants to act together in favor of commercial privilege" (ibid., 73). Kinship ties and formal lineage alliances, however distantly articulated, also bound widely scattered Soninke merchants to a closely followed set of commercial rights and obligations—a necessity of long-distance trading.

Like their cousins the Gajagga Soninke, the Senegambian Jahaanke sought political autonomy, prized Islam as their religion, and practiced commerce. Unlike many of the other groups of the West African trade diaspora, the Jahaanke rejected any use of force and refused to enter into politics. These actions, according to the teachings of Salimu Sware, the Jahaanke spiritual guide, would violate their religious beliefs. "Many traditionalists still claim that Jahaanke caravans moved through the country armed only with the power of prayer" (ibid., 80).

Curtin notes astutely that the various groups of long-distance traders—Soninke and non-Soninke alike—competed commercially. Competition for resources and commodities combined with divergent traditions would create, one would think, both diversity and distance. And yet the trading tradition "laid a very strong emphasis on status solidarity with other merchants. Jahaanke today still insist that they have a bond not merely to other Jahaanke but to other jula [*dyula*], and especially to other jula in the same line of trade. A multinational caravan representing several groups—Jahaanke, Soninke, or Futaanke—would tend to subdivide according to branch of trade, not ethnic identity" (ibid., 83).

Such a long-standing tradition of trading has profound cultural implications for West African traders in New York City, many of whom come from Malinke and Soninke lineages in Senegal and Mali.

Although it is fairly clear that the *dyula* communities of the Senegambia have been—at least in origin—Soninke, careful study of the trading diaspora southward toward Asante reveals a more complex ethnic picture. Claude Meillassoux criticizes the classical historians, particularly the influential Maurice Delafosse, for linking the emergence of professional traders to the dispersal of Soninke populations. Calling this classical position "a rather simplistic view of history," Meillassoux says that the historical evidence suggests no single ethnic origin for *dyula* families. "The proliferation of the jula . . . their spread and their growing influence were the results of an economic conjuncture and not of an accident of history or of an innate predisposition in certain 'races' for trade" (Meillassoux 1991, 56).

25. See Meillassoux 1991, 56.
26. Ibid.
27. Charles Monteil, cited in ibid., 58.
28. See Person 1976; also Roberts 1963.
29. See O'Brien 1971 on the Mourid order and Ebin 1990, Ebin and Lake 1992, Malcolmsen 1997, and Coombe and Stoller 1994 on the Mourids in New York City. See Perry 1997 on Wolof in New York City.
30. Meillassoux 1991, 243.
31. Amselle 1971, 256–65.
32. Gregoire 1992, 54.
33. Interview with El Hadj Soumana Tondi, August 11, 1995.
34. Interview with Issifi Mayaki, November 15, 1996.

Chapter 4

1. Interview with Moussa Diallo, August 17, 1994.
2. There are many fine studies of West African textiles. Among the best are Picton and Mack 1989 and Ross 1998.
3. Picton and Mack 1989, 124.
4. There are several African American enterprises that import handwoven kente strips from Ghana. Among the most important of these is Motherland Imports located in Los Angeles and Atlanta, which sells kente for pastors' robes, church choirs, sororities and fraternities, and for graduations.
5. Ross 1998, 27; also interviews with Moussa Diallo and Sidi Maiga, August 17, 1994.
6. Interview with Samba Soumana, July 24, 1994.
7. Interview with Moussa Diallo, August 17, 1994.
8. Interviews with Moussa Diallo and Sidi Maiga, August 17, 1994.
9. There is a vast literature in economic anthropology. Among the most significant studies, though this list excludes many fine works, are Malinowski [1922] 1961; Herskovits 1952; Bohannan 1955; Mintz 1974, 1985; Nash 1966; Sahlins 1972; Schneider 1974; Wolf 1966, 1982; Bloch 1975; and Godelier 1977.
10. Plattner 1989, 209, 210.
11. Ibid., 211.
12. Interview with Boubé Mounkaila, April 24, 1997.
13. Plattner 1989, 214.
14. Roberts 1996, 66–67.
15. Interviews with Boubé Mounkaila, March 15, 1993, and Garba Hima, August 1, 1994.
16. Interview with Jabar Tall, April 24, 1997.
17. The African art and textile traders had—and have—a warehouse in Chelsea, where shipments from Africa are stored and from which African art and textiles are shipped by van throughout the United States to boutiques, gallery owners, and private clients.

In a future study, I hope to investigate West African traders who sell African art in North America.

18. Interview with Issifi Mayaki, April 24, 1997.
19. See Barnes 1954, 1969; Mitchell 1974, 1989; see also Johnson 1994, 118.
20. See Kapferer 1973, 84.
21. See Walsh and Simonelli 1986, 46; cited in Johnson 1994, 115.
22. Johnson 1994, 132.
23. Noble 1973, 10.
24. See Sokolovsky et al. 1978 and Foster and Seidman 1982 on urban networks; Weisner 1978 on urban-rural ties in Kenya; and for a recent study of a transnational trading network, MacGaffey and Bazenguissa-Ganga 2000.
25. See Mitchell 1973, 20.
26. Ibid., 26.
27. See Johnson 1994, 116–17.
28. See Batton, Casti, and Thord 1995; see also Johnson 1994, 117.
29. Johansson 1995, 287, 305–6. Much of the literature on whole networks is highly technical; it is a key component of what some scholars have called mathematical anthropology. The sociological and economic literature on social networks is perhaps more mathematical than that of anthropology (see Batton, Casti, and Thord 1995). Many of the abstract models, sampling schemes, and computer programs used to locate network clusters seem rather far removed from the ground-level dynamics of network interactions. Plattner criticizes some of this abstract modeling, suggesting that while some models "were . . . intellectually and graphically elegant" many of them "were not shown to be truly descriptive of real-world situations" (1989, 195). Bax (1978) criticizes much of the literature on social networks for its almost exclusive focus on modeling and statistical techniques.
30. There is a long history of ethnic enmity in Niger. As a consequence, there is much rivalry and bitterness between the Songhay, Hausa, Fulan, Kanuri, and Tuareg peoples. Considering the ethnic politics of the Republic of Niger, these deep-seated conflicts are far from disappearing. See Stoller 1995; Charlick 1991.
31. In the years since their founding in 1898, Mourid wealth and influence in Senegal have grown exponentially. The order's founder, Ahamadou Bamba, preached that hard work constituted the path to pious salvation. Adepts worked hard for the *cheik* and provided him a percentage of their earnings. This practice continues today among Mourid adepts, who make up a substantial percentage of the Senegalese population in New York City. See O'Brien 1971; Malcolmsen 1997.
32. See Jacobson 1971, 641. Jacobson's essay is an attempt to understand the social processes involved in the construction of "kin"-based networks in urban settings, not unlike New York City, where social relationships are fleeting and filled with uncertainties. He writes: "Urban populations are typified by geographical mobility, which is often described as producing uncertainty and, potentially, social instability. Social stability, by contrast, requires an expectation of future interaction or continuity. One strategy, therefore, for coping with uncertainty in urban social life is to generate or confirm social continuity in social relations, a process which requires the actors' social perception of factors and circumstances affirming their future interaction" (ibid., 630).
33. Interview with Boubé Mounkaila, August 14, 1996.
34. Interview with Boubé Mounkaila, August 16, 1994.

35. Ibid.

36. Interview with Boubé Mounkaila, April 24, 1997.

Chapter 5

1. Interview with Boubé Mounkaila, March 17, 1993.

2. Asante 1993, 29.

3. Stoller 1989a; Coombe and Stoller 1994, 258.

4. Coombe and Stoller 1994, 261–62.

5. Sullivan 1992, 136.

6. Ibid.

7. Coombe and Stoller 1994, 262.

8. Interview with Boubé Mounkaila, March 17, 1993.

9. Asante 1993, 2.

10. Asante seemingly overlooks the fact that critiques of European constructivism have a long history along the side roads of social theory. One thinks here of the critical philosophies of Montaigne, Nietzsche, Heidegger, and their philosophical successors, especially Merleau-Ponty (1962, 1964) and Foucault (1970). In one way or another, these thinkers challenged the hegemony of European constructivist and positivist philosophy. Asante's critique, in fact, shares much substance with poststructuralism and postmodernism. Following the work of Jacques Derrida, especially in *Of Grammatology* (1976) and *The Post Card* (1987), there has been a sustained critique of a modernist philosophical edifice that has been founded on what Derrida calls logocentrism. In the United States, the work of Richard Rorty, especially his monumental *Philosophy and the Mirror of Nature* (1979), has powerfully deconstructed the very epistemological edifice that Asante critiques. In essence, a postmodern critique, like that of Asante, underscores the complexity of thought and social life as well as the need to recognize, if not embrace, the fragmented nature and particularistic richness of contemporary and past social thought and social life. From the vantage of a critical philosophy, one could see the development of Afrocentrism as part of a growing identity politics that has emerged in the space of the "condition of postmodernity" (Harvey 1989)—itself a result of the unleashing of the forces of globalization (see also Keith 1997; Appiah 1992; Harvey 1989). For the past twenty years, in fact, anthropologists have seriously questioned the Eurocentric bias of their discipline, which has had many ramifications in the practice of fieldwork as well as in representational strategies (to cite only a few of many titles, see Marcus and Fischer 1985; Clifford and Marcus 1986; Tyler 1988; Stoller 1989b, 1997). From an epistemological vantage, then, it is wrong to think or imply that Afrocentrism is a lonely, isolated reaction to or corrective of Eurocentric modernist philosophies. It is, rather, part of an ever-growing disenchantment with the philosophical legacy of the Enlightenment.

11. The emergence of Afrocentrism has created much scholarly and public controversy. Scholars and journalists—European Americans, African Americans, and Africans—have charged that Afrocentrism is racist and separatist. Afrocentrists, for their part, have stated that their critics have often failed to read, let alone understand, their works. They say, moreover, that Eurocentric scholars, bound by European epistemologies and rules of methodology and evidence, are blinded to the truth of things African. So far

this argument is not unlike the unending debate in anthropology between relativists and universalists. Indeed, many contemporary anthropologists, trying to avoid that quagmire, argue that the sociocultural lives of peoples should be assessed through multiple perspectives—including their own theoretical categories (see Stoller 1989b, 1997, 1998). Few anthropologists would agree completely with Asante, however, in suggesting that one perspective—Afrocentrism—be used to the exclusion of all other scholarly interpretations.

Afrocentrism is a curious mixture of orientations. On the one hand, Afrocentrists espouse a particularistic approach to things African, an approach that jibes with philosophical orientations in postmodernity. On the other hand, they also argue for a universal set of African values, suggesting that these values form the foundation of African and African American sociocultural life. This position is derived from the diffusionist work of Cheik Anta Diop. For diffusionists, there are cultural epicenters—ancient India for Indo-Europe; Kemet (ancient Egypt) for Africa—from which culture spreads over time. In the nineteenth century, many scholars employed a diffusionist model to support a racist polygenist theory of evolution, claiming that the races constituted separate and distinct species. Using this framework, Herbert Spencer argued that race was the key factor that distinguished civilized peoples (whites) from barbarians and savages (peoples of color). In essence, nineteenth-century diffusionism promoted a hierarchical and exclusionist view of social evolution and cultural development. It is ironic, then, that Afrocentrists, who criticize Eurocentric epistemologies, employ diffusionism, which is not only Eurocentric, but exclusionist as well.

There are many other problems associated with diffusionism. Diffusionists, like Afrocentrists, use historical linguistic analysis to argue for protolanguages and proto-cultures. In the nineteenth century, the aim was to find the key elements of a proto-Indo-European language and culture, which diffusionists believed could be reconstructed from comparisons of Indo-European languages to Sanskrit. They believed that the essence of sociocultural things might be discovered in the search for origins. Based on the putative lexical similarities demonstrated, for example, in Grimm's law, the diffusionists argued that the presence of lexical similarities demonstrated an original cultural influence that through time spread like ripples on water. The diffusionism found in books like Asante's *Kemet* or in Bernal's *Black Athena* rests on foundations of historical and comparative linguistics.

Historical linguistic analysis can be curiously intoxicating, especially when one discovers similar lexical items or cultural concepts in societies greatly separated in time and space. And yet linguists like Greenberg (1970) have written elegantly on the difficulties and uncertainties of linguistic reconstruction. Just how much influence can be attributed to reconstructed protolanguages and -cultures? Is it possible for there to be what Boas (1911) long ago called parallel development, which opposes unlineal diffusionism and speaks to local creativity?

The greatest danger of Indo-European as well as Afrocentric diffusionism is that it essentializes. In the case of Afrocentrism, African culture is considered a hermetic whole. In the index to Asante's *The Afrocentric Idea,* for example, the following specific African peoples are listed: Akan (which is a language group, not a people), Asante, Ga, Hausa, Ibo, Mandingo, Shona, and Yoruba. Elsewhere in the text, Asante mentions a few other peoples, like the Dogon. By and large, though, the specific practices of specific African peoples, which vary widely even within the same region, are not described. Instead of specific and nuanced descriptions of intracultural variation among the Ibo or the Yoruba, the author attempts to argue for a pan-African culture, based on "historical analysis" that somehow stands outside of the specific historical forces that gave rise to specific social histories and distinct social and cultural practices. Although African social practices often shine with harmony, they are also marred by conflict. From an anthropological vantage, the delimitation of any specific culture is at best a slippery enterprise. What is Songhay culture? Whose version of Songhay history is correct? To espouse a pan-African culture on a continent famous for its diversity is at best a scholarly enterprise open to question.

12. Asante 1990, 93–94. In *The Afrocentric Idea*, Asante uses "nommo" as "the generative and productive power of the spoken word" (1987, 17), considering it a kind of "word-force" that is present in African discourse. The Dogon concept of *nummo*, not specifically mentioned in Asante's corpus, is central to discussions in the elaborately annotated ethnographic descriptions found in Marcel Griaule's *Masques dogons* (1938) and *Conversations with Ogotemmêli* (1965), in Genvieve Calame-Griaule's *L'Ethnologie et langage: La parole chez les Dogons* (1972), and in Genvieve Dieterlen's *Les ames des Dogons* (1941). From these texts, it is clear that the Nummo were the original Dogon ancestors—a pair—that came into being when God, Amma, had sexual relations with the excised Earth. The Nummo felt sorry for their mother, the excised Earth, and brought her fibers that would cover her exposed parts. The fibers were filled with the moisture of the Nummo, which contained the vapors of the first language, which was used to organize the world (see also Stoller 1992). This Dogon myth is quite culturally specific and quite nuanced—more nuanced than the origin myths of many other West African societies. Greater mention of these concrete and specific African ideas in Asante's work would be felicitous. What is clear, though, is that the sociocultural importance placed on the power of the spoken word varies within and between African societies. To imply that the generative power of the spoken word is intrinsically African is to give short shrift to both the historical and ethnographic record.

13. Riley 1995, 3.

14. Ibid., 20–27. The seven symbols are (1) *mazao*, the fruits, nuts, and vegetables representing the family labor celebrated in African harvest festivals; (2) *mkeka*, the placemat that expresses African history and culture; (3) *vibunzi*, the ear of corn that stands for fertility and family viability; (4) *misumaa saba*, the seven candles symbolizing the sun and its light; (5) *kinara*, the candleholder, representing the ancestors, the source of life; (6) *kikombre cha umoja*, the unity cup, for the libation on the sixth day of the festival; and (7) *zawadi*, gifts, are exchanged on the seventh and final festival day.

15. Ibid., 4.

16. Cited in Wilde 1995, 69.

17. Woodward and Johnson 1995, 88.

18. Wilde 1995, 70–71.

19. Ibid., 71.

20. Ibid.

21. Early 1997, 56–57, 61.

22. Wilde 1995, 70.

23. Ibid., 71; see also "Only in Afro America" 1994, A32.

24. Interview with Issifi Mayaki, January 28, 1998.

25. Woodward and Johnson 1995, 88.

26. Wilde 1995, 71.

27. Brown 1997, A6.

28. Interview with Boubé Mounkaila, December 17, 1994.
29. Wilkinson 1996, 72.
30. Ibid., 73.
31. Ibid., 74.
32. Ibid., 75, 76.
33. Jenkins 1995, 4.
34. See Baudrillard 1983, 1986; Harvey 1989; Coombe 1996, 1998; Connor 1989.
35. See also Benjamin 1968, 1978. Although Afrocentrism is a serious attempt to construct a distinct epistemology, if we examine it from a broader vantage, it is clear that it, too, is part and parcel of the mimetic faculty. From Maulama Karenga to Molefi Asante, Afrocentric scholars have isolated what they consider core pan-African values (Karenga's seven principles of Kwanzaa and Asante's five principles of Ma'at). Applied to scholarship, the creation of rituals, or the promotion of social policy, these Afrocentric principles are, like many Afrocentric products, reproductions, copies of dense and nuanced African systems of thought. They are copies that take on the character of the original, which in the case of Asante's system, existed in the distant past; they are copies, following Taussig 1993, that influence the original. Given the power of the copy in the globalized context of postmodernity, Afrocentrism operates as a system of signs and becomes a kind of simulation of a potential reality. Like so many contemporary social movements, Afrocentrism becomes hyperreal. In Baudrillard's language, Afrocentrism may "no longer be a question of imitation, nor of reproduction, nor even of parody. It is rather a question of substituting signs of the real for the real itself, that is, an operation to deter every real process by its operational double, a metastable, programmatic, perfect descriptive machine which provides all the signs of the real and short circuits all its vicissitudes" (1983, 4).
36. Coombe 1996, 205.
37. Ibid.
38. See Baudrillard 1983; see also Castells 1997.
39. Bhabha 1984, 126.
40. The sale of trademarked goods—both original and counterfeit—is a major feature of informal economic activities in inner-city urban neighborhoods in North America. New York City is no exception. For example, West African street merchants sell hats, T-shirts, and sweatshirts emblazoned with "Timberland." In 1993, the proliferation of Timberland products, which are associated with the American mythos of a vast and clean outdoors, greatly increased the company's sales. West African merchants, who have always recognized the sales potential of new "hot" items, have also offered Karl Kani hats, which feature heavy metal tags on which the designer's name is engraved. A card attached to the hats reads: "Inspired by the vitality of the streets of Brooklyn, New York, Karl Kani the young African-American owner/designer of Karl Kani jeans encourages you to follow your dreams to accomplish your goals. Wear the clothing that represents the knowledge of African-American creativity and determination. Recognize the signature that symbolizes African-American unity and pride . . . Peace, Karl Kani" (cited in Coombe and Stoller 1994, 267).
41. Interview with Idé Younoussa, March 17, 1993.
42. Interview with Soumana Harouna, March 5, 1995.
43. Interviews with Amadou Bita, Issifi Mayaki, Idrissa Dan Inna, and Moussa Boureima, March 5–6, 1995.
44. Coombe and Stoller 1994, 265.
45. Ibid.
46. See Clifford 1988.

47. Coombe and Stoller 1994, 269–70.
48. Baudrillard 1983, 5.
49. Ibid., 146.
50. Ibid., 148.
51. Ibid., 14.
52. Castells 1997, 11.
53. Baudrillard 1983, 14.
54. Asante 1990, 93–94.
55. Interview with Issifi Mayaki, January 4, 1997.

Chapter 6

1. On the migration of Senegalese traders, see Conor Cruise O'Brien's history of the Mourid brotherhood (1971). See also Donald Carter's ethnography (1997) on Senegalese traders in Italy. Papa Demba Fall (1997, 1998), a demographer, has analyzed population shifts and trends among Sengalese who have immigrated to Italy.
2. Ebin and Lake 1992, 35.
3. These observations are based on systematic field observations between 1992 and 1997 at 48th Street and 6th Avenue as well as Broadway and 46th Street, 53rd Street and 7th Avenue, and 42nd Street near Grand Central Station.
4. See Stoller 1996. For parallel studies of quasi-legal trade among African merchants, see MacGaffey 1987, 1991; MacGaffey and Bazenguissa-Ganga 2000.
5. See Dickens 1992; Harvey 1989; Mitter 1987; Mittelman 1996; Mollenkopf and Castells 1991; Portes, Castells, and Benton 1989; Sassen 1991a, 1991b, 1994a, 1994b, 1996.
6. Coombe and Stoller 1994, 251.
7. See Bourgois 1995 for a particularly poignant case study of how deindustrialization affected the Puerto Rican community in East Harlem. Writing of such social upheavals, Coombe and Stoller (1994, 251–52) state:

> New social cleavages emerge in these cities due to the same forces that attract capital and labour. As demands for more specialized services for those corporations engaged in the global economy draw more and more professionally educated people into these cities, new markets for goods and services are created, and new sources of supply emerge to meet these demands. Whereas economic growth in the post–World War II era sustained the growth of a middle class, through capital-intensive investment in manufacturing, mass production, and the consumption of standardized products, which in turn created conditions conducive to unionization and worker empowerment (Sassen 1991a, 83), today's new urban elites demand gentrified housing, specialized products, small full-service retail shops close to home, catered and pre-prepared foods, restaurants, and dry cleaning outlets (Sassen 1991a, 86). These are labour-intensive rather than capital-intensive enterprises in which small-scale production and subcontracting are obvious means of increasing profits. Whereas middle-class suburban growth in the Fordist period depended upon capital investments in land, road construction, automobiles, large supermarkets, mass outlets, and nationally advertised goods (all things which require large workforces in large workplaces), today's professional elites create markets for goods and services produced in small scale enterprises— subcontractors, family enterprises, sweatshops and households (Sassen 1991a, 86). Such low-wage workers are paid minimum wages, have no job security, and by virtue of their working conditions, are often isolated and unable to organize.

These workers, in turn, also require goods and services, thus creating markets for lower priced goods than even the mass retail chains can provide. The needs of low-wage workers are met by lower-waged workers, often immigrants, and increasingly women and children subject to patriarchal family restrictions, and isolated by language barriers and fear of deportation. The management and servicing of a global network of factories, service outlets, and financial markets has also had consequences for the spatial organization of North American cities, resulting in situations that might be described as emergent urban apartheid, in which housing becomes more expensive, there are more and more homeless, and densities in low income areas increase. Those low wage workers who take advantage of the opportunities afforded by the informal economy find it very difficult to afford to live in the cities that afford these opportunities (Sassen 1991b, 329). The deeper and deeper impoverishment of larger and larger sectors of the population is exacerbated in precisely those cities that contain increasingly affluent elites.

8. Coombe and Stoller 1994, 252. See also Sassen 1991a, 1991b, 1994b, 1996.
9. Castells and Portes 1989, 12.
10. Tierney 1997, 22.
11. Sontag (1993, A1) writes that New York City has a long history of street peddling. Street peddlers were first licensed in the 1880s. Just before World War I, the number of peddlers had grown so much that city hall limited their number to six thousand, which brought on an explosion of "illegal" street vending. In the 1980s peddling once again expanded on the streets of New York City, but city hall issued only 853 licenses for general peddling, a number frozen in 1979 by the city council. There are currently about three thousand licensed food peddlers. Booksellers and traders in religious artifacts do not need a license. In 1997, city hall permitted traders to sell art objects without a vending permit.
12. Coombe and Stoller 1994, 255.
13. Interview with Boubé Mounkaila, August 14, 1996.
14. Ibid.
15. See Baudrillard 1983; for analysis of the mimetic faculty, see also Taussig 1992, 1993. Although the original is here higher in price than the copy, vendors sell more copies than originals, which means that copies bring them more money. Put another way, copies have a higher market value. Making these distinctions enables the vendors to adhere—at least in theory—to their Islamic principles.
16. Sullivan 1992, 136.
17. Coombe and Stoller 1994, 265; see also Nelson 1989.
18. Coombe and Stoller 1994, 265.
19. Purchased by author on August 8, 1994, on 125th Street in Harlem.
20. See Stipp 1996, 131. Most counterfeit merchandise is produced in Asia. The replicability of merchandise has been enhanced, moreover, by the dislocation of manufacturing. When U.S. companies move their manufacturing sites to Korea or the Philippines, advanced technology falls into the wrong hands, which makes it easy for Asian entrepreneurs to reproduce originals—at very cheap prices. The knockoff industry is also good for the local economies of Asian countries. In 1994, for example, Chinese compact-disk factories produced three million legitimate CDs, but also produced seventy million pirated copies (ibid., 132). Consider also the case of counterfeit Tiger Woods products. They demonstrate how entrepreneurs in the counterfeit mar-

ket quickly exploit perceived opportunities. In April of 1997, when Tiger Woods was winning the Masters Golf Tournament, police in Augusta, Georgia, arrested four men and seized tens of thousands of dollars in illegal Tiger Woods goods—and this before Woods had officially won the championship. Speaking of Tiger Woods products, one licensing agent said: "Just about everything out there is a fake. . . . It isn't like Tiger is desperate to go into this business. . . . The only thing we can do is try to educate golf clubs and fans to watch out because when demand exceeds supply by this degree, the worst element moves in to take advantage of it" ("Chasing Tigers" 1997, 48). Most of the items, it should be noted, come with certificates of "authenticity."

21. Interview with Garba Hima, July 14, 1994.
22. Roberts 1996, 66.
23. "Video Ring Is Broken" 1994, B5.
24. Ibid.
25. Roberts 1996, 66.
26. Ibid.
27. Interview with Garba Hima, July 14, 1994.
28. Observations and interviews, Malcolm Shabazz Harlem Market, December 8, 1997. The decision of the Masjid Malcolm Shabazz to forbid the sale of counterfeit videos, audiocassettes, and CDs may also be the result of a more widespread effort by the state to regulate copyright, trademark statutes, and licensing agreements. According to officials of the Recording Industry Association of America, however, the key to antipiracy efforts is not so much in seizure, but in creating deterrents—stiffer penalties and amended penal codes, as in New York, where in November 1995 it became illegal not only to manufacture counterfeit music and film, but also to distribute and sell it (see "RIAA Releases Piracy Statistics" 1996, 6; "RIAA: Bootleg Seizures Soar" 1997, 6).
29. Interview with Boubé Mounkaila, March 12, 1998.
30. Observations and interviews with Boubé Mounkaila and Sala Fari, December 8, 1994.
31. Observations in midtown Manhattan, February 4–5, 1997.
32. Observations on 125th Street, August 23–27, 1994; and at the Malcolm Shabazz Harlem Market, December 8–9, 1997.
33. On this second wave of immigration, see Stoll 1996, 1; also Borjas 1996, 72; Foner 1995, vii; and Foner 2000.
34. See Sassen 1991b, 1994b. In *The Global City,* Sassen writes, "The notion that New York City keeps receiving immigrants because it has been a city of immigrants is simply insufficient. Migrations are produced and this requires specific conditions. . . . It would seem that two of the basic processes identified in this book—the internationalization of the economies . . . and the causualization of the employment relation—contribute to producing new migrations and facilitating their absorptions" (1991b, 319).
35. Stoll 1996, 2.
36. Borjas 1996, 72; Stoll 1996, 2; Halbfinger 1997, 1.
37. Schmitt 1997, 9.
38. Borjas 1996, 73; Stoll 1996, 2.
39. Pear 1994, A1.
40. Firestone 1995, A1. See also "Court Says City Can't Forbid Workers" 1999, B7.
41. Golden 1996, 1.
42. Interview with Boubé Mounkaila, February 25, 1994.
43. Files of the author.

44. Interview with Boubé Mounkaila, May 11, 1994.
45. Interviews and observations in New York City and Newark, May 11, 1994.
46. Interview with Boubé Mounkaila, August 8, 1995.
47. Interviews and observations in New York City, February 8, 1996.
48. Interview with Boubé Mounkaila, November 14, 1996.
49. Sontag 1994, A1.
50. Engleberg 1994, A1.
51. Ibid., B10.
52. Pristin 1996, B1.
53. Branigin and Constable 1997, A1. The IIRIRA comprises five titles that cover various aspects of immigration enforcement and INS processing. Here are some of the major provisions. Title 1 authorizes the INS to hire a thousand new border patrol agents per year for five years (1997–2002), increases the budget for border patrol enforcement, and mandates the construction of a triple-tiered fence near the Mexican-U.S. border near San Diego. Title 2 increases penalties for immigrant smuggling and document fraud.

    Title 3 alters the manner in which the United States considers and acts on many types of immigrants, both those seeking legal status and those who have arrived in the United States without proper documentation or no documentation. These immigrants can be deported without a hearing before an immigration judge unless they can convince a low-level immigration officer of a bona fide fear of persecution or that they are seeking asylum in the United States—not an easy task. Title 3 also limits judicial power to review a questionable or erroneous INS decision.

    Title 4 concerns the relationship between immigrants and employers. Under the IIRIRA provisions, it becomes much more difficult for employees to establish their identities as the law reduces the number of documents one can use to establish identity. It has become more difficult for employees to prove employer discrimination; they now have to prove employer intent to discriminate.

    Title 5 has made it much more difficult for immigrants—legal and illegal—to qualify for public benefits. In most circumstances, it has made them ineligible for Social Security, food stamps, Medicaid, and Medicare. For legal immigrants to qualify, they must prove that they have worked in the United States for a minimum of ten years.

    Title 5 also requires those who sponsor immigrant family relatives (and certain employment-sponsored immigrants) to have an income 125 percent of the poverty level, which for a family of four is $19,500. If the sponsor is unable to show the required support, another person who meets the minimum fiscal requirements can cosign. Once sponsors qualify, they must sign an affidavit of support that is legally binding until the sponsored immigrant has worked in the United States for ten years or has obtained U.S. citizenship (see "The Illegal Immigration Reform and Immigrant Responsibility Act" 1997, 45; see also Estevez 1997, 86).
54. Fisher 1997, 35.
55. Ibid.
56. Levy 1997, 43.
57. Ojito 1997, A1.
58. Branigin 1997, A9.
59. Ibid., A1.
60. Branigin 1998, A13.

61. Ibid.
62. Interview with Issifi Mayaki, October 8, 1997.
63. Ibid.
64. Interview with Issifi Mayaki, November 12, 1997.
65. Interview with Issifi Mayaki, January 28, 1998.

Chapter 7

1. Interviews on 125th Street, October 12, 1994, and October 14, 1994.
2. Interview with Moussa Boureima, October 14, 1994.
3. Interview with Idrissa Dan Inna, August 1, 1994.
4. Interview with Idrissa Dan Inna, October 11, 1994.
5. Hull 1976, 45; see also Lévi-Strauss 1967, 128–59, and Griaule and Dieterlen 1954.
6. Merleau-Ponty 1962, 243–44. For the phenomenological orientation, see Lynch 1960; see also Lefevre 1974; Davis 1990; Soja 1989; and Stoller 1980, 1989a.
7. Gupta and Ferguson 1992, 7, 9.
8. See Harvey 1989.
9. Gupta and Ferguson 1992, 17.
10. Interview with Boubé Mounkaila, October 17, 1994.
11. This description and dialogue are based on firsthand observation and informal interviews in Harlem on October 17, 1994.
12. See Bluestone 1991.
13. Interview with Sala Fari, March 8, 1993.
14. Files of the author.
15. Interview with Issifi Mayaki, August 19, 1994.
16. One year into the Giuliani-Bratton tenure, crime fell dramatically in New York City. By the second year of Bratton's term as police commissioner, journalists were hailing him as a brilliant hero who had crafted a policy that had made New York City one of North America's safest cities and, more important, one of its most desired tourist destinations. Bratton's notoriety—and his swagger—may well have upstaged Mayor Giuliani. After two years on the job, he tendered his resignation. Giuliani could now accept all the credit for reducing crime in New York City. In 1997, New York City was voted the safest city in the United States. Following Bratton's tenure, the Giuliani administration sought to pass more city legislation to improve the quality of life in New York. One such measure, passed in June 1996, effectively banned aggressive panhandling, defined as begging that is "threatening, involves physical contact or blocks a prospective donor's path" (see Toy 1996, B1).
17. See Kaufman 1994, A18.
18. Castells and Portes 1989, 12.
19. See Sassen 1991a; Coombe and Stoller 1994, 253–54; Stoller 1996, 1997.
20. Hicks 1994b, A43.
21. Interviews with Amadou Adamou and Boubé Mounkaila August 19, 1994.
22. Interviews with Boubé Mounkaila and Issifi Mayaki August 19, 1994.
23. Interview with Sala Fari, August 19, 1994.
24. The key political groups that supported the mayoral crackdown constitute the Harlem business and political establishment. Morris Powell has been a street vendor in Harlem for more than thirty years. His association's estimated membership of five hundred vendors consists mostly of African American merchants but also includes a contingent

of West Africans. Members are asked to pay a fee of twenty dollars a month to finance a newsletter and promote peddling. Powell has long been an advocate of the self-determination of black people in Harlem and has long been at odds with the Harlem business and political establishment. One could say that social class seems to be a significant political determinant in this case. For more detailed information on Morris Powell, see Barry and Hicks 1995; for other analyses of the African market's demise, see Thomas 1995 and Zukin 1995, 230–47.

25. Files of the author.

26. Interview with Moussa Touré, October 15, 1994.

27. See Hicks 1994b; interviews with Boubé Mounkaila and Issifi Mayaki, October 15, 1994.

28. Interview with Garba Hima, October 15, 1994.

29. Hicks 1994a, B3.

30. Policano 1994a, 2.

31. Ibid.

32. Interview with Boubé Mounkaila, October 15, 1994.

33. Interview with Issifi Mayaki, October 17, 1994.

34. See Bohannon 1962; Clark 1994.

35. Policano 1994b, 9.

36. Shipp 1994, 15.

37. Sinclair 1994, 27.

38. "Protecting Harlem's Merchants" 1994, 23.

39. Finder 1994, B1. Race became the centerpiece of a deadly political dispute that erupted in Harlem in December 1995, slightly more than one year after Mayor Giuliani's dispersal of the 125th Street market. A part-time vendor on 125th Street burst into a Jewish-owned store waving a revolver and carrying a container of flammable liquid. He ordered the African Americans in the store to leave. He then shot four people: the Jewish manager of the store, two construction workers, and a Guyanese employee. He set fire to the store and shot himself in the chest. The issue behind the deadly attack was whether a Jewish leaseholder had the right to increase the rent of a black businessman who sublet space in the store building. The shootings and fire followed several weeks of demonstrations, like those following the demise of the 125th Street market.

40. "Walking on 125th Street" 1994, A21.

41. Kleinfield 1995, 51.

42. Interview with Issifi Mayaki, December 11, 1994.

43. Ibid.

44. Interview with El Hadj Harouna Souley, December 11, 1994.

45. Interview with Garba Hima, June 14, 1996.

46. Interviews with Issifi Mayaki and Boubé Mounkaila, March 12, 1998.

47. Interview with Issifi Mayaki, April 13, 1998.

Chapter 8

1. Interviews with Moussa Boureima, August 15 and October 4, 1997.

2. Interview with Issifi Mayaki, August 11, 1995.

3. Firestone 1995, A1.

4. Dugger 1996b, A1; 1996c, A1.

5. Dugger 1997, A10.

6. According to Celia Dugger, asylum seekers are detained "in part because of a quirk

in the law that treats people entering the country illegally at an airport more severely than those who are caught within the nation's borders" (1996b, A1). Detained asylum seekers are placed in prisons far from their lawyers and families. The detainment centers are also poorly supervised by the INS, which leads to the kinds of abuse reported by Kasinga and Bulus.

7. Interview with Sala Fari, May 10, 1994.

8. Interview with El Hadj Soumana Tondi, August 15, 1994.

9. In the Republic of Niger, Islamic healers study Islamic medicine, but they also employ techniques used by pre-Islamic healers. In the most prominent families of sorcerers in western Niger, for example, learned Muslim clerics and pre-Islamic practitioners engage in similar therapies. There are, of course, practices that Muslims will not publicly acknowledge, but in my experiences in Niger between 1976 and 1990, I found a remarkable melange of healing traditions.

Some of the plants brought to New York by Alpha Turi have been classified scientifically. *Kobe* is *Ficus platyphylla*, a principal plant used by Songhay sorcerers. *Nine baso* is *Walteria indica*. *Yulumendi*, the love potion, remains unclassified. For more information on medicinal plants in Niger, see Peyre de Fabregues 1979.

10. Interview with Boubé Mounkaila, April 22, 1994. SROs have long been the way that poor people have been housed. In New York City, many homeless people have been moved into city-subsidized SROs. In 1960, New York City had 142,000 SRO units. Between 1960 and 1985, this number declined precipitously to 42,000. That, combined with the fact that in 1974 the State of New York began to release two hundred thousand psychiatric patients into the community, increased exponentially the population of homeless people on the streets of New York City. "Now the city is helping non-profit agencies create new SROs once more. City-provided loans for the units have reached a total of $262 million. The state has chipped in a subsidy to pay for support services, such as TB testing and employment assistance. The city now has 10,500 beds in 'supported' SROs, and around 35,000 private rooms" ("Room at the Top" 1996, 24).

11. Interview with Boubé Mounkaila, April 22, 1994.

12. Interview with Boubé Mounkaila, March 29, 1995.

13. In Songhay and Hausa families, there is a strict code of respect accorded to the oldest brother in a family. Because age denotes rank and prestige, the oldest brother can make serious and substantial requests of his younger brothers. If younger brothers refuse these requests, it brings them great and irrevocable shame.

14. Interview with Boubé Mounkaila, March 31, 1995.

15. Nossiter 1995, B1.

16. Ibid., B23.

17. Ibid.

18. Ibid.

19. See Hodgson 1974. The model for the Islamic notion of community is Medina in the seventh century under Muhammad's delineation of individual responsibility before Allah, to the community, and the community's responsibility to the world. "It was the mission of the community to bring God's true ways to all the world; hence the rule of the Muslim community should be extended over all infidels" (ibid., 322). And yet peoples brought under the hegemony of Islam were allowed to practice their religions as long as they didn't defame Allah and as long as they accepted Muslim authority. The Shari'ah code of law was an attempt to extend these principles of a small-scale society to a caliphal state.

20. Interview with Issifi Mayaki, March 12, 1998.

21. Ibid.

22. See Mirowski 1995; Mirowski and Ross 1991; Krause 1990; Rodin 1986; Kahn and Antonucci 1980.

23. Zukerman et al. 1996; Baltes, Wahl, and Reichart 1992; Krause 1990; Rodin 1986.

24. Dugan and Kivett 1994.

25. Mirowski and Ross 1991.

26. Nwadiora 1996, 118. For a more nuanced consideration of so-called collectivist cultures, see Matsumoto et al. 1997.

27. Interview with El Hadj Moru Sifi, August 1, 1994.

28. Interview with Boubé Mounkaila, March 12, 1998. A *kountigi* is a single-stringed lute.

29. Interview with Issifi Mayaki, January 4, 1997.

30. Interview with Abdou Harouna, March 12, 1993.

31. Interview with Sidi Sansanne, August 8, 1995.

32. Interview with Moustapha Diarra, March 12, 1998.

33. See Inglehart 1990; Maffesoli 1996. In recent years, considerations of communities have shifted to the study of new social movements. In *Culture Shift in Advanced Industrial Society*, a massive study based on European and North American survey data, Ronald Inglehart argues that relative economic security in advanced industrial societies has prompted a shift from material values, which focus on physical security and sustenance, to postmaterialist values, which emphasize belonging, self-expression, and the quality of life. Inglehart argues that this shift "seems to be one aspect of a still broader process of cultural change that is reshaping religious orientations, gender roles, sexual mores and the cultural norms of Western society" (1991, 66). The shift from materialist to postmaterialist values, he suggests, has also given rise to a wide variety of new social movements, like the West German Green Party, that are focused squarely on improving the quality of life. In another study, *The Time of the Tribes: The Decline of Individualism in Mass Society*, Michel Maffesoli uses elegant philosophical reflection to extend the insights of Inglehart's study. Accepting Inglehart's premise on the widespread shift to postmaterialist values in advanced industrial society, he introduces the concept of "the emotional community," in which "the community is characterized less by a project (*pro-jectum*) oriented towards the future than by the execution *in actu* of 'being-together'" (1996, 16). The need to "belong" gives rise to what Maffesoli calls "tribes," which are delocalized microgroups that arise "as a result of a feeling of *belonging*, as a function of a specific *ethic* and within the framework of a communications *network*" (ibid., 139). From Maffesoli's vantage, a wide variety of ephemeral social groupings become "neo-tribes": being a regular on a commuter train or joining a sports club; belonging to an association of hobbyists or participating in crowd behaviors at festivals or sports events; taking part in community policing groups or working for single-issue pressure groups.

These examples of new social movements are impressive but they do not take into consideration the sociocultural hybridity of contemporary social life in advanced industrial societies. In the case of Inglehart and Maffesoli, the subject of investigation is strictly limited to European and North American sociopolitical formations. Immigrants to North America, for example, have created new social formations, but have usually left home for decidedly materialist—not postmaterialist—reasons. Inglehart and Maffesoli, moreover, do not address the cultural resources that non-Western peoples use to construct hybrid social formations in European and North American contexts. Their theories of culture shift and the formation of "neo-tribes" are therefore partial.

34. See Lewis 1951.
35. Ortner 1997, 63–64.
36. Ibid.
37. Ortner 1997, 68–75; see also Connerton 1989.
38. See Hodgson 1974. Hodgson is careful to point out the social and political tensions generated—from the classical to the modern periods in Islamic civilization—by the clash of deeply rooted Bedouin egalitarianism and state absolutism. The Ummah is most definitely a community of equals who submit to the authority of Allah, but in Islamic authoritarian states, some people have always been more equal than others have. Deeply religious adepts decried the fall of the egalitarianism of early Medina; Muslim rulers have backed religious interpretations that supported strict social stratification. Throughout the history of Islamic civilization, this schism has provoked much political debate, military action, and social change.
39. Interview with El Hadj Harouna Souley, December 14, 1995.
40. Interview with Ali Zerma, February 26, 1994.
41. Ibid.
42. Chomsky's *Syntactic Structures* (1957) and *Aspects of a Theory of Syntax* (1965) are classic works in linguistic theory. They moved linguistics from the rather dry compilation of non-Western grammars theoretically framed by stimulus-response theory to a theory of cognitive competence based on a universal, innate structure of syntactic rules that Chomsky believed to be the foundation, the deep structure, of human cognition. Work in child language acquisition provided much evidence to reinforce Chomsky's ideas about the universal applicability of his theory. In the late 1960s, Chomsky's students extended his ideas about syntax to what they called generative semantics. Chomsky and the generative semanticists based their theoretical assumptions on the premise of a relationship between an ideal speaker and hearer. "Linguistic theory," Chomsky wrote in *Aspects*, "is concerned primarily with an ideal speaker-listener, in a completely homogeneous speech-community, who knows its language perfectly and is unaffected by such grammatically irrelevant conditions as memory limitations, distractions, shifts of attention and interests, and errors (random or characteristic) in applying his knowledge of the language in actual performance" (1965, 3). Later on, Chomsky defined linguistic competence as this speaker-hearer's knowledge of the language. This position, which completely ignores the contextual ramifications of language use, was criticized by sociolinguists and linguistic anthropologists who argued that one cannot overlook how social contexts influence both linguistic competence and linguistic performance.
43. Among the classic studies of child language acquisition is Roger Brown's *A First Language* (1972) and Carol Chomsky's *Acquisition of Syntax in Children from Five to Ten* (1969).
44. William Labov (1972a, 1972b) was one of the first linguists to extend Chomsky's notion of linguistic competence to social contexts. Using data from a massive study of Black English Vernacular in New York City, Labov suggested that variation precipitated by shifts in social context needed to be accounted for in linguistic theory. Accordingly, he developed what he called variable rules that would predict how social constraints might alter the production of sentence strings. Dell Hymes (1974) approached the same problem from a more anthropological perspective. Rather than positing an extension of the theory of linguistic competence, Hymes advocated ethnographies of speaking in which scholars would painstakingly describe how social context and cultural principles affected language usage. Following Hymes, scholars began to talk about sociolinguistic competence.

45. See Theodore Schwartz (1982) on the acquisition of culture. The argument is simply a logical extension of the theory of language acquisition. Since most cultural categories, logical relations, attitudes, and beliefs are embodied in language, Schwartz argued, one could logically extend the model of language acquisition to culture.

46. Goffman is the most prominent of the sociologists who analyzed social interaction. Indeed, an entire movement within sociology, ethnomethodology, was developed to analyze the behaviors of people interacting. Through microscopic documentation and analysis of social interaction, especially its conversational aspects, the ethnomethodologists hoped to uncover backgrounded, taken-for-granted rules that shape everyday life. They continue to believe that theories should modestly emerge from painstakingly gathered and minutely analyzed data. They have spent an inordinate amount of time developing methods and analytical systems that guard against interpretive bias. Among many others, see Garfinkle 1967 and Sudnow 1972.

47. Goffman 1981, 74.

48. Sue 1998, 440.

49. See Binet and Simon 1908; Piaget 1972; Sansone and Berg 1993.

50. Sansone and Berg 1993, 217.

51. Interview with Idrissa Dan Inna, August 2, 1994.

52. See Millman 1997; Malcomsen 1997; Stoller 1996, 1997.

53. See Mennan 1986.

54. Interview with Sala Fari, October 25, 1995.

55. Perry 1997, 236; see also Malcolmsen 1997; Millman 1997; Ebin 1990; Ebin and Lake 1992.

Epilogue

1. The ritual incantation that speaks to these points of misfortune comes from Djibo Mounmouni, who in 1976 was a *sorko* (a praise-singer to the spirits and a river magician) in the village of Mehanna. The incantation says:

> I must speak to N'debbi and my words must travel until they are heard. N'debbi was before human beings. He showed the human beings the path. Now human beings are on the path. My path came from the ancestors (my teachers and my teacher's teachers). Now my path is beyond theirs. The path is war. When there is war, men have 30 points of misfortune; women have 40 points of misfortune. A person has many enemies along the path, enemies who will seek him/her out. The evil witches can search a person out with evil medicine, and a few of them will be overcome. They say that the evil genies will search a person out, and a few of them will be overcome. They say the devil's children and the spirits of the cold will search a person out, and they too can be overcome. All of them are on the path, and some of them will be overcome, some of them will be misled. (Stoller 1980, 127)

This text is recited over a gourd that contains water mixed with pulverized tree bark and certain perfumes. Once the incantation has been repeated three times, and the *sorko* has spit into the ablution after each recitation, the bowl is given to a victim of witchcraft, a person whose soul has been stolen by a witch. The magical pungency of the ablution is supposed to attract the victim's soul back to his or her body, which theoretically eradicates witchcraft illness. The numbers associated with male and female points of misfortune derive from Islamic numerology, in which the number 3 is associated with men, the number 4 with women.

2. Issifi's father had been caught up in mass fears of penis-snatching sorcery. Accusations of penis snatching that resulted in mob violence have been reported twice in Africa, once in the Cameroon in 1996 and once in Côte d'Ivoire in 1997. In both cases, angry mobs beat and in some instances lynched foreigners who were suspected of having the power to make male genitals disappear by simply shaking a person's hand. In Côte d'Ivoire, Hausa from Niger and Nigeria were prime suspects. A mob stopped Issifi's father's car. Suspecting correctly that he was Hausa, they pulled him from his automobile and beat him senseless. See Jackson 1998, 49–51.

3. See Sassen 1991b for an exposition on the relationship between the growth of economic informality and the spread of postmodernity. Recent works in urban anthropology have focused on transnational trading communities similar to those described in *Money Has No Smell*. Among the most notable of these is Janet MacGaffey and Rémy Bazenguissa-Ganga's *Congo-Paris: Transnational Traders on the Margins of the Law* (2000). Although there are significant differences between the Central African traders found in Paris and the West African vendors in New York City, the traders in both cities are members of dispersed communities and face a bevy of social problems. As in *Money Has No Smell*, MacGaffey and Bazenguissa-Ganga demonstrate how macrosociological forces affect the social lives of individual traders.

4. There is no shortage of cultural critics who have predicted the demise of anthropology. Clifford (1988) sees anthropology reverting to thickly described travel accounts. Other accounts have underscored the anthropological sins of the past (see Torgovnick 1990; Mihn-ha 1988; Rony 1996). Few of these studies, though, have considered the noteworthy advances made by urban anthropologists who have written about transnational spaces.

5. Recent works in urban studies have been both theoretically profound and methodologically creative. Among these, the most notable are Bourgois 1995, Desjarlais 1997, and Duneier 1999.

References

Amin, Samir, ed. 1971. *Modern Migrations in West Africa*. London: Oxford University Press.

Amselle, Jean-Loup. 1971. Parenté et commerce chez les Kooroko. In *The Development of Indigenous Trade and Markets in West Africa*, ed. Claude Meillassoux, 253–66. London: Oxford University Press.

Appadurai, Arjun. 1990. Disjuncture and Difference in Global Cultural Economy. *Public Culture* 2 (2): 1–24.

———. 1991. Global Ethnoscapes: Notes and Queries for a Transnational Anthropology. In *Recapturing Anthropology: Working in the Present*, ed. Richard G. Fox, 191–210. Santa Fe, N.M.: School of American Research Press.

———. 1996. *Modernity at Large: The Cultural Dimensions of Globalization*. Minneapolis: University of Minnesota Press.

Appiah, Kwame Anthony. 1992. *In My Father's House*. London: Oxford University Press.

Asante, Molefi Kete. 1987. *The Afrocentric Idea*. Philadelphia: Temple University Press.

———. 1990. *Kemet, Afrocentricity, and Knowledge*. Trenton, N.J.: Africa World Press.

———. 1993. *Malcolm X as Cultural Hero and Other Afrocentric Essays*. Trenton, N.J.: Africa World Press.

Baltes, M. M., H. A. Wahl, and M. S. Reichart. 1992. Successful Aging in Long-Term Care Institutions. In *Annual Review of Gerontology and Geriatrics*, vol. 11, ed. K. W. Schaie and M. P. Lawton. New York: Springer Publishing.

Bandele, Gabriel. 1993. *Annual Small Business Guide to African-American Multicultural Events: Conferences, Festivals, and Shows*. 1993–94 ed. Washington, D.C.: Bandele Publications.

Barnes, John A. 1954. Class and Committees in the Norwegian Island Parish. *Human Relations* 7:39–58.

———. 1969. Graph Theory and Social Networks: A Technical Comment on Connectiveness and Connectivity. *Sociology* 3:215–332.

Barry, Dan, and Jonathan P. Hicks. 1995. Protestor Is Caught in Fatal Fire's Glare: New Look at Harsh Message. *New York Times*, December 15, B1, B4.

Batten, David, John Casti, and Roland Thord, eds. 1995. *Networks in Action: Communication, Economics, and Human Knowledge*. Berlin: Springer-Verlag.

Baudrillard, Jean. 1983. *Simulations*. New York: Semiotext.

————. 1986. *America*. New York: Semiotext.

Bax, Mart. 1978. Figuration Analysis: A Better Perspective for Networks, with an Illustration from Ireland. *Anthropological Quarterly* 51:221–30.

Benjamin, Walter. 1968. *Reflections*. New York: Schocken.

————. 1978. *Illuminations*. New York: Schocken.

Bernal, Martin. 1987. *Black Athena*. New Brunswick, N.J.: Rutgers University Press.

Bhabha, Homi. 1984. Of Mimicry and Man: The Ambivalence of Colonial Discourse. *October* 28:125–33.

————. 1994. *The Location of Culture*. New York: Routledge.

Binet, Alfred, and Theodore Simon. 1908. Le development de l'intelligence chez les enfants. *L'Annee Psychologique* 14:1–90.

Bloch, Maurice, ed. 1975. *Principles of Marxist Anthropology*. New York: Academic Press.

Bluestone, Daniel. 1991. The Pushcart Evil: Peddlers, Merchants, and New York City's Streets, 1880–1940. *Journal of Urban History* 18 (1): 68–92.

Boas, Franz. 1911. *Handbook of American Indian Linguistics*. Washington, D.C.: U.S. Government Printing Office.

Bohannon, Paul. 1955. Some Principles of Exchange and Investment among the Tiv. *American Anthropologist* 57:60–69.

————, ed. 1962. *Markets in Africa*. Evanston, Ill.: Northwestern University Press.

Boissevain, Jeremey, and John Clyde Mitchell, eds. 1973. *Network Analysis: Studies in Human Interaction*. The Hague: Mouton.

Borjas, George. 1996. The New Economics of Immigration: Affluent Americans Gain; Poor Americans Lose. *Atlantic Monthly* 278 (5): 72–79.

Bourgois, Philip. 1995. *In Search of Respect*. New York: Cambridge University Press.

Bovill, E. W. [1958] 1995. *The Golden Trade of the Moors*. Princeton, N.J.: M. Weiner.

Branigin, William. 1997. Amid GOP Discord, House Approves Extension of Immigration Provision. *Washington Post*, October 23, A9.

————. 1998. Immigration Advocates to Seek Softening of Laws. *Washington Post*, January 30, A13.

Branigin, William, and Pamela Constable. 1997. Immigration Law Altered Once Again. *Washington Post*, November 14, A1.

Braudel, Fernand. 1972. *The Mediterranean and the Mediterranean World in the Age of Phillip II*. New York: Harper and Row.

Brenner, Louis, ed. 1993. *Muslim Identity and Social Change in Sub-Saharan Africa*. Bloomington: Indiana University Press.

Brown, DeNeen L. 1997. Mainstream Marketing of Kwanzaa Worries Black Entrepreneurs. *Washington Post*, December 23.

Brown, Roger. 1972. *A First Language: The Early Stages*. Cambridge, Mass.: Harvard University Press.

Calame-Griaule, Genvieve. 1972. *Ethnologie et langage: La parole chez les Dogons*. Paris: Institut d'Ethnologie.

Callaghy, Thomas, and John Ravenhill, eds. 1993. *Hemmed In: Responses to Africa's Economic Decline*. New York: Columbia University Press.

Carter, Donald M. 1997. *States of Grace: Senegalese in Italy and the New European Immigration*. Minneapolis: University of Minnesota Press.

Castells, Manuel. 1997. *The Power of Identity*. Oxford: Basil Blackwell.

Castells, Manuel, and Alejandro Portes. 1989. World Underneath: The Origins, Dynamics, and Effects of the Informal Economy. In *The Informal Economy*, ed. Alejandro Portes et al., 11–37. Baltimore: Johns Hopkins University Press.

Charlick, Robert. 1991. *Niger: Personal Rule and Survival in the Sahel*. Boulder, Colo.: Westview Press.

Chasing Tigers in Unlicensed Woods. 1997. *Brandweek* 38 (23): 48.

Chomsky, A. Noam. 1957. *Syntactic Structures*. The Hague: Mouton.

———. 1965. *Aspects of a Theory of Syntax*. Cambridge, Mass.: MIT Press.

Chomsky, Carol. 1969. *Acquisition of Syntax in Children from Five to Ten*. Cambridge, Mass.: MIT Press.

Clark, Gracia. 1994. *Onions Are My Husband: Survival and Accumulation by West African Market Women*. Chicago: University of Chicago Press.

Clifford, James. 1988. *The Predicament of Culture*. Cambridge, Mass.: Harvard University Press.

Clifford, James, and George E. Marcus, eds. 1986. *Writing Culture*. Berkeley: University of California Press.

Cohen, Abner. 1969. *Custom and Conflict in West Africa: Hausa Migrants in Yoruba Towns*. Berkeley: University of California Press.

Connerton, Paul. 1989. *How Societies Remember*. London: Cambridge University Press.

Connor, Stephen J. 1989. *Postmodern Culture*. London: Basil Blackwell.

Coombe, Rosemary J. 1996. Embodied Trademarks: Mimesis and Alterity on American Cultural Frontiers. *Cultural Anthropology* 11 (2): 202–25.

———. 1998. *Cultural Appropriation: Authorship, Alterity, and the Law*. Durham, N.C.: Duke University Press.

Coombe, Rosemary J., and Paul Stoller. 1994. X Marks the Spot: The Ambiguities of African Trading in the Commerce of the Black Public Sphere. *Public Culture* 15:249–75.

Court Says City Can't Forbid Workers to Tell of Immigrants. 1999. *New York Times*, May 29, B7.

Curtin, Phillip. 1975. *Economic Change in Precolonial Africa: Senegambia in the Era of the Slave Trade*. Madison: University of Wisconsin Press.

Davis, Mike. 1990. *City of Quartz*. London: Verso.

Derrida, Jacques. 1976. *Of Grammatology*. Trans. G. T. Spivak. Baltimore: Johns Hopkins University Press.

———. 1987. *The Post Card: From Socrates to Freud and Beyond*. Chicago: University of Chicago Press.

Desjarlais, Robert. 1997. *Shelter Blues*. Philadelphia: University of Pennsylvania Press.

Devish, Réné. 1995. Frenzy, Violence, and Ethnic Renewal in Kinshasa. *Public Culture* 7 (3): 593–631.

Dickens, Peter. 1992. *Global Shift: The Internationalization of Economic Activity*. New York: Guilford Press.

Dieterlen, Germaine. 1941. *Les ames des Dogons*. Paris: Institut d'Ethnologie.

Dugan, Elizabeth, and Vera Kivett. 1994. The Importance of Emotional and Social Isolation to Loneliness among Very Old Rural Adults. *Gerontologist* 34 (3): 340–46.

Dugger, Celia. 1996a. Queens Old-Timers Uneasy as Asian Influence Grows. *New York Times*, March 31, A1.

————. 1996b. Woman, Seeking Asylum, Endures Prison in America. *New York Times*, April 15, A1.

————. 1996c. US Frees Asylum Seeker Who Fled Ritual Mutilation in Africa. *New York Times*, April 25, A1.

————. 1997. After "Kafkaesque" Ordeal, Seeker of Asylum Presses Case. *New York Times*, April 1, A10.

Duneier, Mitchell. 1999. *Sidewalk*. New York: Farrar, Strauss and Giroux.

Early, Gerald. 1997. Dreaming of a Black Christmas. *Harper's* 294:55–62.

Ebin, Victoria. 1990. Commercants et missionaires: Une confrérie musulmane senegalaise à New York. *Hommes et Migrations* 1132:25–31.

Ebin, Victoria, and Rose Lake. 1992. Camelots à New York: Les pionniers de l'immigration senegalaise. *Hommes et Migrations* 1160:32–37.

Engleberg, Stephen. 1994. In Immigration Labyrinth, Corruption Comes Easily. *New York Times*, September 12, A1.

Estevez, Mareza J. 1997. Immigration Rules Have Changed: Cuidado! *Hispanic* 10 (7–8): 86.

Fall, Papa Demba. 1997. Place et rôle "à distance" de la femme *lébou* dans la migration internationale. Manuscript.

————. 1998. Exode et identité: Le modèle migratoire des lébou de Thiaroye (Sénégal). Manuscript.

Finder, Alan. 1994. Bratton Joins Watch over Harlem Boycott. *New York Times*, October 21, B1.

Firestone, David. 1995. Giuliani Criticizes a US Crackdown on Illegal Aliens. *New York Times*, August 23, A1.

Fisher, Ian. 1997. Love for Country, If Not for the Betrothed: An Illusory Deadline Drives Immigrants in a Rush to Marriage. *New York Times*, March 9, A33.

Foner, Nancy. 1995. General Editor's Introduction to *Salvadorans in Suburbia: Symbiosis and Conflict*, by Sarah Mahler. Boston: Allyn and Bacon.

————. 2000. *From Ellis Island to JFK: New York's Two Great Waves of Immigration*. New Haven, Conn.: Yale University Press.

Foster, B. L., and S. B. Seidman. 1982. Urban Structures Derived from Overlapping Subsets. *Urban Anthropology* 11:177–92.

Foucault, Michel. 1970. The Order of Things: An Archaeology of the Human Sciences. New York: Random House.

Garfinkle, Harold. 1967. *Studies in Ethnomethodology*. Englewood Cliffs, N.J.: Prentice-Hall.

Gergen, Kenneth. 1991. *The Saturated Self*. New York: Basic Books.

Gilroy, Paul. 1993. *The Black Atlantic: Modernity and Double Consciousness*. Cambridge, Mass.: Harvard University Press.

Glick Shiller, Nina, Linda Basch, and Christina Szanton. 1992. Transnationalism: A New Analytical Framework for Understanding Migration. *Annals of the New York Academy of Science* 645:1–24.

Godelier, Maurice. 1977. *Perspectives on Marxist Anthropology*. Trans. Robert Brain. Cambridge: Cambridge University Press.

Goffman, Erving. 1974. *Frame Analysis*. New York: Harper Colophon.

————. 1981. *Forms of Talk*. Philadelphia: University of Pennsylvania Press.

Golden, Tim. 1996. California Governor Cuts Off Aid for Illegal Immigrants. *New York Times*, August 28, A1.

Greenberg, Joseph. 1970. *The Languages of Africa*. Bloomington: Indiana University Press.

Gregoire, Emmanuel. 1992. *Alhazai of Maradi: Traditional Hausa Merchants in a Changing Sahelian City*. Boulder, Colo.: Lynne Rienner.

———. 1993. Islam and the Identity of Merchants in Maradi (Niger). In *Muslim Identity and Social Change in Sub-Saharan Africa*, ed. Louis Brenner, 106–16. Bloomington: Indiana University Press.

Griaule, Marcel. 1938. *Masques dogons*. Paris: Institut d'Ethnologie.

———. 1965. *Conversations with Ogotemmêli*. London: Oxford University Press.

Griaule, Marcel, and Germaine Dieterlen. 1954. The Dogon of the French Sudan. In *African Worlds*, ed. Darryll Forde, 83–111. London: Oxford University Press.

Gugler, Josef, and William Flanagan. 1978. *Urbanization and Social Change in West Africa*. Cambridge: Cambridge University Press.

Gupta, Akhil, and James Ferguson. 1992. Beyond "Culture": Space, Identity, and the Politics of Difference. *Cultural Anthropology* 7 (1): 6–24.

Halbfinger, David. 1997. New York Continues to Be Shaped by New Immigrants, Study Finds. *New York Times*, December 1, B3.

Harvey, David. 1989. *The Condition of Postmodernity*. London: Basil Blackwell.

Herskovits, Melville. 1952. *Economic Anthropology*. New York: Knopf.

Hicks, Jonathan. 1994a. Police Move Illegal Vendors from Harlem Thoroughfare. *New York Times*, October 18, B3.

———. 1994b. Vendors' Ouster and Boycott Divide Harlem. *New York Times*, October 23, A1.

Hodgson, Marshall G. S. 1974. *The Venture of Islam*. 3 vols. Chicago: University of Chicago Press.

Holston, James, and Arjun Appadurai. 1996. Introduction: Cities and Citizenship. *Public Culture* 8 (2): 187–205.

Hopkins, A. G. 1973. *An Economic History of West Africa*. London: Cambridge University Press.

Hull, Robert. 1976. *African Cities and Towns before the European Conquest*. New York: Norton.

Hymes, Dell. 1974. *Foundations in Sociolinguistics: An Ethnographic Approach*. Philadelphia: University of Pennsylvania Press.

Ibrahim, Mahmood. 1990. *Merchant Capital and Islam*. Austin: University of Texas Press.

The Illegal Immigration Reform and Immigrant Responsibility Act of 1996. 1997. *Migration World* 24 (1/2): 42–46.

Inglehart, Ronald. 1990. *Culture Shift in Advanced Industrial Society*. Princeton, N.J.: Princeton University Press.

Jackson, Michael. 1998. *Minima Ethnographica: Intersubjectivity and the Anthropological Project*. Chicago: University of Chicago Press.

Jacobson, David. 1971. Mobility, Continuity, and Urban Social Organization. *Man* 101:630–44.

Jenkins, Timothy J. 1995. Misguided "Authenticity." *American Visions* 10 (2): 4.

Johannson, Borge. 1995. The Dynamics of Economic Networks. In *Networks in Action: Communication, Economics, and Human Knowledge*, ed. David Batten, John Casti, and Roland Thord, 287–309. Berlin: Springer-Verlag.

Johnson, Jeffrey C. 1994. Anthropological Contribution to the Study of Social Networks: A Review. In *Advances in Social Network Analysis*, ed. Stanley Wasserman and Joseph Galaskiewicz, 113–52. Thousand Oaks, Calif.: Sage.

Kahn, R. L., and L. C. Antonucci. 1980. Convoys over the Life Course: Attachment, Roles, and Social Support. In *Life-span Development and Behavior*, ed. P. B. Baltes and O. G. Brim Jr., 3:254–86. New York: Academic Press.

Kantner, Rosabeth Moss. 1995. *World Class: Thriving Locally in the Global Economy*. New York: Simon and Schuster.

Kantner, Rosabeth Moss, and Todd L. Pittinsky. 1996. Globalization: New Worlds for Social Inquiry. *Berkeley Journal of Sociology* 40:1–21.

Kapferer, Bruce. 1973. Social Network and Conjugal Role in Urban Zambia: Toward a Reformulation of the Bott Hypothesis. In *Network Analysis: Studies in Human Interaction*, ed. Jeremy Boussevain and John Clyde Mitchell, 83–110. The Hague: Mouton.

Karenga, Maulena. 1977. *Kwanzaa: Origins, Concepts, Practices*. Los Angeles: Kwaida Publishers.

Kaufman, Michael T. 1994. Squeegees and Hope: New Peril, Men Who Wash Car Windows on Street Targeted by William J. Bratton. *New York Times*, December 8, A18.

Keith, Nelson. 1997. *Reframing International Development: Globalism, Postmodernity, and Difference*. Thousand Oaks, Calif.: Sage.

Kleinfield, N. R. 1995. Pursuing the Biggest Emigré Tax Evaders. *New York Times*, June 16, A1.

Krause, Neil. 1990. Perceived Health Problems, Formal/Informal Support, and Life Satisfaction among Older Adults. *Journal of Gerontology: Social Sciences* 45:193–205.

Labov, William. 1972a. *Sociolinguistic Patterns*. Philadelphia: University of Pennsylvania Press.

———. 1972b. *Language in the Inner City*. Philadelphia: University of Pennsylvania Press.

Lamphere, Louise, ed. 1992. *Structuring Diversity: Ethnographic Perspectives on the New Ethnography*. Chicago: University of Chicago Press.

Lefevre, Henri. 1974. *La production d'espace*. Paris: Editions de Minuit.

Lévi-Strauss, Claude. 1967. *Structural Anthropology*. Garden City, N.J.: Doubleday.

Levy, C. J. 1997. Giuliani Eases Marriage Rules for Immigrants without Visas. *New York Times*, March 16, 43.

Lewis, I. M., ed. 1980. *Islam in Tropical Africa*. Bloomington: Indiana University Press.

Lewis, Oscar. 1951. *Life in a Mexican Town: Tepotzlan Revisited*. Urbana: University of Illinois Press.

Lynch, Kevin. 1960. *Image of the City*. Cambridge, Mass.: MIT Press.

Lynd, Peter S., and Helen M. Lynd. 1929. *Middletown: A Study in Modern American Culture*. New York: Harcourt Brace Jovanovich.

MacGaffey, Janet. 1987. *Entrepreneurs and Parasites: The Struggle for Indigenous Capitalism in Zaire*. Cambridge: Cambridge University Press.

———. 1991. *The Real Economy of Zaire*. Philadelphia: University of Pennsylvania Press.

MacGaffey, Janet, and Rémy Bazenguissa-Ganga. 2000. *Congo-Paris: Transnational Traders on the Margins of the Law*. Bloomington: Indiana University Press.

Maffesoli, Michel. 1996. *The Time of the Tribes: The Decline of Individualism in Mass Society*. Thousand Oaks, Calif.: Sage.

Mahler, Sarah. 1995. *American Dreaming: Immigrant Life on the Margins*. Princeton, N.J.: Princeton University Press.

———. 1996. *Salvadorans in Suburbia: Symbiosis and Conflict*. Boston: Allyn and Bacon.

Malcolmson, Scott. 1997. West of Eden: The Mourid Ethic and the Spirit of Capitalism. *Transition* 79:24–44.

Malinowski, Bronislaw. [1922] 1961. *Argonauts of the Western Pacific*. London: Dutton.

Marcus, George E., and Michael M. J. Fischer. 1985. *Anthropology as Cultural Critique*. Chicago: University of Chicago Press.

Matsumoto, David, et al. 1997. Context-Specific Measurement of Individualism-Collectivism on the Individual Level: The Individualism-Collectivism Interpersonal Assessment Inventory. *Journal of Cross-Cultural Psychology* 28 (6): 743–68.

Mbembe, Achille, and Janet Roitman. 1995. Figures of the Subject in Times of Crisis. *Public Culture* 7 (2): 323–53.

McCay, Claude. 1940. *Harlem: Negro Metropolis*. New York: Dutton.

Meillassoux, Claude, ed. 1971. *The Development of Indigenous Trade and Markets in West Africa*. London: Oxford University Press.

———. 1991. *The Anthropology of Slavery*. Chicago: University of Chicago Press.

Mennan, M. A. 1986. *Islamic Economics: Theory and Practice*. Boulder, Colo.: Westview Press.

Merleau-Ponty, Maurice. 1962. *The Phenomenology of Perception*. London: Routledge and Kegan Paul.

———. 1964. *L'oeil et l'esprit*. Paris: Gallimard.

Mihn-ha, Trinh T. 1988. *Woman, Native, Other*. Bloomington: Indiana University Press.

Millman, Joel. 1997. *The Other Americans: How Immigrants Renew Our Country, Our Economy, and Our Values*. New York: Viking.

Mintz, Sidney. 1974. *The Worker in the Cane*. New York: Norton.

———. 1985. *Sweetness and Power*. New York: Random House.

Mirowski, John. 1995. Age and the Sense of Control. *Social Psychology Quarterly* 58 (1): 31–34.

Mirowski, John, and C. E. Ross. 1991. Eliminating Defense and Agreement Bias from Measures of a Sense of Control: A 2 x 2 Index. *Social Psychology Quarterly* 54 (2) 127–45.

Mitchell, James C. 1974. Social Networks. *Annual Review of Anthropology* 3:279–99.

———. 1989. Algorithms and Network Analysis: A Test of Some Analytical Procedures on Kapferer's Tailor Shop Material. In *Research Methods in Social Network Analysis*, ed. L. C. Freeman, D. R. White, and A. K. Romney, 319–65. Fairfax, Va.: George Mason University Press.

Mitter, Swatsi. 1987. *Common Fate, Common Bond: Women in the Global Economy*. London: Pluto Press.

Mittleman, James, ed. 1996. *Yearbook of International Political Economy*. Vol. 9. Boulder, Colo.: Lynne Rienner.

Mollenkopf, John, and Manuel Castells, eds. 1991. *Dual City: Restructuring New York*. New York: Russell Sage.

Nash, Manning. 1966. *Primitive and Peasant Economic Systems*. San Francisco: Chandler.

Nelson, Joyce. 1989. *The Sultans of Sleaze: Public Relations and the Media*. Monroe, Maine: Common Courage Press.

Noble, Mary. 1973. Social Network: Its Use as a Conceptual Framework in Family Analysis. In *Network Analysis: Studies in Human Interaction*, ed. Jeremy Boissevain and John Clyde Mitchell, 3–15. The Hague: Mouton.

Nossiter, Adam, 1995, A Shabby Welcome Mat. *New York Times*, February 11, A21.

Nwadiora, Emeka. 1996. Therapy with African Families. *Western Journal of Black Studies* 20 (3): 117–25.

O'Brien, Conor Cruise. 1971. *The Mourids*. London: Oxford University Press.

Ojito, Mirta. 1997. Painful Choices for Immigrants in US Illegally. *New York Times*, September 25, A1.

Only in Afro-America. 1994. *Economist* 333 (7894): A32.

Ortner, Sherry. 1997. Fieldwork in the Postcommunity. *Anthropology and Humanism* 22 (1): 61–81.

Osofsky, Gilbert. 1971. *Harlem, the Making of a Ghetto: A History of Negro New York, 1900–1920*. New York: Harper and Row.

Painter, Thomas. 1988. From Warriors to Migrants: Critical Perspectives on Early Migrations among the Zarma of Niger. *Africa* 58 (1): 87–100.

Pear, Robert. 1994. Federal Panel Proposes Register to Curb Hiring of Illegal Aliens. *New York Times*, August 4, A1.

Perry, Donna L. 1997. Rural Ideologies and Urban Imaginings: Wolof Immigrants in New York City. *Africa Today* 44 (2): 229–60.

Person, Yves. 1976. *Samori: Une revolution dyula*. 3 vols. Dakar: IFAN.

Peyre de Fabregues, B. 1979. *Lexique des plantes du Niger*. Niamey: Institut National de la Recherche Agronomique du Niger.

Piaget, Jean. 1972. *The Psychology of Intelligence*. Totowa, N.J.: Littlefield Adams.

Picton, John, and John Mack. 1989. *African Textiles*. London: British Museum.

Plattner, Stuart. 1989. Economic Behavior in Markets. In *Economic Anthropology*, ed. Stuart Plattner, 209–22. Palo Alto, Calif.: Stanford University Press.

Policano, Christopher. 1994a. Showdown Today on Rudy Plan to Evict Harlem Vendors. *New York Post*, October 17, 2.

———. 1994b. Twenty-two Busted in Melee at Vendors' March. *New York Post*, October 18, 9.

Portes, Alejandro, Manuel Castells, and Lauren Benton, eds. 1989. *The Informal Economy*. Baltimore: Johns Hopkins University Press.

Pristin, Terry. 1996. Immigration Official Falsified Papers for Illegal Aliens, Authorities Say. *New York Times*, August 1, B4.

Protecting Harlem's Merchants. 1994. *New York Post*, October 19, 23.

Redfield, Robert. 1941. *The Folk Culture of Yucatan*. Chicago: University of Chicago Press.

———. 1955. *The Little Community: Viewpoints for the Study of a Human Whole*. Chicago: University of Chicago Press.

RIAA: Bootleg Seizures Soar 1,300 Percent in '96. 1997. *Billboard* 109 (13): 6–7.

RIAA Releases '95 Piracy Statistics. 1996. *Billboard* 108 (12): 6–7.

Riley, Dorothy Winbush. 1995. *The Complete Kwanzaa: Celebrating Our Cultural Harvest*. New York: HarperCollins.

Roberts, Johnnie L. 1996. Buyers Beware: Those Curbside Movie Videos May Be Cheap—But They're Pirated and Illegal. *Newsweek*, October 14, 66–67.

Roberts, Stephen. 1963. *History of French Colonial Policy, 1970–1925*. London: F. Cass.

Rodin, Judith. 1986. Aging and Health: Effects of the Sense of Control. *Sciences* 23:1271–76.

Rony, Fatimah Tobring. 1996. *The Third Eye: Race, Cinema, and Ethnographic Spectacle.* Durham, N.C.: Duke University Press.

Room at the Top: Housing for the Poor. 1996. *Economist* 339 (7968): 24–26.

Rorty, Richard. 1979. *Philosophy and the Mirror of Nature.* Princeton, N.J.: Princeton University Press.

Ross, Doran. 1998. *Wrapped in Pride: Ghanaian Kente and African American Identity.* Los Angeles: UCLA Fowler Museum of Cultural History.

Rouch, Jean. 1956. Migrations au Ghana. *Journal de la Société des Africanistes* 26 (1/2): 33–196.

———. 1964. *Jaguar.* Paris: Films de la Pléiade.

Sahlins, Marshall. 1972. *Stoneage Economics.* Chicago: Aldine.

Sansone, Carole, and Cynthia A. Berg. 1993. Adapting to the Environment across the Life Span: Different Process or Different Inputs? *International Journal of Behavioral Development* 16 (2): 215–41.

Sassen, Saskia. 1991a. The Informal Economy. In *Dual City: Restructuring New York,* ed. John Mollenkopf and Manuel Castells, 79–101. New York: Russell Sage.

———. 1991b. *The Global City: New York, London, Tokyo.* Princeton, N.J.: Princeton University Press.

———. 1994a. Regulatory Fractures in the Global City. Paper presented at the American International Law Society Conference "Interdisciplinary Perspectives on International Economic Law," Washington, D.C., February 25–27.

———. 1994b. *Cities in a World Economy.* Thousand Oaks, Calif.: Pine Forge/Sage.

———. 1996. Whose City Is It? Globalization and the Formation of New Claims. *Public Culture* 8:205–23.

———. 1998. Swirling That Old Wine around in the Wrong Bottle: A Comment on White. *Urban Affairs* 33 (4): 478–82.

Schildkrout, Enid. 1978. *People of Zongo: The Transformation of Ethnic Identities in Ghana.* Cambridge: Cambridge University Press.

Schmitt, Eric. 1997. Illegal Immigrants Rose to Five Million in '96. *New York Times,* February 8, A9.

Schneider, Harold. 1974. *Economic Man.* New York: Free Press.

Schwartz, Theodore. 1982. The Acquisition of Culture. *Ethos* 9 (1): 4–18.

Shaw, Karen. 1997. New York City Mayor Rudolf Giuliani Campaigns for Immigrants. *Migration World* 25 (4): 15–18.

Shipp, E. R. 1994. Cool It, Face Facts in Harlem. *New York Daily News,* October 19, 15.

Sinclair, Abiola. 1994. Boycott of 125th Street? *New York Amsterdam News,* October 15, 27.

Soja, Edward. 1989. *Postmodern Geographies.* London: Verso.

Sokolovsky, Jay, et al. 1978. Personal Networks of Ex-Mental Patients in a Manhattan SRO Hotel. *Human Organization* 37:5–15.

Sontag, Deborah. 1993. Unlicensed Peddlers, Unfettered Dreams. *New York Times,* June 14, A1.

———. 1994. Aspiring Immigrants Misled on Chances in Visa Lottery. *New York Times,* June 20, A1.

Soto, Hernando de. 1989. *The Other Path: The Invisible Revolution in the Third World.* New York: Harper and Row.

Steiner, Christopher. 1993. *African Art in Transit.* London: Cambridge University Press.

Stipp, David. 1996. Farewell My Logo: A Detective Story. *Fortune* 133 (10): 130–40.

Stoll, David. 1996. The Immigration Debate. *In Focus.* Vol. 31. New York: Institute for Policy Studies and the Interhemispheric Resource Center.

Stoller, Paul. 1980. The Epistemology of Sorkotarey: Language, Metaphor, and Healing among the Songhay. *Ethos* 8 (2): 117–32.

———. 1989a. *Fusion of the Worlds: An Ethnography of Possession among the Songhay of Niger.* Chicago: University of Chicago Press.

———. 1989b. *The Taste of Ethnographic Things: The Senses in Anthropology.* Philadelphia: University of Pennsylvania Press.

———. 1996. Spaces, Places, and Fields: The Politics of West African Trading in New York City. *American Anthropologist* 96 (4): 776–89.

———. 1997. Globalizing Method: Doing Ethnography in Transnational Spaces. *Anthropology and Humanism* 17 (1): 81–95.

Sudnow, David. 1972. *Studies in Social Interaction.* New York: Free Press.

Sue, Stanley. 1998. In Search of Cultural Competence in Psychotherapy and Counseling. *American Psychologist* 53 (4): 440–48.

Sullivan, R. Lee. 1992. Spike Lee versus Mrs. Malcolm X (Licensed Product Merchandising). *Forbes* 150:136.

Taussig, Michael. 1992. *The Nervous System.* New York: Routledge.

———. 1993. *Mimesis and Alterity: A Particular History of the Senses.* New York: Routledge.

Taylor, Lucien, Ilisa Barbash, and Christopher Steiner. 1992. *In and Out of Africa.* Berkeley: University of California Media Extension.

Thomas, Deborah. 1995. The Removal of Vendors from Harlem as a Social Drama: Illuminating Economic and Racial Ideologies in an Age of Global Capitalist Restructuring. Manuscript.

Thomas, Nicholas. 1994. *Colonialism's Culture: Anthropology, Travel, and Government.* Princeton, N.J.: Princeton University Press.

———. 1996. Cold Fusion. *American Anthropologist* 98 (1): 9–16.

Tierney, John. 1997. Man with a Van. *New York Times Magazine,* August 10, 22.

Torgovnick, Marianna. 1990. *Gone Primitive: Savage Intellects, Modern Lives.* Chicago: University of Chicago Press.

Toy, Vivian S. 1996. NYC to Toughen Laws against Aggressive Panhandling. *New York Times,* June 27, B1.

Tyler, Stephen. 1988. *The Unspeakable.* Madison: University of Wisconsin Press.

Video Ring Is Broken, Police Say: Tapes and Recorders Seized in Yonkers. 1994. *New York Times,* July 8, B5.

Walking on 125th Street. 1994. Editorial. *New York Times,* October 21, A21.

Walsh, Anna C., and Jeanne Simonelli. 1986. Migrant Women in the Oil Field: The Functions of Social Networks. *Human Organization* 45:43–52.

Watts, Michael. 1992. Space for Everything: A Commentary. *Cultural Anthropology* 7 (1): 115–29.

Weisner, Thomas. 1978. The Structure of Sociality: Urban Migration and Urban-Rural Ties in Kenya. *Urban Anthropology* 5:199–223.

White, James W. 1998. Old Wine, Cracked Bottle? Tokyo, Paris, and the Global City Hypothesis. *Urban Affairs* 33 (4): 451–78.

Wilde, Anna Day. 1995. Mainstreaming Kwanzaa. *Public Interest* 119:68–80.

Wilkinson, Deborah M. 1996. Afrocentric Marketing Is Not Just a Niche. *Black Enterprise* 26 (12): 72–77.

Wolf, Eric. 1966. *Peasants.* Englewood Cliffs, N.J.: Prentice-Hall.

————. 1982. *Europe and the People without History.* Berkeley: University of California Press.

Woodward, Kenneth L., and Patrice Johnson. 1995. The Advent of Kwanzaa: Will Success Spoil an African-American Feast? *Newsweek* 126 (24): 88.

Zukerman, Miron, et al. 1996. Beliefs in Realistic and Unrealistic Control: Assessment and Implications. *Journal of Personality* 64 (2): 435–64.

Zukin, Sharon. 1995. *The Cultures of Cities.* London: Basil Blackwell.

Index